THE THEOLOGY OF MERCY AMBA ODUYOYE

Notre Dame Studies in African Theology

*Series co-editors: Rev. Paulinus Ikechukwu Odozor, C.S.Sp.,
and David A. Clairmont*

DE NICOLA CENTER
for ETHICS AND CULTURE

Under the sponsorship of the de Nicola Center for Ethics and Culture, and
in cooperation with the Notre Dame Department of Theology, this series
seeks to publish new scholarship engaging the history, the contemporary
situation, and the future of African theology and the African church. The
goal is to initiate a global and interdisciplinary conversation about African
theology and its current trajectories, with special attention to its interreli-
gious and multicultural context on the African continent and in the African
diaspora. The series will publish works in the history of the African church
and in African perspectives on biblical studies, liturgy, religious art and
music, ethics, and Christian doctrine.

THE THEOLOGY
OF
Mercy Amba Oduyoye

Ecumenism, Feminism, and Communal Practice

OLUWATOMISIN OLAYINKA OREDEIN

University of Notre Dame Press
Notre Dame, Indiana

University of Notre Dame Press
Notre Dame, Indiana 46556
undpress.nd.edu

Published in the United States of America

Library of Congress Control Number: 2022951518

ISBN: 978-0-268-20526-3 (Hardback)
ISBN: 978-0-268-20527-0 (WebPDF)
ISBN: 978-0-268-20525-6 (Epub)

To Aunty Mercy:
May these words do your life, work, and voice—justice.

To my ancestor and dearest Mommy,
Chief Iyabo Olayinka Oredein:

We share a name and an unfettered fierceness;
and I am incredibly proud to be your daughter.

CONTENTS

ACKNOWLEDGMENTS

A project like this would not be possible without an inspiration: Mercy Amba Ewudziwa Oduyoye's courage to be herself in a world not yet ready for her fortitude and wisdom has most certainly made the world better. Thank you, Aunty Mercy; I am always learning from you!

If it had not been for Esther Acolatse, I would not have been introduced to Aunty Mercy's voice. Brilliant in her own right, Esther has my deep gratitude for her constant encouragement to see this work through. It is hard being a West African woman in the academy. Esther, thank you for showing me how it's done!

Willie Jennings and Eboni Marshall Turman are the mentors I did not know I needed. Willie, thank you for teaching me to always sound like myself. Eboni, thank you for showing me exactly what this looks like in an academic world that has no idea what Black women can do!

Esther, Willie, Eboni, and Jay Kameron Carter were crucial in suggesting ways to turn my initial research into a book. Thank you all for pushing a timid Duke Divinity doctoral student into a scholar who stands proud in her unique standpoint and who owns her words.

The earliest iterations of this project would not have been written without colleagues along the way crafting their own words ready to meet the world. To everyone who partook in dissertation writing with me in Perkins Library at Duke, I am excited to see where our words will take us!

To writing and accountability partners since: Kathryn House, Kamilah Hall Sharp, Grace Vargas, Julie Morris, and Natalya Cherry, your showing up consistently has shown me what collegiality, love, and friendship looks like. Thank you for being a part of this journey and allowing me to be a part of yours!

To colleagues from Brite Divinity School and Memphis Theological Seminary who shared wisdom, encouragement, book proposals, advice, and kind words, thank you! The heartiest thanks to Natalya Cherry, Jeremy Williams, Wil Gafney, Francisco Lozada, Bar McClure, Jeff Williams, Michael Miller, and Newell Williams at Brite Divinity School for cheering me on. Gratitude and thanks to Janel Bakker, Courtney Pace, Michael Turner, Pete Gathje, and everyone from Memphis Theological Seminary who helped make my first teaching experience such a joy!

Thank you organizations such as Louisville Institute and the Forum for Theological Exploration: the former granted me a postdoctoral fellowship in which to begin this journey, and the latter surrounded me with friends and mentors who look like me and root for me.

To my sister in the world-altering journey of scholarship and teaching, Amey Victoria Adkins-Jones, thank you for being my unofficial adviser, friend, cheerleader, and big sister ever since our time at the University of Virginia! Your encouragement has lifted my spirits more times than I can count; and your brilliance is still a model for me of what can truly be.

To one of the most brilliant souls I have had the pleasure to teach, Jonathan Cabrera, thank you for your brilliance, curiosity, love for learning, and editorial prowess. Your (often thankless) service of turning a series of words and ideas into a cohesive composition is a gift.

And finally, to my family: thank you for always being excited about the twists and turns of this journey. I am beyond grateful that you always affirm me and always make me feel like I am on the right path. To Gbenga (Daddy), Iyabo (Mommy), Gbemi, and Tumi—thank you for being a light! To Kai, Mo, and Emi—know that a better world is possible. Go get it!

Mommy, this work is dedicated to you, is for you. Please know that I will always find a way to tell your story. This is only a start. Please walk with me as I venture into the rest.

INTRODUCTION

The Theology We All Need

Theology and Story

My family permanently moved to the United States from Nigeria in 1987, my siblings and I all under five years old. My parents were determined to build a life in America they would be proud of, one that would support my siblings and me and demonstrate to us that creating a new life was possible. The successful-immigrant narrative was one they believed in wholeheartedly and passed along to their children; it was what had driven my parents to leave the certainty of their country and culture, enter into the unknown world of America, and make it their home.

This trust in rooting themselves away from their first home was fed by the belief that if they worked hard and had faith, all would be well. The precepts of Christianity, that God would not leave nor forsake them, would be an important factor in their stay and sense of purpose in the U.S. If we worked hard, we would make ourselves into something in this country; we believed that God loved us enough to bestow good fortune upon us. Having faith in God and backing up that faith by doing the work would ensure that our circumstances would reflect the measure of our faith, a faith that grounded our ambitions.

In my upbringing, our Christianity was Nigerian, Yoruba specifically. Attributes of Yoruba culture made their way into how we talked

1

about God. Our cultural values blended with Christian principles, such as devotion to a higher power, revering elders, serving others, and living morally. Christianity elevated what we already knew was required to be a good and contributing part of the Yoruba community. But my curious mind also wondered: Was the inverse possible? In a culture that traditionally elevated men above women, could some of the adverse practices I witnessed in Yoruba Christianity be corrected by certain values of the Christian faith overall? Could Yoruba Christian culture learn from subversive Christian assertions such as that in Christ, power structures are inverted? In an African Christianity, which had the upper hand: traditional views enforced by ethnic culture or the radical pillars of the faith? Could the two coexist well? Not yet introduced to concepts like feminism, I often wondered what the mutual influence of Yoruba culture and Christian values would look like in my own formation, how they would work themselves out in my expression of Christianity as a Nigerian-American Christian female.

Raised in part in Nigerian churches, I repeatedly saw how we Africans practiced Christianity in a way that disproportionately benefited and elevated African men or, at the very least, overlooked African women outside of assigned service roles. My question about Christianity's influence on culture intensified: Could the core values of this faith tradition—radical demonstrations of love, intentional inclusivity, and overturning notions of power—address the inequalities embedded and normalized in my own culture? Could Christian values reform or reframe how oppressive ideas and actions entangled themselves into the lives of many Africans, especially women? Could Christianity teach my grandmother, my mother, my aunts, and me myself what freedom in Christ looked like from within the culture that formed who we were?

The church settings of my upbringing did not provide clear answers. My experiences in white, African American, and African churches illumined the complicated reality that African women were at the same time unseen and hypervisible, a foreign and exotic figure in non-African churches. In the African church, these women were both oppressed *and yet* presented with small opportunities for leadership in peripheral areas of service, such as hospitality and children's or women's ministry. What were African women supposed to make of these mixed responses to their capabilities and leadership, determined in large part by how others saw and responded to their bodies?

My questions about where to locate African women's voices in Christian theology took me toward graduate studies, but even in the theological academy it was clear that African women were not recognized as critical voices in standard Christian theological conversation. The problem was not that African women were not doing Christian theology, but that Western Christian theology did not make enough attempts to hear voices it had not already decided to recognize.

African women's visibility, or lack thereof, was an intentional disciplinary arrangement. The academy barely had the capacity to recognize and deal with Black American liberationist (largely voiced by African American men) and Womanist theologies already in front of them. Even today these discourses are still fighting to have equal space in standard theological education. It seemed less and less likely that theology from African women would have much space in the academy.

The African voices that were spotlighted, the Desmond Tutus or Nelson Mandelas—those who offered a peaceful, reconciling vision of African Christianity—were often approved by the Western academy's theological gatekeepers. African theology in the theological academy otherwise has primarily been framed and understood as non-Christian. Africans engaged in African spirituality or world religions against which Christianity could, undoubtedly, compare itself; Westerners did true Christianity. The position of African Christianity within the academy has long felt precarious.

But even if not formally recognized as such by the West, an African theological movement was happening on the continent. Critical voices such as Nigerian theologian E. Bolaji Idowu, Kenyan philosopher and priest John Mbiti, Ghanaian theologian Kwame Bediako, and Ghanaian theologian and priest Kwesi Dickson were authoring groundbreaking works about African syncretic, systematic, and contextual theologies, theologies that would compose the core of what would come to be considered modern African Christian theology.

Though they researched, wrote, taught, ministered, and theologized, the theological insights of these African men still did not make the global impression on Christianity they probably should have. Western theology championed by voices from places such as Europe and the United States had too much of a hold on the direction of theological conversation. Thus although they generated theology from the perspective of their respective peoples and cultures, African (male) theologians were not given the same recognition or respect as their European male counterparts.

African Christian theology emerged without the scholastic recognition due from those in the West. These men worked to defend their culture against colonial narratives that denigrated African identity; they worked hard to illustrate the theological nuance their peoples and cultures brought to the stories and ideas of Christianity. They worked diligently to show the world how they had made Christianity their own and how Christianity could be enhanced by the voices and experiences of Africans.

While vying for visibility, these men, unfortunately, overlooked their own women. African women were largely spoken for but not included within the scholastic representation of African theology. While representation would be a major concern of African women's theological visibility, so too would be the content of the theological ideas advanced by the African male representative voices. Many of these men, seeking to prove their ideas worthy of conversation with European (and continental African!) church fathers and theological giants such as Aquinas, Augustine, and Barth, deliberately conversed with such figures. They privileged European and Eurocentric scholarship and voices as dialogical partners, all the while arguing for the relevance of African perspectives and voices in theological study and education. African women would not miss the irony.

Though contextually proximate and ideologically working from similar starting points, African women would not be male African theologians' primary interlocutors. They would instead have to forge their way into conversations European men and African men were content to have without them. Idowu, who made a splash in the African theological scene in the 1960s, mentored a spirited Ghanaian student of Akan descent whose theological analytical prowess was undeniable.[1] Her name was Mercy Yamoah—later known as Mercy Oduyoye. Early in her studies one of Mercy's university professors, Noel Q. King, would encourage her to further her education around her theological interests. She did; and by utilizing her experience as an African woman as her primary lens, she found a way to impact how African theology is done and recognized on a global scale.

The Importance of African Women's Theology

Mercy's knack for identifying blind spots in African (men's) theology and Christian theology created a way for her to join systematic, contextual, African, feminist, and womanist theological conversations. Her greatest contribution, however, would be a theological hermeneutical genre she would help create out of the need for new interlocutors and content—a perspective that centered the experiences and wisdom of African women.[2] This genre of theology, African women's theology, sometimes called African feminist theology,[3] would be the corrective to African men's theology, encouraging African (men's) theology in a more inclusive direction, but it would also expand the conceptual bounds of Christian theology. African women were not only present in Christian theological conversation, her theological presence would insist, but they were also identifying new angles through which theological truths could be explored. African women's theology would be the representative voice of Oduyoye and countless other African women in need of a platform from which to vocalize their theological insights and push theology forward.

African women's theology creates room for African women not only to declare their voice and work as valid contributors to theological conversation but also to affirm African women's experiences as sound lenses through which one can know and describe the divine. It asserts that African women's voices are worth hearing and that the owners of those voices should be welcomed to pull up a chair at the table of theological exploration and join as equal contributors to the discussion. African women's theology reminds theologians of all stripes that Christian theology is broader than initially imagined and getting broader still. In order for Christian theology to scratch the surface of its findings, it must hear from itself, fully.

African women are Christians. They are theologians. Thus, African women bring contributions about God talk that no other people group will understand through their bodies in the way that these women do. African women's theology is a discourse of insightful, liberative, and prophetic charge. It represents a theological perspective every person involved in the scholastic and communal study and practice of Christianity needs. The inclusion of African women's theology in the dialogical canon of theological inquiry puts into practice the scriptural truth about the efficacy of the Christian body espoused in 1 Corinthians 12:20: "As it is, there are many members, yet one body."

For African women, the discourse of African women's theology became a place where they could feel included in conversations about what mattered in Christian theology. Theologizing attentive to African women's lives is not an armchair enterprise but fleshes out the movement of God in the world with actual lives in mind.[4] Christian theology, these women argue, at its core, connects well with the experiences of African women, women who know the stakes of having certain bodies in this world.

African women theologians, led by Oduyoye's charge, make it their task to put theology not only "on the ground" but also into the hands of women the rest of the world has forgotten. By inserting themselves into the conversation of how Christian theology is to be known and heard on the African continent and in the world, African women's theology is calling Christianity to higher account, for the message is not truly gospel if it is not for and from everyone.

Why *This* Story?

Often, people revere the contributions of a theological figure without examining the life events that brought them to such insights. To understand someone's theology, we must first sit at the feet of a life. African women's theology has a story of a life embedded in its founding, that of Mercy Amba Oduyoye. Outside of her own writing, few texts have done a full treatment of Oduyoye's life—this is a mistake, for telling her story can clarify the small details, insights, and tensions that sit at the heart of her theological beliefs.

The details of Oduyoye's story illumine what Christianity has taught her, what it has done for her, and what she insists it can do. Aspects of her cultural identity as an Akan woman of Southeast Ghana clarify why she positions God or Jesus in certain ways, how she argues that human beings' treatment of one another is at the heart of sound theology, and what she imagines the Christian church's task to be in the world. Her doctrinal interests are fed by her story.

Her life's details illuminate her understanding of how the divine works in tandem with the ordinariness of life. Her mother's identity connected to sentiments, feelings, and ideas that frame her God-talk. Oduyoye's educational background matters. The cultural and political messages she heard, from childhood through adulthood, contributed to the shape of her theological beginnings. Oduyoye's story begets her theological standpoint and reveals her attention to certain gaps in Western Christian (men's and women's) and African men's theologies.

Within Oduyoye's story are the beginnings of African women's theology, a theological position that rightly particularizes theology as reflecting African women's circumstances. Hearing Oduyoye's story helps those who are not African women know where to enter this conversation. Stepping into it encourages readers to suspend certain beliefs until they hear and learn the details of where her foundational truths were born.

The Scope of This Project

For too long African women have been at the bottom of the Western and African theological hierarchy. Less concerned with permission to exist in the theological conversation, African women's theology asserts that African women's voices are critical in the canon of Christian thought. It claims space at the theological table, rightly asserting the expansiveness of Christian theology, and its contributing voices must be given a platform.

Oduyoye formed a space for African women thinking theologically in 1989. This sacred and much-needed gathering allowed African women of various ethnicities and faiths to theologize about how the divine moves in and through their lives. This Circle of Concerned African Women Theologians—or the Circle, as it would be affectionately called—helped African women's theological voices grow in prominence and stature.[5]

In the formation of African women's theology and creating the Circle to affirm and grow such theological positions, Oduyoye helped African women not only pull a chair up to the table but fashion their own chairs! Since 1989, African women's theology, in its many shades, has boldly claimed its presence as necessary for doing theology from the African continent in a holistic way. Its sharp awareness of the lives and contributions of *all* persons in African communities affirms the African value system of appreciating the humanity of all persons in the community.[6]

African women bring modes of thought that only experience can invoke to the world of theological discourse; their daringness in assuming equal voices and parts for themselves in the Christian community is necessary. The promise of Christian theology requires the voices of its underside to speak. This is what makes Mercy Oduyoye's work so crucial. Oduyoye's work has made way for the stories of the marginalized to be heard. Her work provides correction to Christian and local cultures and also challenges these entities to operate with depth and awareness.

Oduyoye's work impresses on her readers questions about their own context and formation. She draws our attention to *our* theological location and asks about our proximity to others. Are we aware of where are we located, theologically, in relation to each other? To bridge the gap and close the distance, her work demonstrates, we must be open to hearing theology from voices for whom it deeply matters. We must hear from African women.

The Theology of Mercy Amba Oduyoye: Ecumenism, Feminism, and Communal Practice is my attempt to follow Oduyoye's cultural and theological journey toward *her* particular vocalizing of African women's theology. Her voice carries her stories, life lessons, and theological conclusions, as well as those of the women and men she has encountered, learned from, and mentored over the course of her lifetime. Her life's work reflects her theological journey.

This project explores Oduyoye's attempts to address African women's omission from African male and Western Christian theology, but it also explores her own constructive turns. I unpack four of Oduyoye's Christian doctrinal stances and in doing so illumine Oduyoye as a prime example of how African women are arbiters of practical theological ideas.

Oduyoye fully lives into that which she claims as theological foundation and truth—that women matter just as much as men to theological discourse, that African voices unveil theological truth just as prominently as Western voices do. Throughout her life she has worked to convince men and women alike that this stance reflects God's truths since the foundation of the world. Inclusion should be humanity's theological starting point; anything else is yielding to misdirection. Oduyoye's work proves that Christian theology is made richer when it includes and centers all of its members, especially African women.

Chapter 1 carefully examines Mercy Oduyoye's story, thus privileging story and narrative. From her birth story to her experiences in higher education, various details of Oduyoye's life foreground her interest in women's equality, an evolving form of African Christianity, and her eventual movement toward what she would call African women's theology.

Chapter 2 traces Oduyoye's feminist formation through the lessons of her culture and family. Narrative tone is important here as well. While chapter 1 overviews her life events, this chapter further unpacks what these lessons and moments meant for Oduyoye ideologically. Throughout her life, the women in Oduyoye's upbringing provided her the blueprint for imagining a world where African women would be heard and respected. In this chapter I explore some of the details of her matrilineal culture, but in doing so I reflect not only on how these cultural ideas illuminate barriers to women's autonomy but also on how they uncover places of empowering possibility. It is within Oduyoye's Akan culture where the women before her create and expose gaps and holes for Oduyoye to escape to and write a different life for herself and for those after her. The ideas and subversive practices of the women in Oduyoye's life cleverly frame a vision for women's empowerment that informs Oduyoye's theological thinking.

Chapter 3 begins to explore the effects of such thinking. I look closely at the timeline of Oduyoye's ecumenical work in order to connect these moments to the formation and practice of African women's theology. Her growing presence and influence in international circles led Oduyoye to create and dedicate her life to the flourishing of a circle of her own, the Circle of Concerned African Women Theologians. In this chapter, I tell the story of Oduyoye's ecumenical work toward her initiative to create and develop the Circle.

Chapter 4 steps into the content of African women's theology, directly examining Oduyoye's conception of the doctrine of God. For Oduyoye the question of God must be approached both from her African culture and through the narrative of colonialism in Africa. For an African Christian God to be possible, Western conceptions of a European God must be exposed and countered. Oduyoye positions the African context as one that, far from being a barrier to God as colonialism purports, affords rich opportunities for better understanding God, because in it African women can develop their own God talk. Central in exploring Oduyoye's doctrine of God are the problem of positioning God as Eurocentric, the use of gender in one's God talk, God's place in debates around plurality, and what lessons the Christian church can learn from the God who knows and sees African women.

Chapter 5 assesses another doctrinal area crucial in the life of Oduyoye and African women's theology as a whole: Christology. In studying the life and impact of Jesus, Oduyoye highlights similarities between Jesus' life and African women's lives. Jesus Christ is important to African women because of how his body and message were received and rejected in the world. African women know this all too well and emphasize Jesus as a figure in solidarity with them. Oduyoye's doctrinal emphases include women's role in naming Jesus Christ and communicating his charge to his followers, Jesus' marginalization as a point of contact with other marginalized communities, especially African women, and Jesus' means of subverting the systems, practices, and peoples who dismissed or sought to destroy his ministry. The parallel between African women's conditions and Jesus' hardships is convincing. African women have not missed the significant correspondence between a suffering savior and a silenced segment of marginalized peoples.

Chapter 6 looks at Oduyoye's theological anthropology as it relates to traditional Akan (Ghanaian, West African) conceptions of God, the self, and others. Within this frame, Oduyoye reflects upon divine order: in order for humanity to understand itself, it must understand its Creator. The fact that identities such as class, gender, race, culture, or ethnicity are allowed to cause a rift between human beings, alienating them from one another and from the earth, suggests that the core truths of theological anthropology must be revisited. Oduyoye's theological anthropology distinctly emphasizes coharmony among all members of the creation.

Chapter 7 wrestles deeply with questions of living as the Christian church. It focuses on Oduyoye's doctrine of ecclesiology. She centers African voices in order to construct a clearer picture of what a holistic ecclesial vision looks like, one that values the voices of its women. Women understand how notions of solidarity and connection matter for a sound ecclesiology. Inclusivity is not only a Christian enterprise. A Christian vision for the church must consider not only marginalized Christian voices but also non-Christian voices. Non-Christian voices must be part of the conversation about what God's creation could look like in the world today. An African woman's ecclesiology affirms that Christians need to learn from everyone in order to discern their purpose in the world today.

In Chapter 8 I ask further questions about what African women's theology can continue to teach the Christian church and Christian theology about itself and the world. I discuss areas of further conversation, including where questions of sexuality, male accountability, and African diasporic identity fit into the conversation of African theology and Christian theology, wholly. I ask where ethics fits in the scope of African women's theology and summarize Oduyoye's impact and legacy in the field of religious and Christian theological studies.

In the conclusion I reflect on how best to read Oduyoye. Her work urges the Christian church in the West to take off its blinders, understand its cultural and social systems, and open itself up to learn from marginalized voices. The challenge in reading Oduyoye is not in the concepts and ideas she offers, but in her call to readers to recognize the cultural conditions in which *their* respective theologies are formed. Oduyoye holds a mirror up to her readers and asks them to describe what they see.

For a collective, holistic Christian theology to exist in the world for everyone, the imagination of the Christian church must be stretched. Oduyoye's theology can contribute new ideas to how Christians typically engage Christian theology. Her theological voice must be made a standard part of the Christian theological canon.

Oduyoye's presence and impact in theological discourse is enormous. Entire swaths of voices would neither be heard nor recognized without her life's work and continuous efforts for theological equality, voices like Isabel Apawo Phiri and Sarojini Nadar. Because of Oduyoye's story, many other stories can be told. *The Theology of Mercy Amba Oduyoye* seeks to gather the stories of Oduyoye's life, the unfolding of her ministry, the content of her doctrine,[7] and the impact of her legacy in one place. A text of this sort is overdue. Oduyoye has forever changed the face of African theology for the better and has enhanced the influence of Christian theology in the world, and she has done so through being true to herself.

A credible lesson can be learned here: no matter how looming, intimidating, or scary, the truth deserves to be in the room—in discourse, in traditions, and in ideas. The truth carries within it realities that only make the world better. If this is not the heart of the gospel, the intention of life in God and life in Christ, then nothing is.

THE LIFE OF MERCY AMBA EWUDZIWA ODUYOYE

Entering a World: A Birth Story

On October 21, 1933, in rural south Ghana during cocoa harvest, a full-term Mercy Yaa Dakwaa Yamoah labored.[1] She continued working in her father's cocoa fields that day. Time passed and her labor intensified; Mercy Yaa was unsure she would make it. Her fortitude, however, was unyielding. She was determined not only to survive, but that her baby girl would, too.[2] Mercy Yaa safely delivered that Saturday, and, as is Akan cultural custom, eight days later the baby was named.[3]

Mercy Amba Ewudziwa Yamoah, bearing her mother's first name, was born amid labor and harvest. Her middle name, Ewudziwa, loosely translated to "strength," honors her paternal grandfather, Kodwo Ewudzi Yamoah, on whose property she announced herself to the world. Six months later, she was baptized.

"Mercy" and "strength" were names fitting for this girl. With a harrowing arrival, it was clear she was destined for a life of challenge, risk, and courage.[4] Mercy Yamoah, who would later become Mercy Oduyoye, arrived in the world under her own terms, her courage foreshadowing the force of her life's work. Her impact on both the Christian theological and African cultural landscape would be undeniable, even if overlooked.

The cultural parameters that helped determine Oduyoye's theological rationale—from her parents' viewpoints, her schooling journey, and the political moment surrounding Oduyoye during adulthood—all contributed to the women-centered voice around which she would anchor her theological message and catalyze the emergence of African women's theology.

Early Messages

Mirroring the fortitude and wit of her mother, Mercy Yaa Dakwaa Yamoah, and following the vocational footprints of her minister father, Charles Kwaw Yamoah, the daughter decided to craft a vocational direction that best suited her.[5] Her parents imparted a twofold message about the path to success: be attentive to the contours of the Christian faith, and be aware of the power of education to help create the life you want. Observant and keen, Mercy took in what they told and showed her.

For Charles, dedication to the Christian faith was principal. A Methodist pastor and theological educator, he prioritized his ministerial work, moving the family to multiple parishes in which he served. The mobility of the Yamoah family, living in as many as four or five mission houses during her childhood, proved fruitful for expanding his daughter's worldview.[6] Exposed to different tribes of Akan people from a young age, Mercy not only gained knowledge about, but also developed a keen appreciation for, the range of Ghanaian culture and heritage.[7]

Fervent dedication to both European and African Christianities also taught Mercy subtle lessons about the inner workings of gender, a lesson she would carry with her throughout her life. Though her father believed in gender equality and practiced it openly, her mother, Mercy Yaa, was impacted by Christianity differently. Mercy Yaa said that Christianity affected her life in such a way that, as a woman, she felt "lesser" than men. She "entered completely" into her husband's life, losing the distinctiveness of her own.[8] As his wife, Mercy Yaa became embedded in Charles's pursuits and interests.

Mercy Yaa was not properly recognized in the churches in which she served; though she served the Methodist Church as faithfully as her husband, she routinely received less recognition than the men—both European and African—in the church. In hope she thought that becoming Westernized would free her and other women from what Oduyoye calls "African sexism,"[9] but this would not be the case. The sexism was embedded too deeply.

Attuned to women's marginalization in their culture and church, Mercy Yaa imparted to her daughter an informal education about gender in the African church. Paired with Akan culture, the supposed values of the Christian church did not help Akan women but further subjugated them. This clash between a matrilineal, mother-centered Akan culture that did not always adhere to its claims and a European-patriarchal Christianity that wandered from its message of love for all taught Mercy Amba a harsh lesson in African women's (in)visibility in the Christian church and in African culture.

Though her mother continued to serve faithfully in the church, in many instances starting ministries within which women in the church could participate, the resultant experience clearly demonstrated how easy it was to erase Akan Christian women from the church's narrative.[10] Mercy Yaa and other women who served in critical ministerial capacities felt and named the danger of colonialism's influence on their culture. Christianity's arrival had brought something into Akan culture from which these women were afraid it could not recover. They lamented how "Westernization was teaching Africa the advantage of keeping women invisible"[11] not only through European men but also through African men. In dutifully practicing their spirituality, these women saw how African men were ignoring the core cultural principles of their Akan community—namely, in honoring their women. Mercy Amba watched this and learned early on that Christianity was not a salve for many of the African women of her mother's generation; it was a foe to be wary of and yet to be kept close.

Both Charles and Mercy Yaa imparted knowledge about their daughter's place in the world. While Mercy Amba internalized her mother's strength and experiences, her father's dedication to the faith fascinated her. A multilayered identity, attentive to gender and faith, helped the girl develop a firmer understanding of what it meant not only to be an Akan woman who was Christian but also an Akan woman privy to the benefits of certain systems, like education.

Educational Journey

The eldest of a Yamoah clan of six girls and three boys, Mercy Amba was encouraged to go to school. Education was too important to the Yamoah children's futures for each child *not* to have the opportunity.[12] Mercy Yaa knew this the most; her daughter recognized how the "sacrifices of [her] mother and her age-mates for their daughters' education paid off."[13]

Most of the Yamoah children went on to university.[14] All "grew up into key positions in church and society," later boasting careers in medicine, security, business, and the academy.[15] The Yamoah clan understood that access to a sound education could open doors to the life one wanted; with this in heart and mind, a young Mercy steered herself through the complex waters of school.

School for Mercy Amba was a door her parents had opened for her, but the details around access to education were most telling. While she would immerse herself in the educational opportunities presented to her, Mercy quickly learned that the social details surrounding the world of education piqued her curiosity most. Questions of educational and monetary access, the cultural diversity of Akan culture, and the life choices that women had in a postcolonial Ghana would all help forge her educational path.

Mercy attended elite Methodist schools as a young girl. She began at a Methodist primary school, then later matriculated to a presecondary Methodist school, Mmofraturo, in Kumasi, Ghana. It was in secondary school where she gained significant exposure to the culture of the Asante people, a large cultural subgroup under the umbrella of her Akan culture.[16] The school's curricular incorporation of Asante cultural knowledge helped Oduyoye increase her awareness of the range of Akan identity and culture.

She later attended the Methodist Girls Boarding School and went through secondary education at a boarding school in southeast Ghana, Achimota School, finishing in 1952.[17] Attention to Ghanaian culture was also an important emphasis at Achimota School. It stressed educational excellence through diverse curricular offerings and granted students the opportunity to learn the native Gã language (a Niger-Congo dialect known across Southern Ghana, including among the Akan). The observation that a "broad perspective of Ghanaian culture grounded the curriculum" stayed with Mercy Amba Yamoah and affected her deeply.[18] At Achimota School she learned to see all peoples, even within her cultural group. People of different backgrounds were not only important but also worth learning about and living among.[19] Shaped by African cultural practices and Christian ideals, she found that as her education progressed, so did her value system.

After secondary school Mercy Amba wrestled with her career choices, ultimately deciding to continue into higher education on the path to teaching. At the prompting of her father, "she attended the Teacher's Training College at Kumasi College of Technology (now the Kwame Nkrumah University of Science and Technology) in Kumasi" from 1953 to 1954.[20] After completing her Post-Secondary Certificate of Education (Teachers Certificate A, Ministry of Education, Ghana), she took a teaching position at Asawase Methodist Girls' Middle School in Mamfe, southeast Ghana, where she served from 1954 to 1959.[21]

For her undergraduate education, in 1959 she moved south and attended the University of Ghana in Accra. In 1963 she became the first woman to receive her bachelor's degree in religious studies from the university.[22] During this time, in 1961, she also received an intermediate bachelor of divinity degree, a divinity focus within the bachelor of arts degree, from the theology department of the University of London.[23] Mercy Amba chose this academic route out of a growing interest. Initially she had intended to study geography and economics,[24] but Noel Q. King, her church history professor at the University of Ghana, encouraged her to study theology. Motivated to understand Christian theology further, Mercy Amba studied for the Tripos Part III (a one-year master's-level program in the Cambridge educational system) in dogmatics at the University of Cambridge. In 1964 she graduated from Cambridge with her bachelor's degree.[25]

After Cambridge, Mercy Amba continued on the teaching path, gaining experience in the community. In 1965 she taught religious studies at Wesley Girls' High School in Cape Coast, Ghana (on the southern coast of Ghana). This teaching assignment was both challenging and edifying. She was inspired to think through and address issues concerning "the education of girls, teenage pregnancy, early marriages, rumours of abortions and occasional drop-outs for no apparent reason."[26]

Girls and women continued to be at the forefront of Mercy Amba inquiries. She often found herself asking about education's impact and purpose. She wondered what the church's role was in providing education for those on the fringe. Because the function of theology continued to be a burning focus, Oduyoye pursued another BA, this time in theology, graduating from Cambridge University in 1965.[27] She earned a master of arts in Christian theology from the same university in 1969, the year after she married Modupe Oduyoye.[28]

Having witnessed African Christianity's response to social ills, Oduyoye knew she had questions that needed answers: What was the Christian church's response to the plight of the poor? What did African Christianity have to say about Africa's problems, especially the concerns of its women? She spent significant time in academic spaces providing reflective and thoughtful responses to Africa's issues. She subsequently created scholarship to better express the difficulties her people were facing.

Oduyoye's search for answers allowed for an impressive yet unconventional intellectual journey and academic career. For decades she created theological content in local African and international spaces without having formally receiving a doctorate! Practical in focus, Oduyoye does not frame her work as an intellectual exercise but as a concrete, realistic response to crises faced by real people and communities, especially crises felt acutely by African women. Her academic and scholastic placements include a visiting lectureship/research position at Harvard Divinity School from 1985 to 1986,[29] the Henry Luce Visiting Professorship at Union Theological Seminary in New York from 1986 to 1987, a visiting position at Princeton Theological Seminary, and a visiting scholar position at Union Presbyterian Seminary in Richmond, Virginia.

Not earning a terminal degree has not slowed Oduyoye down nor dampened the growing force of her message. The ecclesial and academic worlds seem to agree. She has been awarded ten honorary doctorates: in September 1990 from the Academy of Ecumenical Indian Theology, in January 1991 from the University of Amsterdam, in 2002 from the University of Western Cape, and in 2008 from Yale University, as well as from institutions such as Chicago Theological Seminary, Stellenbosch, and the University of the Free State.[30] Oduyoye used and still uses education platforms to name and discuss the ideas and realities that matter to African women.

But the pursuit of education could only do so much for African women. Patriarchal cultural realities would still influence Oduyoye's ideological path. Growing up, she recalls, she experienced "discrimination both from her own Akan culture and from the Christian church."[31] Education alone would not be enough to effect change on multiple levels. It would, however, sharpen her awareness around the interconnectedness of issues and problems embedded in "African culture, Islamic norms, Western civilization, and the church's traditional antifeminism piled on African women."[32]

Stories of her upbringing helped determine Oduyoye's theologically inclusive approach. The memories of worrying about her financially insecure grade-school peers would stay with her throughout her life.[33] Critically assessing the notions of access and opportunity grew Oduyoye's consciousness. She realized economic and political opportunity were joined; she understood how gender dynamics and social practice worked in tandem. The political revolution in twentieth-century Ghana caught the attention of higher education students of Oduyoye's day. Many saw the issues present in their country as traceable to conflicting ideas of authority and its influence on social change. Political action and protest became the norm as students "demanded to know why they should not be involved in the processes that determined their lives and shaped the world."[34]

Oduyoye's own self-determination proved critical to where life would take her. She found herself a beneficiary of Ghana's political education programs; it was not lost on her that she was chosen to study at Cambridge as part of the government-initiated developmental efforts under the regime of Kwame Nkrumah, the president and prime minister of Ghana.[35] Her educational journey had political ties; the regime's focus on education training as a means of national influence provided her and others with a rare opportunity. Recalling the story of this revolutionary occasion, she notes: "The Kwame Nkrumah government was so focused on education, a lot of us got our secondary education more or less for free. Nkrumah always insisted that Ghana's independence meant nothing if the rest of Africa was not independent."[36] The impetus behind this education boom was that it would strengthen Ghana's continental and global influence. It would prove Ghana's success at self-management and demonstrate its ability to alleviate educational deficits in the country and around the African continent.

Oduyoye's expanding educational horizons were directly tied to a Pan-African effort. President Nkrumah offered free educational opportunities if the recipients taught anywhere on the African continent. Able to attest to the importance of a diverse worldview, Oduyoye took advantage of this offer, pursuing a few short teaching stints in neighboring country Nigeria.

Ghana was fighting for independence as Oduyoye came of age. Within this struggle, she witnessed the message of liberation not only in her mother's and Akan Christian women's concerns but also on a national and continental scale. Oduyoye recognized how this same energy for liberation and inclusion, especially of Ghana's women, could translate into matters of Christian discourse.

Oduyoye would receive an opportunity to test the union of Christian study with a message of liberation. Soon after moving to the Cape Coast of Ghana in 1966, she was invited to attend a conference sponsored by the World Student Christian Federation at the University of Ghana. Her presence was felt, and she would later become the first woman and first African to serve as president of this student organization.[37] From there her influence would grow to international proportions. Oduyoye would be invited by a representative of the World Council of Churches to attend its upcoming meeting in Switzerland. The objective of the meeting would be to explore the role of Christian education in encouraging ecumenism. These conference opportunities would be the seeds of Oduyoye's eventual and lifelong international and ecumenical work around the message African women had wanted the Christian world to hear for so long.[38]

Ghana's Political Climate

Oduyoye's longing for women's liberation had cultural, economic (in terms of educational access), and political components. The independence movement in Ghana would be a critical model to watch: Could

Ghana's restlessness on one side of history yield reward on the other? What did this independence movement have to do with how Ghana wanted to understand itself? What did it have to do with how the world would understand Ghana?

In order for "the powerless" to exist as themselves in the world, change had to happen. Ghana sought freedom from British colonial power to determine its own identity, to name itself and its contributions in the world. The country's fight for voice on a global stage was not too far off from African women's fight for visibility. Having a picture of Ghana's political path, then, is helpful in recognizing a model for Oduyoye's own pursuits.

To best understand Ghana's pursuit of independence we have to turn to the events of mid-twentieth-century Ghana, where the motions of an independence movement were well under way. This narrative, however, must first be appropriately positioned in the history of Ghana's original systems of governance. The spirit of independence emanating from the Gold Coast (which would later become Ghana) reflected an attempt to return to native practices of shared governance and communal responsibility.

Like many other precolonial West African societies, Ghana primarily functioned in tribal relational systems of governance. Members of tribes operated under certain beliefs around communal relations. This blueprint of relationship was often modeled through the home. Tribal life "represented, in Africa, a way of life in which certain kinds of relationships—the family, the lineage, or the clan—formed the bedrock of significant social interactions."[39] In precolonial Africa, one's tribal beliefs and rhythms constituted personal, familial, and social identity.

European models of political life, introduced through colonialism, would alter this tradition of centering communal relationship. These political structures in West African societies led to Africans practicing less self-government in the ways to which they were once accustomed. To be sure, Africa was not monolithic; its people largely lived and moved in ways particular to their context. But a reality that many Africans across the continent historically had in common was the impact of European rule in African social life. The domino effect of European political impact was one that political scientist David Apter describes as "a gradual redefinition of social life . . . occurring throughout the continent." He continues, "What happens in one area has its repercussion in others. People are less bewildered and less passive to European rule."[40] In other words, European forms of governance affected African societies in sequence.

Europeans, however, brought certain benefits with them to Ghana. Building schools, like Achimota, which Oduyoye attended in her childhood, was a primary one. But even assets like these had their liabilities to the Ghanaian people. Initiatives like Achimota School were founded upon forgetting or erasing the tradition and life of the people who once lived in the area on which a given school was built. Education of this nature more often than not expunged history and served as "the colonial government's attempt to compete with religious denominations in providing a first-class educational institution for its colonial subjects."[41] This meant that Achimota School, though a progressive example in some of its curricular choices, had a marred history. Achimota's conflicted presence proved that some educational institutions could, in the long run, be a source of harm and erasure.

With the spread of colonialism, tribal life in Africa would take a back seat to new modes of rule. Apter describes in detail the shift through which Africans, in being taught a new mode of governance, would adopt the governmental attitude of their colonizers:

> Authority patterns the West had established in Africa have succeeded in bringing forth new images as well as new gods. These new images increasingly reflect concern by African groups for greater freedom of action. Political autonomy has become an insistent theme. As the desire for autonomy sharpens, two great cultural traditions clash with one another. One points to the past, when tribal freedom represented a period of dignity and independence within the traditional pattern of life. The other points to a national future: instead of the tribe, the state; instead of the colonial administrator, the African politician; instead of the mission school, public secular education; instead of colonial status, parliamentary democracies.[42]

These political institutions would capture the imagination of some Ghanaians toward harmful ulterior ends. Political scientist David Kimble claims that economic development was a creative force by which the "individualist, competitive, acquisitive attitudes and values of the West were introduced into African society."[43] He reminds us that "the early European traders brought new means to wealth and power: their guns and gunpowder profoundly altered the balance of power among the coastal States with which they came in contact."[44] Colonialism's benefits were counterbalanced with violent agendas. This did not go unnoticed. African men witnessed how power was a means of creating change. Thus, many sought political power; some sought such power in order to liberate their people from colonial rule. This desire for power birthed numerous Ghanaian national political parties, many led by African men focused on the goal of Ghana's full independence from Great Britain.

Though the effects of Western colonial governmental power were felt all over the continent of Africa, I will focus on Ghana and one of its most influential leaders: nationalist political philosopher Kwame Nkrumah. Though his efforts would be short-lived, his tireless work to liberate Ghana and Africa from colonial rule would have an important effect on Oduyoye. His pursuits would have a major impact on Ghana's mentality of independence, especially on its women. For many Ghanaians and other Africans, Nkrumah modeled the path to liberation.

The Bearing of Kwame Nkrumah

Kwame Nkrumah reflected a swath of leaders who resisted Western colonialism and racism in hopes of reclaiming their country's autonomy and self-governance. Various voices and ideologues would arise, but one would emerge from the field as most influential. Leader of the Convention People's Party (CPP), the first prime minister of Ghana, and Ghana's eventual first president, Kwame Nkrumah appealed to Ghanaians because of his inclusiveness. He extended a unifying message of strength and solidarity in Ghana as well as across Africa.

Nkrumah sought the affirmation of Ghana's global greatness. In his presidential acceptance speech after Ghana gained independence, he stated, "My last warning to you is that you are to stand firm behind us, so that we can prove to the world that when the African is given chance [sic], he can show the world that he is somebody!"[45] He claimed a new

African in the world, an African "ready to fight his own battle and show that after all, the black man is capable of managing his own affairs."[46]

Curiously enough, theological messages were tied into the political movement of the time. Many in Ghana assumed Nkrumah's and others' liberative efforts to be God's will and intention.[47] No doubt, Nkrumah leaned on this theological help. For many in Ghana in the midtwentieth century, political action would be the means for God-ordained liberation to come about. Though Christianity came coercively with British colonizers to spaces like Ghana, liberation efforts showed how Christianity would later be contextualized to help Ghana's situation—turned around to be the interpretive force pushing back against British colonial presence and values. The Christianity brought to Ghana would soon be integrated into the life and desires of Ghana's people, eventually bearing a different message than its original colonial form. As the British imagined, their Christianity did not "take" in Ghana, since, as Ghanaians perceived it, Ghanaian cultural perception of Christian principles would become the very impetus for resistance against colonizers in Ghana's gospel message.

The political and social awakening in Ghana carried a tone of deliverance and redemption, evoking the biblical narrative of ancient Israel's exodus from Egypt. Many Ghanaians saw parallels between the liberation they were pursuing and the liberation of ancient Israel. Nkrumah claimed, "Nothing in the world can be done, unless it has the support of God."[48] Ghana came to feel that it needed—and to read itself as needing—its own exodus event. And the person who would bring Ghana out from under colonial rule, Nkrumah, was considered an agent in God's liberating action. Recognized as God-sent, Nkrumah saw the suffering of God's (Ghanaian) people and was, for the most part, given the good faith and permission of the people to lead Ghana out from under oppressive rule.

The "prince of African nationalism" fused Ghana's liberative claims with religious invocation: the inscription on a statue of him "stepping forward with one arm raised in salute and greeting"[49] read, "Seek you first the political kingdom and all other things shall be added to you."[50] The political message fused itself to a theological one: political influence could be utilized for and toward African progress under God, for Ghana's liberation was perceived to be God's desire.

Women's Empowerment under Nkrumah

Nkrumah's platform urged Ghanaians to govern themselves as they were capable. Under Nkrumah "foreign rule was overthrown in order to enable Africans to build up a new society."[51] Historian Ousman Kobo discerns the pattern of Ghana's political transition this way:

> The Gold Coast's political landscape was changing rapidly between 1948 and 1956. As the colony, now united with the Northern Territories, moved closer to independence, regional identities began to shape political configurations and identities of newly founded political parties. The National Liberation Movement and its predecessor, the United Gold Coast Convention, came to be dominated by Ashanti people, while the Northern People's Party (NPP) derived support primarily from the north. Only Kwame Nkrumah's Convention People's Party (CPP) transcended regional affiliations and drew significant support from all regions.[52]

On March 6, 1957, Ghana—the country formerly known as the Gold Coast—would gain its independence from Great Britain and join other African nations in organizations such as the Organization of African Unity "in order to break the monopoly and dominance of the North Atlantic in political and economic affairs of the world."[53] Nkrumah's decision to "form his own party to agitate for independence" helped give rise to a new political culture.[54] One thing he did was especially unheard of: he incorporated women into government through the parliament.[55] This strategy was intentional; he seized upon the political potential of the country and established a totalitarian regime toward socialist and emancipatory ends by unconventional means. And he included women in this vision toward Ghana's prosperity. Ghana's women certainly took notice.

Nkrumah's policies were designed to reach many. Ghana's empowerment led to a surge in new initiatives and inclusive measures, ones that involved the people most overlooked in Ghanaian society. African studies expert Takyiwaa Manuh explains, "Indeed, the CPP and Nkrumah introduced a new paradigm in Gold Coast politics when they implemented strategies to involve the youth, the grassroots, and women in mainstream politics."[56] The pattern, however, was telling of the complex dynamics of

gender in Ghana—a man ruled over a country in which some of his fierc-
est supporters were its women. Nkrumah saw and incorporated women
into the political vision of Ghana's emancipation, but his initiatives could
only reach so far. It remained to be seen if the radical action of one man
could change cultural perceptions of Ghana's women for good.

Women supported Nkrumah's campaign and message because it *appeared* to have made space for them. They were interested in being a part
of the decolonial struggle in seeking "self-government now."[57] Women
were able to hold positions in the party, recruit members to the Convention People's Party (CPP), and sponsor rallies; they did so "inasmuch as
independence sought to end colonial domination and create better conditions of life for the population in the form of more schools and hospitals, better drinking water and greater access to all of these amenities."[58]
Manuh reminds us that women had the most to gain from independence
and that Nkrumah sought to "raise the status of African Womanhood."[59]

Perhaps the greatest impact of this political moment was Nkrumah's
focus on providing educational opportunities to all, especially to girls.
Certainly Oduyoye benefited from such opportunities. Schools and universities received girls and women at record rates. Women's training colleges were opened. By the end of Nkrumah's administration, many women
had professional and governmental positions.[60] Women's empowerment to
work under and alongside Ghanaian men would make a lasting impression on how women would perceive what was possible for them.

However, though his efforts propelled Ghana into social, political, and
economic change and mobilized many Africans continentally and globally,
Nkrumah was overthrown on February 24, 1966. His reign appeared too
unstable and totalitarian for some.[61] Ghana would undergo multiple shifts
in government until civilian rule took root in the early 1990s.[62]

Nkrumah's impact on women would be tremendous and long-
standing, but his support for women would not be enough to overturn
the patriarchal barriers still present to many women within their own
cultures.[63] Women would still have to wrestle with the ills of colonialism
alongside the patriarchal traditions of their cultures and country. Their
world would still primarily be a man's world. The contradictory messages
of empowerment alongside gender hierarchy would color the story of
many Ghanaian women.

Some women, however, took hold of this reality to craft their *own* movements. One such woman is the focus of this work, Mercy Amba Oduyoye. An Akan woman born into a powerful class of self-assured women and to a preaching father, she would consistently raise her voice to insist on men and women's equality in a culture that spoke of but could not properly demonstrate its values of communal care and wholeness toward its own women. Oduyoye's voice would provide a much-needed challenge to a contradictory Akan cultural history claiming to uplift the communal whole while simultaneously yielding to gendered practices of exclusion. Her theological voice would, further, assert the full value of all persons, not solely those whom the Christian church chose to acknowledge or recognize.

As we recall, African women were deeply impacted by and greatly benefited from Nkrumah's rule. He lit a fire of indignation in the people and proved Ghanaian women valuable to social and political change. Mercy Oduyoye would ride and be raised by this wave of empowerment. Under Nkrumah's regime Oduyoye would learn that the message of liberation belonged to African women as much as it belonged to African men. Within this moment in history Oduyoye embraced educational opportunities and clashed with the patriarchal logic still present in her culture and in demonstrations of the Christian faith. She advocated for the well-being of all but would still run up against both colonial and cultural preservationist attitudes and beliefs. This intersection is the place in which we are introduced to matrilineal figures and lessons in Oduyoye's life that would contribute to her feminist formation.

CHAPTER TWO

A FEMINIST EMERGENCE

Ideological Formations

Finding Meaning

We do not learn about gender by ourselves. We learn it from others, *with and because of* others. Gender pedagogy is a communal exercise; we learn what gender is, how it functions, and what it means for our life from those closest to us—from family, from our community, and from our society.

For Mercy Oduyoye the question of gender is one deeply tied to the message of womanhood, as even being a woman is characterized by cultural and ethnic markers. Gender-marked, the question of womanhood only makes sense when asked amid others. Oduyoye's notion of "woman/women" would be complicated and determined by her culture's understanding of women and by which parts she took to heart. Her theology pushes the question and function of gender into another realm: Should women accept the gender narrative handed down to them, or should they trouble its incomplete and limited aspects? How do divine association or implications complicate a gender trajectory? How can women be women the way God sees them? For Oduyoye, gender conversations have always intersected with the theological ones. To best understand the shape of her feminist theological consciousness, we first turn to the conversation on gender within Oduyoye's Akan culture.

29

Akan culture taught Oduyoye the details of her identity as an Akan Christian woman. But the ordering of her identity was not so easy to parse out; certain aspects of her identity superseded, and even determined, others. Oduyoye did not learn she was a woman, then Akan— she learned about womanhood *because of* her Akan identity. She learned the boundaries of gender through Akan culture. She would later wrestle with where Christianity fit into the order of her identity, for Christianity was tertiary to her sense of womanhood and tribal identity.

Akan Cultural Signposts

The Akan people of Ghana hold a fixed, traditional view of gender: biological males, considered men, and biological females, considered women, function in society in particular and customary ways. Women are expected to marry and have children. It is a matter of religious duty.[1] Men are expected to lead in the various facets of their people's lives—in the household, in religious life, and in the community at large.[2] While some could call this ordering assimilation into typical gender roles, it is easy to envision and assume a role-infused understanding of manhood and womanhood within patrilineal and patriarchal social and cultural parameters, especially Western ones. The Akan notion of social relations is not Western. Gender roles are nuanced and made more complex because of matrilineal, or "mother-right," culture.[3]

Matrilineality is "a social system that emphasizes interactions between matrilineal kin, i.e. individuals related only through females."[4] This system includes women's influence in political matters as well as "inheritance of property and descent."[5] The Akan believe that one's descent and one's lineage are traced to the mother's side. A child then, whether male or female, "belongs to the mother."[6] As opposed to patriarchal and patrilineal identity, matrilineality ensures that one's strength and identity are directly connected to the bloodline of one's mother, or "the uterine line," as Christine Okali cleverly describes it.[7] Akan women are primarily honored as crucial members of society through a cultural reality tied to their bodies, for their bodies are extremely critical for the wellness of the community.[8]

Although women are, in this way, admired and relevant, it is important to clarify that matrilineal culture does not necessarily mean matriarchal culture. Women's importance in Akan cultural belief does not include all-encompassing "control" of the people's cultural beliefs or practices as a whole. Though women's influence can be seen in many parts of the Akan community, their presence does not automatically translate into total communal influence or power.

Matrilineal identity must be distinguished from matriarchal practice. The former alludes to kinship structure and its social expressions and impact. It emphasizes "one or more social domains, including the norms regulating inheritance, succession to office, marital residence, authority within the family, and descent."[9] Matriarchal practice refers to overarching cultural structure and its implications for the communities therein. Anthropologist Ifi Amadiume, who has explored matriarchy among members of the matriarchal Igbo tribe of Nigeria, has concluded that matriarchy is culturally determining. It is a means of social kinship that implicates the cultural framing as a whole. Women in matriarchal cultures are "cultural producers and leaders."[10] Among the Akan, the same may not fully be true; this is so because Akan women cannot determine culture. They sit high in it, but Akan men are the dominant cultural decision-makers.[11]

Akan women hold a place of unique genealogical importance among their people, to be sure. This woman-affirming foundation of Akan culture is promising: the full determination of anyone's identity—their family, or *abusua* (house)—grants Akan women immediate and permanent ontological importance. It is significant that they ensure the continued existence of the people as a whole. This cultural relevance empowers Akan women to be viewed as fundamental components to Akan cultural life. Critical figures such as the queen mother, symbolically vital in the social and political affairs of the Akan, announce that Akan women bear importance in the culture equal to that of men, if not greater.[12] Women are arguably positioned as central in the Akan's sociocultural structure. Because of the expressed social order of their importance, Akan women hold to and believe in the heart of their culture, even if they wrestle with its questionable positions. Oduyoye was not exempt from such acceptance and wrestling.

As she grew up, the complex aspects of Akan matrilineality made Oduyoye curious about and suspicious toward matrilineal and patriarchal culture alike. Though her instinct and position in life taught her to consider matrilineal and patrilineal (and subsequently patriarchal) culture to be polar opposites, life events told her differently. Matrilineal culture was more complex than it was initially letting on. Oduyoye saw it—she saw the dual message of Akan women's empowerment and entrapment through the gender lessons of her parents. She would eventually come to better understand women's importance in empowering potential, but she also gained clarity about her theological position through her experience of marrying into patriarchal culture. Her theology would hold these tensions as well. African culture was full of contrasts; her theology would question and hold the tensions of her culture.

The Matrilineal Puzzle

Anthropologist Laura Fortunato explores a mystifying dynamic in matrilineal culture that, it can be argued, Oduyoye found herself facing. Though matrilineal culture elevates its women, it does not fully account for the place of men in the culture. This leads to practices of isolation and discrimination in one's total familial structure and opens the door for patriarchal habits and practices. This phenomenon of the indeterminate place and relevance of men in the culture is called the "matrilineal puzzle." Fortunato explains: "Unlike alternative arrangements (e.g. allocation based on patrilineal kinship), matrilineal kinship organization may involve conflict between the interests and responsibilities of men in their roles as brother/uncle versus husband/father, especially where men hold control of the resources (i.e. resources proceed *between males*, but *via* females). The notion of the 'matrilineal puzzle' . . . captures the potential for tension inherent in the matrilineal arrangement."[13] Akan women's influence only extended so far. Since the men did not know where to consider themselves in the kinship structure, they created their own place and permanence; they would not be forgotten.[14] This led to social practices of imbalance that ultimately left women valued in name alone. Akan men found their value in serving as leaders in the community. This slowly erased women from positions they once occupied and erased the influence they once held.

Although as an adult Oduyoye became a fierce advocate of her matrilineal culture, as a child she saw the cracks in it. She realized that matrilineal culture was not as empowering for women as Akan women originally thought. Patrilineal complications in her own life led Oduyoye to face these cultural questions and concerns firsthand. At times her relationship to her father's side of the family felt isolating. While with them she felt that she and her siblings had no place. She recounts, "Outside the group [of my mother's family line] I was a non-entity, or so I felt."[15]

We see the roots of the "matrilineal puzzle" within Oduyoye's family. The honoring of matrilineal lineage left significant gaps in how to consider patrilineal relations. Her gender further complicated the matter—not that she and her siblings felt unwanted by her father's family, but that the girls were viewed as lesser in the communal imagination. The sexism of matrilineal Akan culture bled through. It expresses preference for male children over female children, so much so that when a woman bears a male child, it is commonly said that she has given birth to a human, but if she bears a female child, no such compliment is extended. The implication is unfortunate: in having a girl, one has birthed a nonhuman.[16] The embedded sexism cannot be ignored.

It became clear pretty early in Oduyoye's life that matrilineal culture was not exempt from falling into patriarchal practice. Growing up, she "had serious questions about how the African principles of complementarity and reciprocity operated in a hierarchy."[17] Were Akan women as valuable as Akan men? It would, however, take time for Oduyoye to openly name and condemn the contradictions in her culture. She wrestled with how a cultural belief that uplifted women could also hold them back. Later in life she would find herself wrestling again; marriage into a patriarchal culture would expose her to this world.

Marriage and Cultural Clashes

Akan culture's puzzling elements did not deter Oduyoye from praising its positive features. Although her matriarchal culture had its blind spots,

Oduyoye's own experience in that culture would not be the worst experience of patriarchy she would know. African patriarchal culture opened her eyes to the critical need for women's autonomy in Africa as a whole.

Oduyoye's feminist consciousness sharpened when she married a Nigerian man. His culture showed her firsthand patriarchy's dangerous effects on women. "Coming into contact through marriage with the patriarchal Yoruba culture of Nigeria was a traumatic experience," she recalls.[18] It was a culture that "counts fathers and ignores mothers."[19]

Mercy married late according to Akan culture, at age thirty-five, to Modupe Oduyoye—a storied linguist, renowned publisher and writer, Yale graduate, and self-identified Anglican, who—most importantly—was a man of Yoruba descent.[20] It was in marriage to Modupe that Oduyoye first witnessed the routineness of severe gender inequality.[21] In the patrilineal and patriarchal Yoruba tribe of southwestern Nigeria, traditions and customs privilege men over women. The starkness of this contrast to the matrilineal cultural values of the Akan not only shocked Oduyoye but also appeared to be in direct opposition to her life experiences as an Akan woman.

In Yoruba culture a woman is considered important primarily in subservient roles. She must manage domestic life and know her place "in her husband's house,"[22] whereas in Akan culture, women are considered critical to political life as well as to the home life.[23] Oduyoye was not accustomed to nor interested in succumbing to the expectations for women in Yoruba culture. For her, the positive aspects of the Akan's matrilineal culture—though it had its own challenges—trumped the practices and beliefs of the Yoruba.

While she claims her marriage to a Nigerian man marked an important moment of her feminist awakening, Oduyoye also recognizes her own culture's blind spots, where "boys and men tend to predominate."[24] She maintains that "the identity and autonomy of women fare not much better today under the matrilineal systems of the Akan group than under the overt patriarchies of southern Nigeria, and most particularly, the patriarchal system that operates among the Yoruba."[25] The two cultures were not very distinct in their treatment of women after all.

Oduyoye's awareness of the controversial practices within her own culture was, in many ways, sharpened *through* interrogating the practices of Yoruba culture. Her 1995 work *Daughters of Anowa* explores patriarchy's reach and how she came "to realize that by looking more critically around us, as well as deeper into our history, we can be motivated and empowered to create structures that obviate all that we have denounced in patriarchy."[26] Oduyoye's experience with patriarchal practice in African culture, with its matrilineal and patrilineal iterations, catalyzed her theological mission to discern where women's empowerment in African culture and Christianity could come from and how it might manifest.

Akan Feminism: Foundations of Akan Womanhood

Blood is not thicker than culture. For the Akan, one's gender has the greatest influence in one's social life. Oduyoye learned her place in the world from how her father and mother related to the Christian faith from the space of their identities. Early in life she wrestled with the social role of Akan women in a culture that too often privileged the patriarchal aspects of Akan culture and Western Christianity over the best of its matrilineal sensibilities. It was perplexing that women were being treated as inferior to men in a culture that professed that women were critical to the literal lifeblood of the people.

The challenge Akan women faced was twofold: it was not simply Christianity they were wrestling against, but Akan Christianity. As a young girl Oduyoye learned about Christianity's biased gender practices against African women. The Christian faith did not seem to bring them a message of hope and freedom but to push them further to the margins of their own culture. Though it had opportunity and impetus to eradicate the negative aspects of Akan culture and Christian practice, Akan Christianity did neither, but seemed instead to combine the oppressive aspects of the two.

To Akan women it was clear that the *Akan* Christian faith tradition and practices were no different from Western versions of Christianity that disregarded women of Western cultures. Though women were some of Akan culture's most faithful advocates, they had limited input and impact on what Akan Christian tradition would be. Their matrilineal position did not necessarily generate matriarchal power. Akan men determined the

Akan Christian message and praxis. Even so, other ways for Akan women to consider their personhood existed outside of rigid faith frames. Akan women crafted their own ideas of themselves. This was the case for Oduyoye, who developed her theological prowess in large part by reflecting on lessons from her father, mother, and other women in her life and on the cultural significance of maternal imagery.

What Father Taught: A Childhood Lesson

Oduyoye's mother taught her to hold her relationship to Christianity loosely and in healthy tension. But it was not Oduyoye's mother alone who impacted her analytical eye; her father's faith also influenced her own faith. His passion for the church and the people played a large role in Oduyoye choosing theology as a career path.

Oduyoye became an educator and theologian in large part because of her father. Women were typically limited to the few career choices of becoming nurses, secretaries, or teachers at the time. Mercy decided to listen to her father's advice to pursue teaching—a talent that would later prove helpful to her.[27] A former schoolteacher himself, Charles Yamoah recognized his daughter's potential and encouraged her forward.[28] And Mercy excelled.

Following closely in the steps of her father, Oduyoye became a Methodist mainly because of her paternal grandfather, Kodwo Ewudzi Yamoah, and grandmother, Martha Aba Awotwiwa Yamoah, affectionately known as Maame. They founded a Methodist church in Asamankese.[29] Women came to the church because of Martha's "love for and creativity at weaving Mfantse lyrics"[30]—Mfantse being Oduyoye's native tongue. The Methodist church Charles Yamoah's parents founded would be central to Charles's life and later become critical to his daughter's identity as well.[31]

The child of a minister, Oduyoye saw how the church influenced social identity. One of her earliest, most memorable moments came during a Palm Sunday. Mercy, not quite twelve years old, was tasked to recite the Gospel scripture reading in Mfantse.[32] She succeeded in doing so but was admittedly less interested in the religious meaning of the moment than in the details surrounding it. The "who," not the "what," of that church moment reigned supreme. At the heart was a spirit of achievement; Oduyoye wanted to make her father proud.[33] But I suggest perhaps there was more behind this event. Perhaps this recital moment is etched into Oduyoye's memory because of what her performance signified. The repetition of words in a certain form—her father's word-form, in particular—heightened her socioreligious consciousness, because this moment reflected recognition of a proper (and dominant) form of vocalizing, of Akan voice, in the church.

Oduyoye recalls the minutiae of this memorable moment: she rehearsed the scripture relentlessly, with "the right pauses and intonation," so that she could say it "exactly as Papa would have read it."[34] The entanglement of her faith with the desire to emulate her father rings clear: she wanted to sound like this man. Did she do it correctly? Did she read the passage enough like her father? The message behind the message seems important: Did the young Oduyoye sound authoritatively *male*? Christian enough? African enough? African Christian enough?

Connected less to linguistic analysis and more to cultural commentary, this incident is, I think, a salient moment in Oduyoye's theological path. We must pay attention to why one of her greatest church memories is interwoven with her father's expectations. Or at the minimum, we must be alert to her perception of right church presence being so closely aligned with her father's practice (and performance) of his faith.[35] In this instant, African gendered identity and Christian commitments converge and are intricately woven together. The moment reads as gendered in so many ways. The force of Oduyoye's tongue is pressured to mimic male diction, an African Christian maleness that is, in itself, a mimicry of European Christian maleness.[36] The complexities are profound, and the questions surrounding them critical to acknowledge: Can an African woman achieve such a feat—can she sound like an African man? Questions of whose Christianity, whose tradition, arise. What manner of Akan womanhood is this, that it aims to mimic a maleness that, in many ways, cannot be copied? It is a wonder what message of Christian personhood and theological appropriateness configured itself into Oduyoye's memory when performance and sacred event converged at the site of her father.

The intersection of her father's image and Akan Christian womanhood must be explored; it is an important and early memory of where

African body and voice fit in the function of Christian idea and practice.[37] Oduyoye's performing Christianity in such a way opens up numerous questions. Who was honored more—Akan culture as a whole
or its patriarchal features? Did Charles want his daughter to perfect and
thus honor her mother tongue, or were his aspiration and hers of two different sorts? Was the repetition of word and form an ode to *Charles's* performance of Christianity? What was being perfected in Oduyoye's word?
Did this performance exceed her father, her grandfather, and reach back
into something more ancient? During this moment of recollection and
remembrance, what did Oduyoye's memorization mean to the conver-
gence of colonialism, Christianity, and Akan culture? And where did
Akan womanhood fit in with everything? Was there space for women in
that moment, and if so, where? Could women be lost between the into-
nations of their own mother tongue, or was this recitation a moment for
women to gain their own "pronunciation"? Was this moment an open
door for women to introduce their own mode of Christian voice, or was
it a means to reinforce performances of male Christianity?

Given that some of her earliest church memories include a "white
male image of liturgical leadership" that reluctantly gave way to "African
male leadership," the question of male leadership is an important one. If
African women were not included in leadership as African men began
gaining prominence in African churches, how does this imagery influence a young girl who wants to be like her father? Was the way to beat
the paternalism aimed at African women from both white men and their
own men to act like them—to *become* them?[38]

Questions abound, but overall it is clear that this Palm Sunday moment captured Oduyoye's attention and remained a core memory. In this
moment the question of what or whom Akan women were being dis-
cipled toward came alive. Though enthralled with the Christian faith in
her childhood, Oduyoye was first becoming a believer of inquiry. Her
admiration of the faith did not always mean total acceptance of it—at
least in its limited iterations. The structure of the faith blossomed questions within her. How could Akan girls and women find ways to have
voice in their culture and community?

Oduyoye's message about the weight and place of Akan women's
voice in society and the church would take a different form than her

father's message—in some ways, Oduyoye turned in a more cautious direction. She would pay greatest attention to the influence the women of her family held in *their* Christianity, because these were the dynamics most interesting to her. Remembering their experience, her mother and the women before and around her introduced Oduyoye to a position of healthy skepticism toward Akan and Western Christianity. Oduyoye was taught that when encountering the intersection of faith and culture, she ought to trust her sensibilities as an Akan woman over anything else.

What Mother(s) Taught: On Mothers and Christian Skepticism

In matrilineal culture, the bloodline of one's mother is seen as a literal life force. One's connection to one's mother, in part, determines one's connection to the people.[39] On her mother's side, Oduyoye is linked to the royal Asene family, who later migrated to Akyem in the eastern region of Ghana. Her maternal grandmother, Awo Yeboaa, was given in marriage to Ampofo Amenano, from the Brong Ahafo region in Southern Ghana. They settled in Asamankese, became cocoa farmers, and later converted to Christianity. This conversion, however, would be difficult due to Ampofo's run-in with a particular Protestant denominational sect.[40]

Grandfather Ampofo lived in Asamankese until the Presbyterians, the predominant Christian sect in that area at the time, "enforced a regulation that all who had not converted to Christianity should move out."[41] He resisted valiantly, holding tightly to the Akan traditional belief system, but eventually converted to Christianity of his own accord.[42] He "did not move to the Basel Mission ghetto," the church's designated housing area into which many Brong peoples were syphoned, but relocated elsewhere.[43] Grandmother Awo played a part in this departure as well. It was clear that neither Ampofo nor Awo was going to let the Presbyterians tell them who to be or where to go. They both refused to submit to either Presbyterian command or ideology. Generations later, Oduyoye would follow suit.[44]

Like her maternal grandparents, Oduyoye would control and determine her own Christian identity. She "has refused to become a ghettoed Methodist," religious studies scholar Elizabeth Amoah affirms.[45] Oduyoye would not be displaced like many Akan were. She joined the Christian church to improve it, not assimilate to it or be controlled by it. Her refusal to be told where to live and how to live by Christian forces, missionary or otherwise, colors the feminist nature of her theological ideas.

The resistance posture of the women in her life—from her grandmother to her mother—would teach Oduyoye how to claim her religious agency. It was not lost on Oduyoye's mother, Mercy Yaa, that Akan women were receiving the short end of the stick from both Europeans and Akan men who claimed to be arbiters of the Christian faith. Women would have to make up this ground elsewhere—namely, through their own self-determination.

The women in Oduyoye's life taught her to approach the Christian faith with a lens of skepticism. This "hermeneutic of suspicion" was not taught to her in a classroom or even termed as such; her inclination to question Christian ideas and practice ran through her matrilineal bloodline, a bloodline descending from both Asante and Brong subgroups of the Akan. "The Asante is a very culture-conscious group, matrilineal and not easily impressed by other peoples' way of life, not least the western Christian culture," Oduyoye asserts.[46] Because of her ethnic and tribal identity, Oduyoye learned where to trust and where to question, how to survive and whom and what to resist.

Oduyoye's matrilineality worked in empowering ways for her. She would not be prone to blind acceptance of Christian practices. The women in her life taught her to question and resist them. They showed that although they had welcomed it, the Akan did not need Christianity to lead meaningful lives.

Oduyoye's maternal line is the strength of her identity. Akan women resist the growing patriarchal aspects in their culture by asserting their value as more than wives and mothers. They assert themselves as leaders in every facet of life, able to determine and influence the wellness of a community.

Oduyoye knows that she comes from women who know their value and place, who understand their worth and believe in it enough to act upon it. All the women in her life who nurtured her worldview—her "mothers"—were women who knew who they were and passed their self-affirmation down to their daughters. These women were deliberate in deciding whom they would give themselves to and how. In honor of Akan culture, they practiced valuing themselves. The wisdom from these "mothers" taught Oduyoye to question Akan culture and the Christian faith; and as an Akan woman, she was right to listen to her maternal elders. "My feminist heritage," she offers, "was heightened not only by being my mother's daughter but also by growing up in the Asante and Brong areas in Ghana. . . . I am an African woman who is Christian."[47]

This ordering is noteworthy. Oduyoye's African identity determines her Christian identity, her Akan womanhood (as she exercises it) being the centripetal force of her theological thoughtfulness. Oduyoye actively privileges the wisdom from her mother's ancestral side because of Akan women's problematic treatment in her culture, but also because of her desire for her culture to privilege its women as critical agents.[48]

Her mother's side of her family, historicized as strong-willed, was, quite importantly, skeptical of Christianity because of its colonial practices. Mercy Yaa, never afforded a formal education due to the "elitist educational system set up by the missions," did initially see Christianity as a means of salvation (through educational means and access), but as quite unreachable for herself and for other women like her.[49] Akan women were already culturally directed to invest their lives in their male spouses and children, particularly the male children. This feature of Akan culture saw service to God as above women's well-being. Though they desired their own sense of wellness, Akan women's thriving and wellness were not prioritized in the community.

It is no surprise that the women in Oduyoye's family were dissatisfied—dissatisfied with their place in the Akan cultural order of things and dissatisfied in serving in subservient church roles. Mercy Yaa wanted her daughters to be able to lead a life free of patriarchal and colonial control.[50] She and her generation believed somewhat in the "worthwhileness" of the church, but they also believed in the potential of the women who would come after them to change it.[51]

Oduyoye describes herself as both an Akan woman and a Christian woman, but most notably an Akan woman raised to view Christianity with a watchful and critical eye. This watchfulness is warranted. The colonial Christian faith tradition did not alter Akan women's situation or place in society, but, arguably, further marginalized them. What Akan women's skepticism illustrates is not a divided identity or loyalty, but a multiplicitous identity, and a hybridization. It is illustrative of how many Africans already live into their identities as Christians. Akan culture and its Christian expression required Oduyoye to ask how she could honor her identity as an Akan woman who is Christian.

Oduyoye's mother taught her to protect her Akan womanhood, to keep it distinct from the Christian religious tradition. She learned from the women in her life and lineage that keeping her identity unblemished and unaltered was of the utmost importance; her Akan identity *already was* before Christianity met them. Her identity neither came from nor started with European religious claims on her people. Oduyoye's inherited resistance and theological voice emanate decolonial and feminist practice. Her resistance and voice not only assert the validity of African voice but also move against cultural patriarchal norms.

Theologically Oduyoye is determined to "carry on a tradition of ensuring life-centeredness in the community."[52] What might this life-centeredness look like? Perhaps honoring facets of her culture that respect the entire community, especially traditions that do not erase its women. The least Oduyoye can do is what her mother and the mothers before taught her: refuse your erasure by asserting your presence.

Mercy Yaa taught her daughter to speak for herself.[53] Akan culture's gendered expectations were secondary to Oduyoye's own self-fulfillment and self-actualization. This self-awareness introduced Oduyoye to the notion of mothering herself, a reality I will explore in depth later on. Resisting patriarchal assaults to their maternal-focused culture would be part of this movement. True to form, Oduyoye's theological work resists patriarchal and colonial presence, forces, and pressures. Being an Akan woman meant holding on to a particular sense of agency, apart from cultural postulation.[54] Akan women are autonomous beings with desires of their own; they are critical to Akan culture beyond anatomical expectations alone. Women are important because they are human beings. Oduyoye's mother imparted to her what can be argued to be a sound Akan feminist theological anthropology.

Colonial Christianity pushed back against this. Its message did not sit well with Oduyoye, for the message she received was that to be a viable Christian meant one had to exclude certain aspects of African identity.

Oduyoye's theology would resist this Christianity. She created a different Christian theological viewpoint that pointed toward both a hopeful faith tradition and cultural consideration of all its members.

Wanting to live in the liminal spaces of identity and agency, Oduyoye openly questioned and examined whether her Christian identity and African identity could coexist. She rightly asked: Given the gendered and colonial nature of the faith, what did Akan Christianity mean for Akan women? She reflects on this intersection in her essay "Be a Woman, and Africa Will Be Strong," from *Inheriting Our Mothers' Gardens*: "Living out my Christianized Akan background, I have never ceased to dig around that culture in search of my mother's specifically Asante and Brong backgrounds, the side of the family that was not as completely sold on Christianity as other branches seemed to be."[55] Though they identified as Christian, many Akan women would not be so at the expense of their culture. At her mother's instruction, Oduyoye privileged who Akan womanhood told her to be; she let this facet of her identity inform her relationship to others. For Oduyoye, Christianity's suppression of both African culture and African women was a telltale sign that she ought to engage it cautiously.

Those of us who do not identify as African women would do well to notice what the particularity of identity unveils—notably, the tendency to assume that "African" is to be an adjectival modifier of "Christian identity." Oduyoye's Africanness stands on its own as the most important aspect of her identity. Our understanding of her theology is enriched once we consider that her Akan womanhood determines her Christian identity and practice.

The women in her life taught Oduyoye to be a culturally critical disciple. The descriptor "Christianized-Akan" illumines the source of her worldview. Her Akan identity should order our understanding of her cultural formation as a woman and thinker. In recognizing this order we glimpse the dynamism of her identity. We see Oduyoye's feminist sensibilities most clearly when we keep in mind that her Christian identity grew through both her father and her mother, but that a firm sense of her Akan identity came through her mother(s).[56] An Akan woman who is also Christian and keenly attentive to issues of gender equality, Oduyoye developed a perspective that is distinguishably African feminist.

Ulterior Maternities

Literal bloodlines are not the only way Akan women continue the life of their people; they also mother subversively. The physical childbearing and child-rearing aspects of motherhood are only one such kind of maternity. Broadening the idea of motherhood to women's social connection and impact, however, bears remarkable fruit; it serves as an entryway into more progressive discussions around Akan women's value. A generative conversation is emerging around African women's ulterior maternities. If reconceptualized, the notion of maternity and its influences can serve as a point of women's empowerment. In this maternal reimagining Akan women can dislodge themselves from patriarchal ideologies and determine their own stories. Subverting normative beliefs assigned to Akan women is the substance of what Oduyoye knows as Akan feminism. As a standpoint it actively refutes oppressive aspects of the church and society imposed upon Akan women.[57]

Oduyoye's Akan feminism, in some ways, invites creative reimagining of the maternal. It frees African women to exist in their communities and in the world differently and wholly as themselves. In her theological work, Oduyoye expands the notion of motherhood to include self-and-others-centered care. The idea of maternity embraces women's self-determination and the governing place of maternal figures.[58] Oduyoye's understanding of African women's theology, undergirded by her Akan feminism, creates space for women to mother themselves and to govern their people. Both postures, in the eyes of African women's theology, are viable examples of motherhood. Oduyoye asserts that African women must have a solid understanding of themselves instead of solely being formed by cultural claims.[59] For Oduyoye, the notion of mothering one's self is a self-reflective exercise tied to powerful cultural, political, and maternal figures such as the queen mother.[60]

Mothering One's Self

Oduyoye did not quite fall in line with the traditional timeline assigned to Akan women. Her marriage in her late thirties was already a cultural cause for concern; it signaled that she did not see herself the way her culture saw her—eager to become a mother at as young an age as possible.[61] Physical maternity was not her exclusive goal. Oduyoye instead understood her maternal influence differently. She saw and still sees her influence in being a woman who "inspires community; a woman who prays that the men and women she touches and who touch her will grow and prosper as God would have all humans do; a woman whose life helps effect an earth that is prosperous and at peace."[62] Leading life on her own terms would not shield Oduyoye from the marriage and motherhood expectations placed upon Akan women. It was always in the back of her mind that her status as a mother would culturally cement Oduyoye at the "the center of the kinship unit" and communal life.[63]

But for Oduyoye, motherhood stretched beyond cultural assumptions of childbearing; it was found in the fruit of caring for and influencing another. Akan kinship systems recognize social linkage as being on par with biological connection. Akan people do not parse the language of motherhood as literally as the West. They speak of "younger mothers and older mothers" in place of the terminology of "aunts." For the Akan, mothering can take many forms; their notion of kinship does not translate in the West. In fact, the West's permeation into Akan culture created new language of relationships that did not exist before. Akan women, once considered "mother" in various ways, had to come to terms with the new social realities that kinship language brought.[64]

Oduyoye makes it known that while it was not her sole objective to have a child, she did want to become a mother. Her fierce spirit of independence and self-determination did not preclude her desiring conventional motherhood; as a married woman, she was constantly expected to have this desire.[65] She also simply wanted children. Oduyoye struggled with this, because it proved physically unattainable.

Even though she wrestled with what the absence of children meant in her marriage, Oduyoye learned not to deem herself a failure.[66] She shifted her focus and placed value in the difference her work was making for oppressed women, herself included.[67] If she was not able to fulfill motherhood in the traditional way, she would do it in subversive ways: she would be a maternal figure to others, but only after she learned to care for, to mother, herself.

Caring for her needs and caring for others through mentoring would become a critical aspect of Oduyoye's feminist position, but what is most crucial to keep in front of us is the active tension present in Oduyoye's subversive maternal trajectory. What made it so tensive was her seemingly inverted order of prioritization. Oduyoye attended to her own desires first. For a lot of Akan women (and Yoruba women), cultural expectations are automatically positioned as women's primary desire. Women are expected to care for a spouse, children, and other family members before themselves. Though many African women may desire biological motherhood, it is revolutionary to ask women what *they* desire, outside of cultural assumptions. This is the power of mothering one's self—allowing one's own cares to be on par with the concerns of the culture. It is a means of honoring and extending love toward the personhood of African women.

Of course, mothering one's self does not preclude the desire to biologically mother and rear children. Oduyoye wanted to become a mother, but also made conscious decisions to prioritize her desire and draw to ministry. Oduyoye's understanding of feminism affirms, as a revolutionary expression of motherhood, women's prioritizing their own desires above the "needs" of the culture or people.

This expression of Oduyoye's feminism sought creative alternatives that, for some women, seem impossible. In mothering herself, Oduyoye authors the contours of *her own* womanhood. In expanding the parameters of maternity and motherhood, she is naming herself. She is determining the value of her life to and in her community. An exemplar of Akan womanhood, Oduyoye asserts her value to her community. In this she creates room for women to reimagine their value outside of their biological purposing.

Oduyoye has made it clear that even though Akan women are admired for their ability to maintain the bloodline by becoming mothers, these women are still marginalized.[68] This cultural stance does not prove beneficial to Akan women—it, instead, relegates women to the gender roles their culture claims not to advocate.[69] Yet being aware of this dynamic does not make it less difficult to live with. Growing up, Oduyoye admittedly wrestled with the odd marriage of women's familial and communal roles and expectations. "It seemed to me, however, that the more these women made others comfortable and dependent upon them, the more they felt alive. I absorbed all of this," she states.[70]

Oduyoye puts a name to the dilemma of whom *women are women for* in Akan culture. While the focus on motherhood may have communal benefit, gender roles diminish women's agency, pressuring them into male-determined life goals. Oduyoye took a different road.

In privileging her draw to ministry as a priority in her life, Oduyoye broke the mold of the typical Akan woman's path. She pursued her calling and career first; she married when she wanted and only after having a firm grasp on the direction of her future in ministry. She privileged her own desires, doing life "out of order" and on her own terms. In mothering herself in this way Oduyoye decided to determine her own future. This ironic act of maternal resistance illumined the well-being of the community as a whole, especially its women, as critical to Akan identity. In mothering herself Oduyoye made space for *all* Akan women to be women however *they* chose.

If one must marry and biologically mother in order to be considered human, is Oduyoye a *true* Akan woman?[71] Is there room for ulterior forms of Akan womanhood? Can Akan women be liberated to be someone different in their culture? How do women who determine their own stories honor Akan values?[72] Akan women approach situations with their wellness in heart and mind. As Oduyoye's mother demonstrated through her own life, Akan women can proudly create other modes of being in the world and pass them down to their daughters. Their resistance to the forces that stifle the fullness of their lives reflects their Akan identity and feminist commitments.

Oduyoye came from a line of women of strong resolve who knew the balance of keeping their culture's strengths in front of them while affiliating with the Christian church as needed.[73] Being an Akan woman gave Oduyoye a gender-sensitive and feminist lens that would shape how she moved about in the world as a woman of Akan descent. Her "mothers" taught her her worth. They were figures whose principles she furthered through the events of her own life. In this self-assertion, Oduyoye became a model of empowerment for others. She had influence over the politics of Akan women's lives, much like the revered figure of the queen mother, to whom we will now turn.

The Appeal of the Queen Mother

In the Akan political culture, both men and women hold a measure of power.[74] Representatives oversee the affairs of the people, the chief representatives being two leaders from select royal families, *ϑhene* (male chief/king) and *ϑhemaa* (female ruler). Cultural anthropologist Beverly J. Stoeltje describes the chieftaincy structure in more depth: "Each lineage is a political unit, represented by a head who acts as a representative on larger councils. This form of representation and hierarchy is expanded into larger political units through the village leader, the division chief, the paramount chief and finally to the Asantehene, the chief of all Asante. Parallel to each chief is a female leader known as the queen mother. This system is known as chieftaincy, or traditional rule."[75]

Both chiefs keep harmony and balance in the everyday affairs of the community, but the male chief has primary decision-making power. The queen mother primarily works in the background of communal affairs. She assists in selecting the chief, holds her own meetings, and sits on her own stool, a symbol of authority and importance in the governmental system.[76] Sometimes she works in tandem with the chief, serving as an adviser.

Though her role is primary in conferring political status to male leaders, in Asante circles the queen mother is a figure of political advocacy and regality.[77] She is a staple in the cultural governing bodies of the Akan people.[78] Her presence in any political happening is noteworthy. The *ϑhemaa*, or female ruler, "was theoretically a co-ruler and had joint responsibility with the king for all affairs of the state."[79] In the absence of a male ruler or heir, she can rule alone as the monarch.[80] Her symbolism is important; she is an example of women's importance in their respective contexts. This is in step with Oduyoye's feminist position; women are able to make a difference in the systems and spaces in which they are present and respected.

The queen mother's voice is meaningful, foundational to her community; it is important to remember that often she exists *alongside* the male chief.[81] In the precolonial era she had a role in selecting the male chief (or local high figurehead), who would serve as the political face and primary decision-maker in the governing collective of the community.[82] For the Asante of the Akan, the queen mother was (as she still is) a central character in the structure of this performing culture.[83] The queen mother was elected to choose the community's most prominent voice.[84] For a woman to aid in selecting the most prominent male voice in the community is ironic power, indeed.

More than selecting the male chief, *ðhemaa* serves in her own right as a guardian of the women in her community. Her maternity is more than domestic: it is political, social, and cultural. Since she is literally the embodiment of all those who hold the rights to lineage and blood rights, the matrilineal reality of the queen mother is arguably her *most important* feature.[85]

ðhemaa's partnership with the king has maternal overtones. To be clear, the designation of partner does not diminish the power of the queen mother; it notes the parallels between how, in the past, Asante women have exercised power even amid the limited parameters of women's communal influence and how, in the present, they continue to exercise such power. Being a chief adviser to the chief still yields returns.[86] In living into this counsel partnership, women have gained greater say and influence in the overall affairs of society. This not only benefits the people but should impact women in general positively.

Given the presence and importance of the queen mother, this much is clear: the courts, the style of rule, and the symbolic personhood of the queen mother reinforce the sacred nature of Akan customs. The queen mother's power is, in great part, found in her cultural relevance. The cultural mores would be incomplete without this figurehead. Most powerful or not, the queen mother is an Akan cultural icon.

"The *ðhemaa* is considered to be the mother of the clan in her town and therefore the mother of the chief."[87] Her political role expands outward as the male chief's decisions impact the community as a whole. While living into her role as adviser and counselor, the queen mother expands her meaning into the literal lives of the people. Her role gives the culture staying power. Her impact and longevity in this way create meaning in the culture.

If the Akan people are considered her family, one could argue that the queen mother is considered the "head" of the household. She ensures that all of its members are living optimally. She truly is the mother of her people; this is a uniquely powerful position in the culture.

I. Owusu-Mensah, W. Asante, and W. K. Osew assert that "Queen Mothers must strive to establish and build a cordial and harmonious relationship with the college of kingmakers to define key societal interests which override parochial and personal interest."[88] Their standpoint is far-reaching, all-inclusive, and considerate of the overarching condition of the community, a community of men and women. Thus, gender is quite a critical factor not only in the queen mother's presence but in the content of her leadership.

Ɵhemaa "has responsibilities for women and domestic affairs and for advising the chief in all matters."[89] Stoeltje argues that the offices of both *Ɵhene* and *Ɵhemaa* "represent parallel lines of authority expressing gender. Asante queen mothers then are the legitimate, publicly recognized female leaders in this society that reckons descent through the female line."[90] Stoeltje suggests that this "gender parallel" means a functioning that is joint yet distinctly based on gender identity and roles assigned through such. "As a duality they are expected to consult regularly, even daily, and to cooperate in their leadership, acting always in the best interest of the community whom they represent," she explains.[91]

This small detail is important to examine. Stoeltje makes a compelling case for the equal *recognition* of the male and female chief figures in Asante political structure (all within Akan culture).[92] In Western frames of thought, if ruling influence and power are not parallel, the terminology of parallelism can appear misleading. This dynamic is characteristic of African understandings of kinship—access and ability are not mutually exclusive.

Oduyoye illumines this dynamic in her own observations: the queen mother is established as culturally important; she is most powerful as a *symbol* of a nostalgic cultural system. She rules adjacent to the chief but does not always practice or have the same amount of influence as the male figure. For women looking for opportunities to subvert the system, this distinction is hopeful.[93] Again, access and ability are not mutually exclusive. Though patriarchal leadership still characterizes a matrilineally based understanding of Akan community and self, we also see that matrilineality still has significant weight. Oduyoye most readily works with and highlights what the women do *within* these systems. Where and how women are empowered can provide a liberative starting point.

Queen mothers are a microcosm of what Akan women face in their communities. The small distinction between stated and actual practice, between access and ability, is what is most useful in thinking alongside Oduyoye's deployment of feminism. Working from one's current place in order to gain ground is meaningful, whether in a political role or not. Real power does not have to be tangible power. The queen mother's symbolism is greatly important. Though in many ways the figurehead no longer functions in the same way she did in the precolonial era, the *legacy* of the figure has power. The impact of what she *signals* still showers her with meaning. In the contemporary moment, she signals the potential for women to occupy the space of "more," spaces alongside men, spaces where they hold deep cultural resonance and relevance.

Oduyoye's emphasizing what is true—the relevance of the queen mother to a matrilineal culture—and offering it up as important to consider in modern conversations or in reimagined Akan womanhood (through maternity) is a test case for the expansion of women's voices in African cultural practice and theological thought. This is the fullness of what African vocality could be. The point is not to eradicate the imbalance in the system of African culture (and though this is important, it is a task beyond Oduyoye to dismantle alone) but to assert *new approaches to doing culture* so that in time the cultural makeup will incorporate balanced practices and modes of thought.[94] For Oduyoye the task is to subvert the assumptions and place of power and to activate embers of change.

The maternal legacy of the queen mother is very much alive in the dynamic voices of African women working for African women's equality in their respective societies. We see this in how African women continue to tell their stories, in how they consider their voices to be part of their people's history. Historian and social anthropologist Agnes Akosua Aidoo notes something powerful in her exploration of the authority of the queen mother. She calls the queen mother "the royal genealogist."[95] She is a storyteller, the keeper of the people's history. We see the staying power of *ɔhemaa*. She represents the life of the people. She is mother. She carries the community in her body and in her tongue. She keeps the lineage. She delivers power: subversive, feminine, and collective. And she does so with great subtlety. Fortunately, the tides are shifting. The queen mother and other important female figures are gaining recognition in their respective contexts. Oduyoye informs us, "In Ghana, female traditional rulers are receiving more recognition and becoming more visible."[96] Women are making inroads in political and social matters.

Oduyoye has always been attuned to the importance of empowered women in every facet of Africa's dynamic life. Through a critical lens, Oduyoye's work, standpoint, and claims reveal the powerful ways African women can have agency in their religio-cultural communities. Creative, subversive theological outlooks are one way for African women to continue to gain voice. Oduyoye's approach to doing African women's theology relies on an Akan feminist outlook that creates space and power where none is instinctually perceived.

An African feminist worldview creates new language from the imperfect consonants of culture; it weaves beauty in order to remind the culture of the value it contains within itself. And it challenges those within the fold to think and act expansively and justly. In adulthood Oduyoye continued fashioning ways to bring African women together to exercise such cultural and theological creativity. Her ecumenical fingerprints are quite visible.

CHAPTER THREE

SPHERES OF INFLUENCE

Mercy Oduyoye became involved in ecumenical activity during her time at university. From her brainstorming and organizing genius with the Student Christian Movement, to collaborations and foundational work with the Ecumenical Association of Third World Theologians, to the formation of the Circle of Concerned African Women Theologians, Oduyoye has always kept the most important goal in view: granting African women equal room at the theological table. Her fight branched beyond intellectual ideas into ecclesial and ecumenical spaces. Her efforts gained her invitations to many international ecumenical and African continental efforts; she would later channel this experience and wisdom into generating space of her own.

The Church and Ecumenical Involvement

As a young adult bringing a ministerial message of equality, Oduyoye ran up against the habits of those around her. Her first bitter taste of colonialism in higher education came during her time at Cambridge (from which she graduated in 1964), where she quickly became involved in campus ministry.[1] While at the University of Ghana from 1959 to 1963, she and a former classmate helped form a prayer group for an immobile friend who could not attend the regularly scheduled morning prayers.[2] She brought the idea to Cambridge with her. Some of her Cambridge colleagues would adopt this prayer group, using it for the foundation of what would become the Christian Union, a ministry branching off from the Student Christian Movement (SCM) of which Oduyoye was a part for two years.[3] Unfortunately, the Christian Union proved a contentious space for her. The group ultimately changed, burdening the communal experience with additional demands.[4] Oduyoye wanted space to grow in her faith alongside her colleagues in the community; she did not need spiritual paternalism, the posture she felt was extended to her. She eventually left the group.[5]

A Western missionary mentality colored her time in SCM. It was assumed that Oduyoye (and other nonwhite students) needed to be schooled in ecumenism, a grossly inaccurate conjecture. As an African, Oduyoye was raised in a diverse society; Africans historically have no problem understanding a pluralistic religious reality. Contrary to assumed racist belief, Africans were already well versed in religious coexistence.

Ecumenism was not a problem or challenge for Oduyoye. What the prayer group debacle unearthed was an issue in her British counterparts' understanding of multiplicity, not her own. Most Westerners, Oduyoye is careful to note, lack understanding of religious diversity. "Africa is very hospitable," she offers. "She has played host to both Christianity and Islam."[6] Africa has never *not* known the importance of religion to one's way of life, as African religion has always been "an integral part of African culture and life."[7] The British students of the Christian Union did not need to teach Oduyoye how to be a religious being, let alone a Christian one. Oduyoye was already familiar with the dynamics of a diverse social and religious reality. After graduating in 1964, she went back to her home country to teach.

At the tail end of her teaching tenure at the Wesley Girls' High School in 1965, Oduyoye became involved in the World Council of Churches (WCC). She would become even more involved some twenty years later.[8] In 1966 she attended her first international ecumenical conference in Bolden, Switzerland. She would find herself at another ecumenical event in Nairobi, Kenya, later in that same year with the World Council of Christian Education (WCCE).[9] From 1967 to 1970, she took on responsibility in the WCC's youth department while also working with the WCCE.[10] In 1968 during the WCC Assembly in Uppsala,

Sweden, Oduyoye served as youth department staff.[11] This would be the first out of a few decades' worth of World Council of Churches meetings for Oduyoye.

Moving to Nigeria in 1970 (after her marriage to Modupe Oduyoye in 1968), Oduyoye became the youth secretary of the All African Conference of Churches (AACC) and remained in that position until 1973. It was then that she would develop her first two book publications in pamphlet form specifically designed for youth. These two cartoon books—*Youth without Jobs* (1972) and *Flight from the Farms* (1973)—gave voice to the various conditions that youth in Africa were facing, including work woes, issues with educational access, and the struggle for survival amid the unstable structure of education.[12] Oduyoye worked to draw attention to Africa's troubles through local and global means.

Oduyoye left the AACC shortly thereafter and taught biblical criticism in a majority-Muslim boy's school. She later taught church history, missions, and then Christian theology in the Department of Religious Studies at the University of Ibadan in Nigeria from 1974 until 1986, an impressive feat.[13] At this time, she also served as the assistant editor and then editor of *ORITA*, the Ibadan journal of religious studies.[14] Teaching at the University of Ibadan, an institution with a majority-male faculty, thrust gender dynamics in front of Oduyoye in such a way that she responded progressively, joining efforts for equal pay and equal treatment of women in the academy.[15]

Pertinent to her academic career was its direct connection to her ecumenical focus and passion. Oduyoye describes herself as the practical type, interested in what the church means to and is doing in the world. She served on the staff of the AACC and the WCC. She served a seven-year stint as the WCC's deputy general secretary beginning in 1988—being the first African, male or female, to take up this position.[16]

What has garnered Oduyoye the most attention is her ability to fill in the gaps for underrepresented voices in the ecumenical and theological world. She served as a founder or a founding member of numerous organizations, including the World Christian Federation, the World Council of Churches Ecumenical Decade of Churches in Solidarity with Women, the Ecumenical Association of Third World Theologians, the Circle of Concerned African Women Theologians, and the Institute of

African Women in Religion and Culture at Trinity Theological Seminary in Legon, Ghana, where she served as its director until 2016.[17]

The three ecumenical spaces where Oduyoye has left her most indelible mark are with the WCC (including her initiative with the Ecumenical Decade of Churches in Solidarity with Women), the Ecumenical Association of Third World Theologians (EATWOT), and the Circle of Concerned African Women Theologians (commonly referred to as the Circle), all of which I will overview in this chapter.[18]

Oduyoye searches for the women silenced in the Christian church in order to uplift their voices.[19] While she aims to be a representative voice herself, she has also made it her mission to empower these women to name their realities for themselves. Her ecumenical initiatives reflect this passion.

The World Council of Churches

Oduyoye's experience with the WCC spans decades. Since 1966 she has been present in leadership capacities, urging the WCC assembly forward in helpful ways. While in Nairobi in 1966, Oduyoye was already seen as a force. She was "one of a few specially invited women" who would be chosen to comoderate "the standing committee on Dialogues with People of Other Faiths."[20] In an article written in a text published through WCC, *Voices of Unity: Essays in Honour of Willem Adolf Visser 't Hooft on the Occasion of his 80th Birthday*, she spoke directly to the colonial impact of Christianity on Africa and its people, asserting that African values treasured wholeness and unity, while colonial religious foundations countered these very values.[21] Oduyoye felt it important to name how European influence was reshaping the religious and ecclesial values of Africans.

Oduyoye's greatest asset was her presence in each WCC Assembly meeting. She would serve on the central committee in a Vancouver, Canada, meeting, on the Faith and Order Commission, and on the program guidelines committee of the Canberra assembly in Australia.[22] There were also WCC meetings in Mexico City in 1975; in Copenhagen in 1980; Nairobi in 1985; Berlin; Accra, Ghana; Venice; Klingenthal, France; and

Sheffield, United Kingdom, in which women "met on specialized issues in Christianity and on human rights issues."[23]

At the 1985 WCC meeting in Nairobi, which Oduyoye attended by invitation, she, along with women from all over Africa, interrogated the power struggles women in the Third World faced. She wanted women to be heard and for the WCC to take seriously the global well-being of women. Through Oduyoye's example, African women began to activate their courage, proclaiming their position "on the liberation struggle."[24] Following Oduyoye's lead, a movement of women's voices was gaining significant momentum.

African women were demanding space to address the gender disparities they suffered; Oduyoye was a large part of this inclusive initiative. She created room for women to voice their stories for themselves. Thanks in part to Oduyoye, the intervention and opportunities from the United Nations provided African women, on three separate occasions, with a platform on which to gain a "global voice and . . . dramatic visibility."[25]

Oduyoye and her colaborers did run into an obstacle, though. Even with this new opportunity to claim space in the world, African women still had to fight through Western feminism. Oduyoye explains, "Euro-American women were quick to name women's heightened consciousness as a liberating experience" instead of recognizing the complexity of context.[26] Western feminism was not the same thing as African feminism, for they do not have the same opponents. In addition, Western feminism's assumption that it could speak for all women made it—as unlikely as this might have seemed—an opponent of Third World feminists. Western feminists, mainly white feminists, did not acknowledge that consciousness around gender issues was not enough. Racial, economic, and cultural issues are real factors in the shape of various feminist positions. To African women, white feminist vocalizing of "women's issues" in a racially tone-deaf manner felt colonial. White colonial feminism reinforced the narrow places where many African women were already confined.[27] Oduyoye knew that Western feminist voices and experiences were distinct from her own, so in each ecumenical organization of which she was a part she sought to provide space for herself and women like her to voice their own realities.

The World Council of Churches Ecumenical Decade
of Churches in Solidarity with Women

It is clear that Oduyoye's time with the WCC emboldened her tongue around women's visibility in the Christian church. She decided to create a programmatic response to highlight women's issues. Established in 1988, Oduyoye's initiative—the Ecumenical Decade of Churches in Solidarity with Women—centered its work on the four themes of economic justice, women's participation in the church, and racism and violence against women until its conclusion in 1998.[28] It was a response to and was modeled on a four-year study Oduyoye had conducted, titled "Community of Men and Women in Church and Society."[29]

Later, in her book *Who Will Roll the Stone Away? The Ecumenical Decade of the Churches in Solidarity with Women*, Oduyoye would reflect on the work the Decade of Churches in Solidarity with Women did in its first two years and the impact it had.[30] In it she inquires what sexism has to do with ecumenism. She reflects on how ecumenical action can be taken on behalf of women of the Christian church, urging equal parts care and action from the church at large, not solely from women but from men as well. The responsibility for the well-being of all in the body of Christ must be a corporate responsibility, she asserts. The rights of women are the rights of the Christian church. The hope of the project was to "further the equality and dignity of women throughout the world."[31]

Ecumenical Association of Third World Theologians (EATWOT)

In 1976 Mercy Oduyoye first became involved in the Ecumenical Association of Third World Theologians, or EATWOT. The next year, she attended the meeting in Accra, Ghana. She wanted to draw attention to the injustices women in the Third World were experiencing from Third World men and First World persons.[32] Her connections with scholars such as "Virginia Fabella and Mary John Mananzan from the Philippines, Marianne Katoppo from Indonesia, Sun Ai Park from Korea, [and] Ivone Gebara and Elsa Tamez from Latin America" fueled her commitment to the organization.[33] Her involvement in EATWOT soon increased; she served as its vice president from 1980 to 1984.[34]

EATWOT has a mission of paying "attention to the situation in which Christians struggle to live as the body of Christ and to present the gospel."[35] It has also expressed a commitment to attend to women's issues in the Third World. Oduyoye, thus, created and capitalized on opportunities for collaboration with other women of EATWOT. At the 1981 New Delhi meeting, she and other women began germinating the collective essay work that would become *With Passion and Compassion: Third World Women Doing Theology*, addressing some of the shortcomings found in the gatherings and initiatives of EATWOT. Despite how groundbreaking it was, these women were still highly aware of the injustices that befell them.[36]

In 1983 Oduyoye teamed up with various women to establish the Commission on Theology from Third World Women's Perspective. It was created to be a "sisterhood of resistance to all forms of oppression" and to create accountability for the full hearing of women and their experiences in theology.[37] This women-focused effort was careful to avoid the dangerous assumption that "naming the structures that divide human beings" would be sufficient to address the global problems the entire church, especially women, was facing.[38] Though EATWOT was progressive in its own right, its efforts alone did not reach far enough; African women, for example, had to resist sexism found in Western Christianity and African culture, so they, and others under similar conditions, formed the EATWOT's Women's Commission.[39]

A friend of Oduyoye, Rosemary Radford Ruether, also a feminist theologian, details this initiative. From 1985 to 1986, the Women's Commission would work through a four-stage process that included planning for a national, continental, and then a Third World intercontinental meeting. The fourth aspect involved creating spaces where Third World women theologians and First World feminist theologians could dialogue. This successfully took place in December 1994 in Costa Rica, boasting forty-five women theologians from fourteen different countries.[40]

Oduyoye's voice was resonating with others. She collaborated with those who had similar interests and goals, many in the world of liberation theology's various strands. Giants in the burgeoning field of liberation theology were her conversation partners: James Cone was a great influence on her work.[41] She has worked with Gustavo Gutiérrez and has been included in major book projects with Ada María Isasi-Díaz, Katie Geneva Cannon, and Letty Russell.[42] Even if their contexts and histories varied, their ambitions for liberating their communities were the same. Oduyoye's ecumenical involvement and message of African women's equality increased her visibility in various theological circles. But one of her greatest achievements was yet to come. It, too, would involve a circle.

Creating the Circle

When used unjustly, culture and religion can stunt African women's potential.[43] Cultural traditions and religious ideologies are often used to force women down predetermined paths. The social effects can be detrimental. The strictures of a cultural-religious mindset do not always prioritize African women in the very societies and communities they build and bolster. Aware of this reality, Oduyoye decided to privilege the wellness of African women, challenge the unjust aspects of African society, and resist the colonial characteristics of the Christian church—and she did so through her theology.[44]

Nuancing the concept of "religious-culture," often utilized by Ghanaian theologian Kwesi Dickson, and thinking alongside her Kenyan feminist theological colleague Musimbi Kanyoro, Oduyoye constructively imagines religion and culture together as "culture and religion," or as a *CuRe* to utilize for the good of African women.[45] Aided by this newly coined term, with its intentionally dual meaning, Oduyoye's work intends to "cure the ills of the continent generated by culture and religion," especially culture and religion as they have been imposed on Africa's women.[46] African women academics already surmised that cultural and religious emphases in their communities could be used for good, that they simply had to be mined for their constructive features. But these women lacked a formal setting for tackling these questions and having these conversations together. Oduyoye saw how they needed a place where African women could communally interrogate what culture and religion *do* in women's lives. She desired a place, a gathering, where women with similar experiences could learn from one another, build each other up, and create new conditions for African women's wellness.

Dreamt up in 1970 and ultimately born in 1989, the network internationally known as the Circle of Concerned African Women Theologians, or the Circle, was cofounded by Oduyoye with the help of the first of several international planning committees.[47] Today the Circle is one of the largest African women's networks and communities focused on religious conversation, study, and publication.[48] In it, women examine gender's role in African theological imagination, which is "still shaped by the colonial experience and ongoing neocolonial relations with the Western world."[49]

The existence of the Circle shows that African women, who "had been discussed, analyzed, and spoken about and on behalf of by men and outsiders as if they were not subjects capable of self-naming and analysis of their own experiences," have their own contributions to make to the discourse about the shortcomings of culture and religion.[50] Circle work, then, is *CuRe* work as well; it is an "effort to *cure* Africa of wanton sexism and gender insensitivity," Oduyoye offers.[51] This twofold focus is "crucial . . . for creating a liberative theology that would respond to the needs of women in Africa," Kanyoro adds.[52] The underlying and recurring theme is significant: these women link together to heal themselves from the abusive use of culture and religion against them through communal and scholastic sharing. In their joining together they have committed to heal not only themselves but also the communities around them.

Structure and Function

Void of official headquarters or strict operational structure, the Circle was created to sustain itself through shared ideas and responsibility. In its beginnings, if a task needed to be done, someone attended to it. Refusing a hierarchical structure allowed women to rotate leadership on a case-by-case basis as they were moved to see an idea to completion. Membership was also not pressure filled. To be a member of the Circle, all one needed to do was produce some writing. More valuable than any membership fee, writing ensured an increasing exposure of African women's theology.[53] The Circle's flexible structure was the brainchild of Oduyoye, whose behind-the-scenes work helped the group to grow in number each year.

In terms of values and aims, the Circle seeks to inspire practicality and transformation around how African women and men think in various areas, including biblical hermeneutics, theological frameworks, and church and society at large.[54] With regional chapters (or zones) of the Circle all over West, East, Central, and South Africa as well as in the wider diaspora, the Circle functions as a series of networks within a network. They gather as a whole every seven years.[55] Through their emphasis on communal theology, members address numerous, overlapping, and sometime evolving issues, the chief being women's spiritual, economic, and physical health.[56]

For pastoral theologian Mpyana Nyengele the Circle "has become a milestone in the development, growth, and promotion of African women's theology throughout the continent and abroad."[57] It is a "loose federation of women held together by their conviction that religion is important to their own personal and professional lives, and potentially revolutionary to the situation of women in their church and communities."[58] It is a space created for women in search of kindred spirits who learn by listening to each other.

In her 2001 piece "The Story of a Circle," Oduyoye notes four areas of focus—or "study commissions," as she calls them—on which African women in the Circle focus: (1) religions in pluralistic cultures, (2) biblical and cultural hermeneutics, (3) theological and ministerial formation of women, and (4) biographies and histories of women in religion in Africa.[59] As of 2001, when the Circle had approximately four hundred members, these foci remained nearly the same.[60] Since the Circle is so internationally dispersed, these focus areas help create a sense of unity and sisterhood. They center the similar aims of its members. These study commissions are, however, only one umbrella under which the Circle tries to concentrate its work and focus its intentions.

The Circle is also guided by main objectives toward women's empowerment and representation. Grounded in seven objectives (which swelled to nine), the Circle destabilizes masculinity as the center of theological witness, highlighting instead women's contributions in theological thought.[61] The growing objectives as outlined by Kenyan feminist theologian and Circle founding member Teresia Hinga are as follows:

1. To encourage and empower the critical study of the practice of religion in Africa.
2. To undertake research that unveils both positive and negative religio-cultural factors, beliefs, and myths that affect, influence, or hamper women's development.
3. To publish theological literature written by African women with a special focus on religion and culture.
4. To build a communications network among theologically trained women both in academia and beyond.
5. To promote a dialogic approach to religious and cultural tensions in Africa.
6. To strive toward the inclusion of women's studies in religion and culture in academia and research institutions in Africa, particularly institutions of higher education, including theological institutions.
7. To empower African women to contribute to the cross-cultural discourse on women's issues through engagement in critical cultural hermeneutics.
8. To promote ecumenism and cultural pluralism.
9. To bring African women's theology to the attention of the general public.[62]

While in-person gathering is deeply important to the Circle's fabric, what is arguably most integral is curating a space for African women's scholarship. Since African women are not as favored as their male counterparts in religious studies, they must create their own networks and opportunities to share their work. Kanyoro is straightforward about one of the Circle's main purposes: "The Circle's vision is to encourage African women to write and publish their works. The goal . . . is to promote the wellbeing of African women and all women through theological analysis and the study of the Bible." For Kanyoro, increasing African women's presence in theological studies positively impacts society.[63] Within the Circle, religious and social ideas that matter to African women can finally be explored by those most directly impacted by them. "Taboo" subjects such as sexuality or HIV are not untouched by these inquisitive voices.[64]

The work and ideas encouraged by the Circle are not only Christian projects. The Circle takes seriously "the religious and cultural plurality in Africa"; thus they "embrace African women from all religions resident in Africa" as long as they convey a theological focus in practically living out their faith in the modern world.[65] The Circle takes seriously how men have dominated conversation and determination of what Oduyoye calls the "Triangle of Reality," a worldview often found in African traditional religion composed of "God the Source Being, the world of spirits, and the physical world of our five senses."[66] Oduyoye subverts this reality; her theological approach to understand God, self, and others (categories popular in Christian study) intentionally smooths the edges of "the malestream triangle with its connotations of hierarchy . . . into a circle of relationships."[67] The sharp angles of male-determined religious foundations no longer worked for her; Oduyoye preferred the equitable shape of a circle.

The Circle both resists ideologies of the old guard and fashions new responses welcoming of all. Its main concern is women's wellness and liberation; therefore, as long as African women have been doing theological work against systems of oppression, they have been welcome to join its networking and scholastic mission. The Circle functions as "a theoretical framework," Kanyoro offers. Its emphasis on joinedness and connectiveness is crucial. African women from all over the continent "work together for the empowerment of women and the recognition of human dignity." They are "seated together" and "connected" in a mission for women's unity.[68] The imagery is intentional; in a circle, power in the group will reach all of its members.[69]

Meetings and Purpose

The Circle's inaugural meeting in Accra, Ghana, in 1989 was attended by eighty women scholars from all over the African continent and two hundred churchwomen from Ghana.[70] They met under the theme and heading "Daughter of Africa, Arise!" The biblical mandate "Talitha Cum!" perfectly captures the Circle's origin, purpose, and necessity: the Circle works to affirm that girls and women are, in fact, not dead in their communities, but very much living beings in Christ.[71] Many women relate to the Mark 5 story of two female characters: though both are "nameless, associated with sickness, and . . . not identified through having any professional roles," they are eventually "restored back to life and society."[72] Botswanan feminist theologian Musa Dube asserts that some of these African women are "the bleeding woman who reaches for power." They call out to the generations after them, providing hope that healing is possible; they "are the ones calling out 'Talitha Cum!' to the unfinished business of a young girl's life."[73] In the Circle, the old and young are interconnected, for if one gains name and life, it is so that the other may be privy to the same. African women look out for each other's wellness. They tell stories about their survival and successes.[74]

In providing intergenerational networking and support, the Circle has continued to grow in number and influence. Kenyan religious scholar Nyambura J. Njoroge reports that in August 1996 "the second Pan African Conference of the Circle met in Kenya,"[75] and twice as many registrants showed up for the second meeting as for the first, totaling 140 women from various areas including West Africa, Francophone Africa, and southern and eastern Africa. They gathered to present, listen to, and workshop papers; eventually many of these papers were published—a gift for many of the women, since publishing opportunities were scarce.

Collaboration is a critical part of the Circle's growth and exposure. In 1999, through Oduyoye's leadership and connection, the Circle co-convened a joint theological conference with various organizations, "including the regional and country chapters of the Ecumenical Association of Third World Theologians (EATWOT), the All African Conference of Churches (AACC), the Congress of Association of Theological Institutions (CATI), and . . . the Organization of African Independent Churches (OAIC)."[76] At the conclusion of the conference the participants "issued a joint communiqué naming twenty-two issues that demanded urgent and collective action from all concerned."[77]

The Circle's focus is the ordinary African woman. It provides space in which women can examine the social, political, and theological conditions that have marginalized Africans, whether colonial or cultural, especially in the Christian church. Oduyoye's familiarity with the cultural-religious practices of silencing women jump-started her work with the Circle. She has pressed the question of what the lack of female presence in theological and ecclesial representation means for the welfare of an inclusive African theology—and she does so by naming where women are absent. She then creates a response.

A case can be made that the Circle was catalyzed when Oduyoye wrestled with her position and place as a woman in the academy. She recounts a particular moment as especially impactful. Finding herself the only female theologian among her male colleagues in an institutional meeting, she was asked to fetch drinks for all the men present. She refused, instead summoning the man responsible for providing refreshments at the meeting.[78] It was perplexing how the modifier "African" of African theology primarily came to be affiliated with maleness.[79] These instances and more contributed to Oduyoye's desire to write *Daughters of Anowa*. This book helped spur the initiative of creating spaces for women who were missing in places that affected them.[80] Not being well resourced and adequately supported contributed to the Circle's slow emergence, nine years in the making;[81] but the Circle accomplished and still accomplishes its purpose, serving as a communal place for African women.[82] "Our story is one of letting it be known that African women are awake," Oduyoye asserts.[83]

The Circle encourages theological work from African women's perspective as "a gift to the church and a gift to women." It is a gift because it "calls the Church to repentance for its role in the subordination of women" and has, as Kanyoro argues, "opened our eyes to the fact that the future of society and the future of women depend on our placing our trust in the message of God rather than the message of men."[84]

The Circle offers women of African descent space to be supported, to support one another, and to network.[85] There is something to be said for women creating new spaces in order to feel seen and to understand that *they* usher in their own liberation.[86] The Circle has history and legend because of the commitment and dedication of a group of women whose time and effort helped realize Oduyoye's vision. It reflects the scope of Oduyoye's community-centered and empowering work. It proves that African's women's writing in theology—Christian theology especially—can have a significant impact. The force of the Circle and the impact of Oduyoye's theological work lend weight and importance to her hermeneutical take on Christian theological doctrine.

CHAPTER FOUR

DOCTRINE OF GOD

God is imaged as the one who holds the cosmos together in unity.
—Mercy Amba Oduyoye, *Introducing African Women's Theology*

Framing Christian Doctrines

Taking African women's voices seriously is neither an extreme request nor an impossible task.[1] Mercy Oduyoye has built her theological framework around such truth. The practices of inclusion and exclusion and demonstrations of power in the church play a role in how theological sites of knowledge are developed, especially doctrinal viewpoints. Because Oduyoye is an African woman, inclusion and power frame her understanding not only of God but also of how *others* claim and understand God—how others frame belief about and around God. Oduyoye's voice—reflective of the voices of countless African women who have been historically marginalized in dialogues that have determined Christianity's doctrine of God—inflects differently, announcing African women's right to be co-determinants of Christianity's God-talk. But first, she had to wade through depictions of Christian theology that denounce Africanness, the very fabric of her being. Oduyoye's doctrine of God is part ideation from her African culture and the subsequent response that Africans, including African women, must create to address their religio-cultural denigration. African women view God as cognizant of God's total creation but also view God through a lens of suspicion as a reflex toward European colonialism and the ideas it brought along with it.

Not deterred by the lack of recognition from Christianity's gatekeepers, Oduyoye's doctrinal interpretation shines a light on the nature of Christianity's God-claims over time. Humanity in all its diversity should make for an array of theological emphases, but this is not always the case. Christianity's doctrine of God has been rigidly aligned with its European messengers and those in the African church invested in keeping this alignment as the standard. African women, then, fight for a truer and more holistic framing; they call for a different, more liberative theological premise. A soldier in this fight, Oduyoye argues that the entire Christian church, not men alone, should have a say in how it articulates a doctrine of God. Christianity's doctrinal tongue should be multilingual, not monolingual.

Who gets to "explain" the Christian God in the church? What is at stake in "framing" God in this way? Oduyoye's answer exposes the process of cross-cultural indoctrination. She explores the particularities of God-character from her standpoint as well as the form by which humanity as a whole—existing in hierarchical social tiers—articulates its understanding of the divine. This nuance, of African women's analyzing their own as well as *another's* understanding of God, positions African women's doctrine of God as conscious of the indoctrinators' ties to the process of indoctrination.

God-talk is contextual and based on experience. Recall how Oduyoye's mother and the women around her interpreted the God of Christianity in light of their own lives and the actions of God's followers. African women's theology is aware of this dynamic. It does not ignore the container in favor of the contents, but counts the entirety of the offering as part of the message. Proponents of African women's theology, quite rightly then, interpret the character of God through their experience of God's supposed agents. It would be irresponsible not to include this dynamic as a factor, especially in the force and form of colonial Christianity. How God is understood, whether that understanding be in advocating European over African identity or advocating maleness over femaleness, is a result of how God is packaged and presented.

African women read the conditions of knowing and receiving theology as a theological message in itself. Racism, ethnocentricity, patriarchy, and sexism all inform their understanding and reception of Christianity. Oduyoye's work helps foreground this nuance. Unlike what many African men tend to argue, her African-women-centered timbre does not seek to incite pointless dissension; it, instead, critiques Christianity's practices and points of harm to illumine where its message is ineffective. It frames Christianity's message with these truths in view.

If "God continually calls us [Christians] back to the paths of justice, compassion and humility," Oduyoye writes, then African women must be given space to tell the truth as they have witnessed it.[2] They understand themselves part of the Christian church; thus their emphases must have importance equal to everyone else's. Of the Christian church, African women assert that "women and men are empowered by Christ to breach our broken relationship and transform our human community to become a family of God."[3] But the truth must be desired, and those to whom it is addressed must be willing to hear it.

We already see how Oduyoye has better positioned African women in Christian theological conversations through initiatives such as the Circle of Concerned African Women Theologians and other ecumenical work. Her contributions purposefully rub against the grain and challenge Christianity's colonial history and gender-oppressive habits in order to distinguish its true message of love and inclusivity. "I look for a theology that will bring us in Africa closer to the quality of life of God's children," she says. Oduyoye's theological position honors not only her people but the heart of the gospel.[4] In her eyes, theology must be vibrant and life-giving, not limiting and harmful. Unfortunately for too many Africans, Christian theology has a complex and injurious history. African women have received the brunt of unexamined Christian foundations.

Through the lens of African women's experiences, Oduyoye questions the process of Christian indoctrination. Why should African women accept a mode of belief that puts them on the fringes of their own communities? Why was the point of Christianity to put many down in order to uplift a few? Suspicious, African women knew that other truths lay under the surface of Christianity's presence in Africa. It would take a woman's eye to identify the heart of such discrepancies and to call forth a different, more life-giving understanding of what Christianity can mean in Africa.

Enter Oduyoye. In her doctrinal reflections on God, Christology, theological anthropology, and ecclesiology, Oduyoye does not shy away from places of critique. In fact, she centers them. We must first discuss the problems in order to hear the possibilities. For quite some time African women have had too many barriers placed in front of them in the name of Christian doctrine. To dismantle this theo-cultural fortressing, Oduyoye centers the cultural and spiritual difficulties of inclusion in Christianity. Theology cannot be understood rightly until these barriers are named and broken down.

The barriers African women first and foremost face reflect the nature and issues of the carriers and arbiters of the gospel message. To erase oppression, one must first name it and state that it exists. Leaving women out of theologizing serves no useful purpose. Oduyoye's theological aim, then, is clear: Christian doctrinal reflection is not being done at all if it is not being done with the input of *everyone* in the Christian church. Oduyoye's theology envisions inclusively grounded notions of God in a rich reading of the conditions and processes of how God is named and how beliefs about him are articulated. A firm believer that "religion permeates all life,"[5] Oduyoye focuses on how life shapes one's experience of religion and one's understanding of God. One's theology reflects either the life one leads or the life being imposed upon one. To spend one's life wrestling against theology is not to fight against one's own sinful nature or some sort of deficit, but against a theology forced onto one, a theology that one had no hand in co-determining. Too many African women have spent their lives in a constant state of wrestling.

Context colors one's theological lens. Honoring the experience of African women, Oduyoye theologically reflects on God's meaning and action alongside the tragic realities of colonialism and the function of gender. She reflects on African women's theological affinity for a pluralistic God. She begins to strip the European inflections from the African theological tongue. The lasting legacy of colonialism still troubles African theology today, but this does not prevent Oduyoye from doing theology differently, adding to Christianity's God-talk by engaging the mind and experience of African women. It does not stop her from asserting an African women's doctrine of God unashamed of calling out the messiness of African Christianity and the strength of its potential.

God in Context

What makes God God?

    What constitutes God's work, God's presence?

    How does one talk about God?

    It seems impossible to know the "right" answer to any of these questions, because we each know God through the story of who we are. This is how Christian theology is done as a whole. The specificity of how we each know God is too universal a truth to label "contextual theology" alone. The opening questions prove as much—depending on who one is and the life one leads, one may have a different answer to each question. But even amid a diversity of interpretations, a few universal truths stand: (1) God is complex, exceeding simple category; (2) God moves about freely and, in the midst of that movement, creates the foundations of being; and (3) God simply is, existing beyond but also with humanity.[6]

    This last truth may be difficult to grasp—God exists outside of how humanity understands itself in the world. God is in everything humanity knows and much of what humanity does not know. "God is experienced as an all-pervading reality," Oduyoye asserts.[7] We humans, then, try to narrow the universal truths into tangible features we can grasp. We are eager to name God through holy texts or scriptures, experiences, embodied and rational knowledges, and traditions—a Wesleyan quadrilateral or other model categorizing humanity's means of processing our relationship to the divine. But these models only do so much; they are means of and attempts at exploring how to name God, but they primarily show the cracks in the foundation of our theological houses. They crystallize the reality that in the larger scheme of things God is not the true mystery: *our* knowledge of God, or lack thereof, is shrouded in mystery.

    If "God is a constant participant in the affairs of human beings," the questions we ask about God expose the limits and parameters of our own God-knowledge.[8] How *do* we know the breadth and depth of God's being? How can *we* justify in *our* respective theologizing that we are in fact doing it well, that we are in fact rightly heeding a greater knowledge than ourselves? We do theology in order to "articulate our belief in the divine origin of all that is and its concomitant of the sacredness of being," yet we route our reflections on God's essence through our own existence.[9]

Our first point of theological reference, then, is ourselves, and even in this, we have limited view and vision. According to German theologian Dietrich Bonhoeffer, we exist in limit and as limited creatures; we learn this limit through living among each other as God's created beings.[10] This complexity of a type of shared existence indicates how we should consider God—through examining and ruling out who and how God *is not* within human activity. As we identify our limits, aspects of God/the Creator/the Source Being become clearer.

Naming our own limits helps us generally frame our Christian theology. By understanding our created nature, we can conclude God is Creator. God is divine. God is not humanity, though the Creator of such. But God is also the one who joined human beings in the person of Jesus Christ. God is the gale of holiness in Christian scriptures and in the early and current church inspiring tongues and power and healing. God is Trinitarian. God is God in the way God wants to be God. These truths still return us to an earlier question or perhaps a rhetorical statement of curiosity: How do *we* know *God?*

This question presses directly into Mercy Oduyoye's conception of God. "For me," she asserts, "to seek to be coherent about God is a presumptuous exercise. We are touched and moved differently by the incomprehensible depth of the Spirit of God."[11] God-talk, a doctrine of God, the baseline of Christian theology, is built from the contextual ground up. Beyond a basic Trinitarian framing, Oduyoye does not immerse herself in philosophical inquiries to provide an answer to the question of who God is. For her, God meets us—meets humanity—in our conditions and circumstances. Oduyoye thinks God on the ground, involved in the everyday life of God's creation. God is seen through the particularity of one's life. Oduyoye rightly thinks about God through the life *she* knows, through the truth by which she lives her life. And her practical theological reflective approach resonates with other African women.

How we know God is based on who we are. It is true that how God has proclaimed and named God's self becomes truth about God, but it would be unwise not to believe that our experiences act as a strainer through which we interpret God's truth.[12] Our culture carefully crafts our theological lenses. And it should—it is the experiential framework by which we begin to explore the nature of this being called God. The notion of God being filtered through the "how" of our human experience is normal.

"As theologians we are faced with the challenge of mission and cultures," Oduyoye reminds.[13] The gospel message given to us is discerned through our cultural perspective. Cultures vary; this means that theological perspectives will vary, too. This fact should complicate the narrative that many have been given concerning a right mode of Christianity. Christianity impacted by culture is just that, a cultured iteration of Christianity. Thus, it alone cannot be solely right; it is only one interpretation. Oduyoye's reminder proves both challenging and helpful: there is no one correct cultural viewpoint from which to do Christian theology. Theological uniformity is a myth, for "to seek coherence in terms of a single theological school or thrust would be to work for an exclusive ecumenism."[14] One's context is connected to one's God-talk, and one's God-talk is connected to one's perception of the Christian church. None is singular. Diverse expressions in and of the Christian church are to be expected. However, many European missionaries deployed to the African continent did not hold this view.

If God is seen through the eyes of experience, Oduyoye's work shows us the errors of missionary colonialism. Spreading the gospel was a tactic to forge a singular narrative of cultural experience and thus theological vision. Salvation—through erasure of culture, of language, of identity—became the calling card of colonial Christianity. For Oduyoye, then, it is critical not to bypass the injustice of such an assumption and such events. An African women's doctrine of God does not offer armchair reflections of God's nature, but critiques the nature of evangelism. An African women's doctrine of God calls out the colonial version of the Creator forced into the cultural frame of many Africans. For African women, it is critical to examine what it means to name the Christian God introduced to West Africa over and against how God, or the Source Being, was already known within African culture.[15] It means naming how historically, for Africans, a God-head was not a new concept, but a European God-head was.

The God of the European missionaries illumined a few things about Africa's relationship to Christianity, including how Africans were thinking about divination on a different plane than their European counterparts. Upon Christianity's arrival in West Africa the various religious frameworks, worldviews, and cosmologies of Africans came into contact with colonial Christianity and its questions about the validity of West African religious beliefs. While this religious duality will be attended to in greater detail in Oduyoye's theological anthropology, it is important to name this duality of divinity in order to frame African theology's reception and understanding of the Christian God. For the purposes of examining a Christian doctrine of God through the lens of African women's (Christian) theology, we now turn to European/Western Christian missions.

Mission Statement: The Problem with Christian Missions

For many Africans the Christian God is connected to the complex memory of European colonialism. Oduyoye outlines this directly: "The history of the modern missionary movement in Africa begins with Europeans' attempt to 're-Christianize' or 'Christianize' various areas of north Africa, some of which had been ancient strongholds of Christianity."[16] The absurdity is comical. Missionaries tried to missionize African peoples with already strong religious foundations, with histories associated with the foundations of Christianity. These communities descended from areas where the earliest Christian churches in Africa existed since the fourth-century.[17] We can already see how European missions started on the wrong foot.

The Christian churches that directly and greatly impacted Oduyoye's personal development and growth started in the eighteenth century and had staying power into the nineteenth century.[18] I am indebted to her work *Hearing and Knowing*, in which she outlines her views on the emergence and development of the church in particular African contexts.

According to Oduyoye, evangelism was not the only reason Europeans brought Christianity to West Africa. Their main motivation was accessing and controlling material goods around the continent. After the Portuguese had already made contact and taken slaves and gold from West Africa, Roman Catholics, Anglicans, Presbyterians, Methodists, Baptists, and Mormons and "Protestant nations" joined the clamor for presence on the "dark continent."[19] The gospel would be the cover for a different imperative: European expansion.

The colonial narrative is a complicated one, however, or perhaps it ventures into the area of the miraculous as the European Christian God *was* contemplated and given space in African religious imagination. Religious beings within their own cultures, Africans were open to hearing more about the God of the "second-rate and ne'er-do-well" men who "found their way into colonial and missionary service."[20] Though the message was given a chance, the European missionaries themselves were received differently.[21] These men were foreigners to many Africans.[22] What made them most foreign was not their race (as some "African collaborators" doing translation work and such also could not connect with their peers), but their lack of familiarity with and care for African culture. The actions of these men were confusing. They harped on gender divisions and conveyed a European vision of manhood alongside the message of the gospel. They did not return the hospitality extended to them; they lacked the ability to be with and learn from their African counterparts. They, instead, acted superiorly to the Africans they encountered. What's worse, they believed that their calling from God was justification for such behavior.[23]

Many Africans were quick to notice how the God preached to Africans sounded similar to the European men touting him. What was a European God supposed to mean for African peoples? The men accompanying the gospel message did not help. Their "Western Christian attitudes" felt dominant and paternalistic to their African counterparts.[24] They too readily and too easy entangled message and messenger. "Christianity in Africa began by confusing Christianity and European culture," Oduyoye states.[25]

In hearing the gospel, many Africans, both men and women, sensed a European god complex.[26] Though Western Christianity had planted itself in West Africa, its dissemination methods were not fully accepted nor deemed acceptable. They were seen as reflective of a foreign practice and culture, and a nocuous one at that.

European missionary efforts were "an exercise in cultural occupation,"[27] as they made it impossible for Africans to divorce the Christian message from the European culture that brought it. The missionaries did not advocate for African cultural interpretation of Christianity, but preached cultural assimilation. This would ensure that Christianity was presented in a certain way. To allow Africans to interpret and live into the gospel as Africans saw fit for their culture was too risky. Allowing Africans to indigenize Christianity would have resulted in a reinterpretation and ultimately transformation of European/colonial Christianity. Such a risk was too dangerous. The missionaries brought Christianity as a corrective not only to African religion, but mainly to African culture. This was evidenced in controversial practices such as changing African names to suit the European tongue or granting Africans "Christian" names once they accepted the faith.[28]

European missionaries brought a message of salvation, but salvation set to the tune of denouncing African ways of life. They argued European culture as solely in step with Christian identity. They "arrogated to themselves the power to determine what is to be believed."[29] It became clear to many Africans that the Christian mission was one of cultural replacement. With the presence of the gospel in Africa, the spiritual, psychological, and cultural foundations through which African selfhood was built were slowly being leveled, clearing a path for Africans to become more like Europeans.

Though many Africans did align with the European culture that accompanied the Christian religion, the missionary approach overall was not fully welcomed.[30] It hit a nerve in the African consciousness. As European Christianity tried to uproot them, many Africans held firm to who they were. What they practiced was *already* sacred, rooted, and enough in itself to fulfill their sense of religious belonging.[31] For many their culture would *still* play an important role in their reception of the Christian faith.[32]

Something about Christianity appealed to Africans. It attracted them for various reasons. On the one hand, Africans' desire for the material advantages associated with the faith played a role, but on the other hand, Africans' natural welcome of religious diversity created a space for Christianity's entry. Some Africans outright accepted Christianity for the benefits it could provide.[33] Since African understandings of redemption and salvation are tied to physical and material wellness and being, this logic made sense on a level deeper than simply the accrual of wealth.[34] The benefits of Christianity, which included access to various resources such as hospitals and schools, served as a great incentive for Africans to join the fold.

As mentioned before, the missionizing effort was not entirely onerous; many Africans exercised religious openness as an extension of hospitality and curiosity. Because of their customs of welcome, Africans endured the European missionary presence and were open to receive certain aspects of its message.[35] The points of connection between the Christian faith and African cosmology captured the interests of many Africans—a God-figure, spiritual beings, emphases on elder culture all resonated with African cultural sensibilities.

African Christians lived in this hybrid religious identity, soon forming and joining African churches. It made sense to join aspects of their religious culture with Western Christianity.[36] The values of Christianity seemed to merge well with African ways of life, but soon many Africans would find out that this union would still have mixed results, primarily for the Europeans. Unaccustomed to others taking the privilege to culturally determine their own Christian expression, Europeans tried to demonize African Christian culture and identity.

But Africans were merely trying to make Christianity their own—to see themselves in it. Africans did not replace but rather added Christianity to their preexisting faith traditions and cosmological beliefs.[37] Like in Europe, African Christianity's birth, Oduyoye helps us understand, originated from contextual forms of hearing and understanding. For many Africans Christianity would fit into *their* religious categories.[38] For Africans, "hearing" the gospel-cultural message from Europeans was not the same as "accepting" it as it was extended to them—at least not in the ways Europeans had hoped.[39] Africans were not afraid to take the same liberties as Europeans; they incorporated Christianity into their preexisting African spiritual beliefs, making Christianity African.[40]

Africans lived into their own viable mode of Christianity. Unlike the many scholars who are afraid of the implications of "syncretism" in the force of African Christianity, Oduyoye simply thinks African Christianity as Christianity in its African form.[41] For her it is pertinent to allow Christianity the fullness of its expression; the point and position of African Christianity is toward ownership, not crafting a new religion—to assert that the latter is being done is to assume that European Christianity is the "proper" form of Christianity and that African practice of

Christianity is an offshoot instead of a faith expression that is *also* at the center of Christianity's form.

African identity is a lens through which Christianity is being expressed and enhanced. For Oduyoye, African Christianity is "a Christianity . . . 'cultured' in the African context."[42] In order for Africans to have ownership and claim in Christian history, Christianity had to belong to, not exist apart from or in spite of, African culture. Africans would latch on to some aspects of the European-transmitted Christianity, but ones that aligned with their cultural principles. The affinity the Christian faith had for the sacredness of life and "the quality of life of the whole community" resonated well with African religious identity.[43]

Unfortunately, another area on which European and African culture agreed was the function of gender. Europeans asserted God as male. Almost immediately, African Christian men internalized this hermeneutic, joining it to the preexisting male-privileged ideas in their cultures. This patriarchal foundation became a means to bolster their power in their communities.[44] It has also diminished the already paling role of women in African society. Assigning God a gender is not the problem; it is the interpretation of what one gender means in light of another that sparks a wildfire of confusion. For many, Oduyoye emphasizes, "visualizing God as male and experiencing leadership as a male prerogative have blinded the church to the absence or presence of women."[45] Christian sexism has been used as an excuse to render African women invisible in the Christian church, European and African. In African cultures focused on the wellness of the whole and angered at the audacity of European colonialism, sexism is hypocritical behavior. Once they were able to obtain power, many African men abandoned and ignored the dynamics of context. Context "shapes what one says about God."[46] What are African women to make of African men who choose the side of the oppressor, who adopt the mindset of the opponent? How can African men not see how gender is also important to one's theological foundation—that it, too, is a context?

Oduyoye does not hold back the truth—Christianity does not favor women. "All the varieties of Christianity in Africa are riddled with androcentrism and misogyny," she argues. The misogynistic meeting point between the colonizer and the colonized should be a disgrace and not a point of ally-ship; unfortunately, many Africans do not see it as such. It surely is a wonder African women remain in the church, but they find something promising in the message of Christianity, too. Oduyoye attributes their commitment to Christianity to the gospel's potential to liberate people. As is the African practice, African women adopt that which bestows life and light into their lives; at the same time, they resist its harmful notes. Oduyoye comments, "For women to be at home in Christianity, they suspend belief that it is androcracy that dominates them and not the will of God or their own special innate sinfulness arising out of being women."[47] Even with African women's noble resistance efforts, a woman-hating gospel dynamic still presents a major problem for the integrity of the church in Africa. And this dynamic can be traced to toxic gendered ideas around and about Christian God-talk.

Calling God Father: Gender Language

Originally intended for welcome and inclusion, the Christian church betrays its purpose when it upholds patriarchal and sexist ideas. African women feel this acutely. "As with class and race, on issues of gender discrimination," Oduyoye offers, "the church seems to align itself with forces that question the true humanity of 'the other' and, at times, seems actually to find ways of justifying the oppression or marginalization of 'the other.'"[48] African women face scrutiny in the world on many fronts already; their faith should not contribute to the assault.

Riffing off feminist theologian Mary Daly's famous statement, Oduyoye helpfully reminds us of God's supremacy over gender's naming power. "Saying that God is male does not make the male God" reinforces the distinction that human identity and human language about God are not the same thing.[49] The question of God's gender begets others. For Oduyoye the question of most interest for Africans should not necessarily be "Who is God?" but "What is God?" This inquiry foregrounds the problem many Africans wrestle with when learning to accept the depth of God's identity; it cannot be answered with any certainty.

Gender questions invite us to question the nature of our God-talk. When African women are centered, as they are in Oduyoye's work, these questions bear more weight and rattle millennia-old foundations of Christian thought. They also disturb the rationale that the communal values of African culture, initially not as committed to gendered divine language as they became upon European intervention, should be resurrected. God-talk for Africans should point to the strength of African communal-religious values, not reinforce European ideas about humanity under the guise of Christian theology.

Asking "What is God?" opens us up to the question, "Does a gendered understanding of God in fact positively impact the Christian church?," and then toward the larger question, "Does gender matter in the large scheme of human involvement in the will and action of God in the world?"[50] Ultimately, the last question guides the first. In a world where the dominant mentality tends to win out, the response gravitates toward justifying older systems of thought—gender is humanity's language, not God's. But gender is also the main descriptive form humanity has to articulate details of the faith. When it places people into hierarchies, gender becomes a dangerous tool of demarcating God. Many use gender as a hierarchical map that is then mapped onto God; this, regrettably, implies that God's identity is determined by humanity instead of the other way around. Gender hierarchy tries to fortify a disordered narrative. It argues that if God is described as one particular gender, the existence of those of that same gender must matter most. But this approach signals a war of hierarchical ideologies instead of humanity's collective thought toward God. It honors divisive delineations above cooperative God-talk.

What gender has come to mean among tiered humanity and subsequently in constructing ideas of the divine (and thus in reinforcing such human relationality) must be stripped of its power and wrong usage. African women, considering themselves the custodians of culture,[51] are leading the charge to think communally rather than hierarchically, to think from African culture instead of European culture. It is disappointing that "the sexist elements of Western culture have simply fuelled the cultural sexism of traditional African society."[52]

African theology with critical awareness of African communal values, however, has equalizing potential. There are "unveiled elements in traditional African cultures which, if practised, would have been liberative to

women and the whole community," Oduyoye suggests.[53] If African theology looks to its original principles, it will see that African culture favors
communal balance rather than hierarchy. This shift in perspective can
right the ship of the injurious gender ideas and practices found in Christianity. This begins in language about God.

Oduyoye asserts a controversial point in African cosmological
thought: for Africans, gender is neither the most important nor the defining feature of God. "Most of Africa has no images of God, so where
there are no gender-specific pronouns it has been insisted that God is
supra-gender," she claims.[54] She continues, "Although the gender of God
does not have a big role to play in African religious language, questions
of a gendered or non-gendered understanding of God have become a
crucial point in the global theological dialogue."[55] A just conversation
about God-talk is possible.

Right language about the divine *can* begin in African religious
thought. There is already a proclivity for inclusiveness within African
culture; it understands God in both genders. Oduyoye claims, "The fatherhood of God in the Bible does not confer any special priority on
human fathers; in the tradition the father's role is carefully balanced by
a mother's counterpart." Gender justice to Africans looks not like the
elimination of gender, but rather the full use of gender in describing
God. God as father is also God as mother. African worldviews think
gender together. "Father" and "Mother" are thought together, found
within one another. Gender equality is quite native to African culture, as
"the African mind contains an image of a motherly Father or a fatherly
Mother as the Source of Being," Oduyoye contends.[56]

In an African Christianity God is experienced by many as "the good
parent, the grandparent, *Nana*, a source of loving-kindness, and protec-
tion."[57] God is both maternal and paternal. This signals how gendered
understandings of God have less to do with God and more to do with
particular human cultural conceptions of what one needs the divine to
be. How God is God for all people points back to whom *they need God to
be* in light of their reality.[58] Even the divine gender conversation is about
context.

"In the Source Being, there is no question of male preceding female or
appearing simultaneously in the collective memories of the peoples whose

concern is with the unfolding of individual destinies," Oduyoye notes.[59] An order of gender does not matter when it comes to the Source Being. Africans do not need to consider God in a singularly gendered manner, because God's being exceeds any conversation of God's gender. This hints at a component of African Christian theological anthropology: God is not God because God is male or female, but rather male and female are categories of being because God is God. God does not exist to be male or female but works to guide God's creatures in the details of their lives.

This, then, explains why some Africans, including African women, have no problem with the language of the fatherhood of God being used. It "does not unsettle women in Africa."[60] The fatherhood of God is a description, not a coronation. It does not operate as a means to justify privilege for males but works purely as a naming feature—and one that simultaneously boasts inclusivity. To think "father" as label in itself or alone suggests a contradiction; a father is so because of a mother. The title of "father" is incomplete in itself. "Fatherhood" only *is* in relation to "Motherhood."

Since fatherhood is typically balanced out by motherhood, when God is understood in such terms, what is being suggested is a fuller view of human being, and not a reductionist view of a gendered God.[61] The maternal must always be *directly assumed with* the paternal; the female must be assumed with the male; the woman must be assumed with the man.[62] Paternal labels for God are not emphasizing superiority but suggest joint-ness. Humans can only express God through human terminology as working attempts to understand God in name and to begin understanding God's nature. It is innovative and important to note that in African culture, to assume God as "father" is to assume God as "mother" as well.[63] African culture's holistic values support gender equity.

Oduyoye goes so far as to name gender a theological nonissue, as it does not do the work that it does elsewhere, such as when referring to Christ as male.[64] As with her logic in naming God, women are not excluded from consideration when Christ is mentioned; they are assumed to be included in the work that he is doing in the world. This, in a sense, suggests that the being of Christ and the work of Christ are inseparable. The emphasis is not necessarily about which gender Christ embodied, but about who received the grace his presence in the world generated. This logic can be applicable to God as well—the gender of God is rendered insignificant in light of the reach of God's presence. God presented as Father does not make a statement of male superiority, but illumines the relationality of such a role—that God's children are known, provided for, and protected.

The slippery slope with such thinking about the utility of gender is evident: if used with the wrong intention, gendered language for God can quickly become an exercise in gender hierarchy. Oduyoye's work reminds us, then, that the problem emerges when the roles of the divine become confused with the designation of the divine's creation. When men (and women) in ministry and in the church at large begin to assume that the notion of maleness functions simultaneously as God-likeness, they are not providing divine description but relational disorder. Thinking gender in the wrong way dims the spiritual and comforting power behind God as father/mother. We see this happening already: in thinking God as hierarchically male one diminishes the femaleness/motherhood/womanness of God. God-talk done in this way is diminishing. For African women, the point of the gendered language of any sort, but especially male language, is inclusivity. It is supposed to invoke the presence of the whole unified human self—its femaleness as well as its maleness.

According to Oduyoye's logic, the point of naming God in the paternal parental role and naming Christ as biologically male is to signal the need for an interconnected understanding of gender(ed) expression in theological language. This is already the case if we consider the same, inversely. Oduyoye wisely argues that the motherhood of God and of Christ most likely would not provoke hierarchical understanding—that females are more powerful than males—but invoke the fullness of humanity—where God and Christ are pictured as well-rounded. Both the descriptors of "Mother" and "Father" are invoked in the fullness of pairing and partnership. Unfortunately, since this rationale is not carefully attended to in many Christian churches, at the very least, the exclusivist masculine language of God must be continually discussed, debated, and clarified.[65]

In order to participate in God's creative plan for the world,[66] the church must create a theology and theological language that considers "justice in human relations."[67] It must prioritize full recognition and equal treatment of all of its members, and begin doing so through utterances about God that illumine the divine aspects of the Creator, that are not expropriated by humanity to cause separations. Divine language must not be baselessly appropriated, but carefully considered. African women's theology begins to explore constructive forms of God-talk by using images and ideas close to those women's realities.

Hearth-Holds and Holding God: Knowing God Differently

African women do not believe God can be captured in narrow windows of expression. God-talk exceeds the bounds of Christianity. Since theology is "a reflection on our human experience that begins with our belief in God, the Source Being," God can be known in many ways and through various images.[68] Oduyoye asserts as much. "If there is anything that is commonly affirmed by all theologies it is this," she offers: "God is resolved not to tolerate our distorted human existence."[69] God is found in many religious traditions; to assume or assert the opposite misconstrues humanity's cultural diversity and understanding of God's free movement.

Understanding marginalized identity all too well, African women's theology recognizes religious pluralism as a sign of diverse viewpoints. Since they do not have a monopoly on God-talk, Christians must affirm this reality as well. God cannot be narrated solely in one way.

African women's theology contends that the Christian church must acknowledge religious diversity, especially in Africa. Theology done on the African continent, which is home to multiple religious expressions, can serve as an example of religious welcome and tolerance. In the same ways Africans know God diversely, African women speak about their experiences of God as unique to their stories and contexts.

African women's God-talk centers the home. This resonates with Oduyoye. She has two objectives in creatively rethinking the notion of "home": (1) to name how God is spoken of across various religious traditions and (2) to offer a counterpoint to women's marginalization in the home and social structures like it. Oduyoye gives "home" new meaning, especially for those entrapped by the gendered assumptions built into it. African women do not have to know "home" as a place of rigidity; they can know it as a place of openness and possibility. The literal reference of the "home" provides a symbolic example of where religious diversity can coexist. It can be where and how women express how they know God.

Oduyoye asserts that the Christian church is akin to something like a "hearth-hold" of Christ in God.[70] The hearth, an oven-like structure similar to a fireplace, symbolizes the home or the gathering place of many. For Oduyoye, Christianity is only *one* hearth-hold of religious expression in which God is honored; many other hearth-holds exist on an equal plain with the Christian faith. For women, this image of shared and equal identity under God connects powerfully; it refutes images of the house or home as a constrictive location of women's worth. It also suggests God as present in a space where women are allowed to name who they are, to name *their* place in the home. A hearth-hold insists everyone has equal weight and importance in the eyes of God. It further insists on God's affiliation with the home, the image of the domestic.

God is where the women are. Through hearth-hold imagery Oduyoye revises the Christian church's relationship to God.[71] Positioning African women's place in the theological order in this way—in the home—suggests continuity with God, since "Africans . . . are organized around the hearths of women."[72] In this reframing, women gain not only recognition but also divine importance.

Hearth-hold imagery acclaims both Africanized religious practice and women's position in society and in the world. The image of God is directly aligned with honoring the historical imaging of women's being and work, imaging centered in the home. African women's affiliations with the hearth and the maternal align God as Mother, Christ as the Compassionate One, and the Spirit as Comforter.[73] This alignment suggests a familial and communal character and tone are called for in church and ecclesial life, one honoring the significance of everyone in the home.[74] The hearth-hold of God insists on a level of mutuality. It requires that the entire church take up the mantle to "promote the growth of all into the fullness they see in Christ."[75] It challenges the church to recognize everyone in and around it. Hearth-hold imagery glimpses both the potential and the problems of the Christian church.

Inverting the image of the home toward the divine means that instead of delimiting practice, Oduyoye's hearth-hold imagery encourages women to interpret the home for theological means. She gives women the reins to redefine what certain spaces mean for their own theological reflection. In this, African women can serve as theologians in their own right, blending insight and wisdom with African cultural values. They uncover the potential of the divine in spaces of their historical oppression. They gain subversive power to name what is good and true about God's presence in ordinary life. When African Christian women assert a hearth-hold of God (in Christ), they assert the strength and creativity of their theological voices.

African women believe in the expansiveness of God across religious bodies. The body of Christ is only *one* hearth-hold in the household of God. In African religious thought, all human beings—all hearth-holds, all communities—belong to God. The Christian church is one hearth-hold in the larger household of God.[76] God holds all of God's creatures, whether they are part of the hearth-hold of Christ or not.[77] God is big enough to hold those in Christ as well as those who know God in other ways. In this pluralistic move, Oduyoye affirms religious traditions outside of Christianity as critical avenues through which God can be known and named. She reverses the colonial logic of demonizing religious traditions outside of traditional Christianity, while she simultaneously and subversively asserts how God cannot be captured. In this inclusive theological approach, Oduyoye keeps sociocultural context in the forefront of our theological and ecclesial imaginations.

The "whole cosmos constitutes the *oikonomia* of God"; therefore, African women recognize the Christian church as only one means of honoring God.[78] While Oduyoye identifies as Christian, she also recognizes that one's lens does not and should not negate the reality of another's. African women's theology takes a stand against religious marginalization and practices of harm. It respects the numerous ways God can be invoked and called forth. God is not the property of the Christian imagination. God is found in the fullness of human experience.

A God of Life: How Africans Know God

Oduyoye claims that God is the foundation of life.[79] One's "life is lived in the presence of God and in full view of a spirit world that is in constant communion with our dimension of life."[80] A doctrine of God can be articulated with the wisdom of African wisdom literature and oral tradition as well as the values of Christian ideas. This God is connected to the African peoples in *their* manner of life and expression of culture.

Oduyoye also contends that God is a God of life. God inspires "wholeness, well-being, shalom, healthy living."[81] God is "the source of life and being."[82] African women call God the source of vitality. An African women's Christian theology, then, is a life-giving theology, a vital theology. It is a theology "that invigorates and gives life and hope."[83]

God's creative activity underscores God's vitality. "Creation was a deliberate act of God," Oduyoye claims.[84] To know God is to know life. God is the One who infuses all humanity knows with liveliness. The names of God found in African symbols, myths, proverbs, cultural stories, and sayings proclaim a God of life, a God of creation.[85] Africans experience God as hope and foundation.[86] God is comrade and friend, the "sole creator and sustainer of all things."[87] God is the beginning, the middle, and the end of life; all things move through God. God is implicated in all that exists, including relationships between and among God's creation. Humanity has been called to mimic God's affinity for God's creation. We are tasked to love and respect the earth.[88]

God sees all of creation and wants what is right for it. "The African experience of God is that ultimately God is on the side of justice," she offers.[89] Oduyoye adopts the language of her theological colleague and fellow EATWOT participant James Cone when she claims Africa's experience of God is one of recognition; God takes the side of the oppressed. Through the person of Jesus Christ, God seeks the liberation of God's people from marginalizing conditions.[90] God does not abandon God's people.[91] The fact that God is liberating Africans from oppressive European colonial regimes positions God as the arbiter of freedom. God calls humanity out of oppression "into wholeness of life."[92]

For African women, oppression is not only evident in historical colonial rule but also manifested in gender discrimination and violence. For them God is liberation beyond the surface level. God finds and unfetters those in the trenches of African culture's misgivings as well. If an action is to be called liberative, it must include the voices of women. In Africa, this is no different.[93] African theology has pushed women's voices to the margins for too long. Gender should not be as powerfully repressive as it has been. But if gender does not ultimately define God's worthiness, why should it define the worth and value of God's image, of God's creation?[94] It is time for women to experience God in freedom instead of surrendering to and suffering under the deification of man. Women are creation, too. Women are whom God loves, too. In claiming their humanity and voice, African women claim God as well.

Undoubtedly the most gripping example of God's love for all humanity is found in Jesus Christ. He is the expression of God's love for the entirety of humanity, without caveat. He lives in the world opposite a masculinist vision of God. God enfleshed, Jesus shows God as compassionate, caring, loving, and most important, fully aware of the circumstances of God's creation. He fully includes women in the vision and in-breaking of God's kingdom.[95] He welcomes all into the household of God and claims all of God's children as significant. They bear God's image.[96] This affirmation is salvific for African women. It is the freedom that saves—women are known and loved by God in Christ. Now we will take a closer look at how Oduyoye asserts this claim as true, through her communal and careful look at who Christ is *for* African women.

CHAPTER FIVE

CHRISTOLOGY

For many women who go to church, Christ the Word comes as a story.
—Mercy Amba Oduyoye, *Introducing African Women's Theology*

Beginnings

Christians know Jesus through words. Words echoed across podiums and pulpits, on street corners, in living rooms, and elsewhere tell the story of the divine Word. Words contain religious ideas and moral principles; they unearth the truth about divine and ordinary encounter. "As human constructs of experience," words "are the places where doctrine and life meet."[1] Words translate experience, relate context, artfully craft accounts. Words name moments—and serve as experts in telling. They are sacred. The Christian tradition bears witness to their holiness in referring to Jesus Christ the Word of God. Because words carry power and sacred movement, where they live is imperative to note.

For this reason, Mercy Oduyoye examines and tells the story of Jesus Christ through the words of African women. Though well versed in discourses in Christology—examining the person, nature, and role of Jesus Christ—Oduyoye grounds her understanding of Jesus in her own experiences and those of women like her. Her Christology unfolds through the words of women. For Oduyoye, women's words can be trusted—women's words are faithful to do theological naming.

We have already seen how important context is to naming the shape of one's belief. Africans interpret Christian tenets and doctrinal ideas in ways familiar to them.[2] As with the doctrine of God, one expresses one's Christology contextually.[3] African women especially believe this; they interpret Jesus through the lens of their fringe existence. Women accustomed to being marginalized, unheard, and made to feel invisible connect with Jesus on both an experiential level and a hopeful one. Jesus knew marginal identity: this is the experiential connection in African women's Christology. He also overcame the forces of oppression: this is the hope of African women's Christology. African women feel close to the story of Jesus because his place in the world—of being peculiar in so- cial status, leading an ostracized life, and fighting for a just world—mir- rors their own.[4]

Oduyoye boldly asserts that Jesus is found in the "everyday experi- ences of the women of Africa."[5] Since African women are this connected to Jesus' life and message, their words about Jesus carry different weight. Women know cultural estrangement very intimately. Their accounts of these painful schisms differ from how their African male and white Eu- ropean male and female counterparts speak of the entanglement of Jesus' ministry and his social reception.

African women know Jesus through their cultural invisibility and so- cial marginalizing; "Christ is the liberator from the burden of disease and from taboos that restrict women's participation in their communities."[6] They know not only that Jesus reaches people like them but also that he may have experienced life in ways similar to how they have experienced it. Jesus presents a different way to be human in this life. He offers the possibility of inclusion, affirmation, and freedom. For African women, the novelty of Jesus' message of freedom toward God is seen in scripture's stories of healing and solidarity. This is the clarion call of the Christian church, a church that includes African women. We must pay close atten- tion to this. If Jesus is the church's word to the world and women are also the church, then Jesus is in women's words.[7]

In sitting with women's words about Jesus and exploring African women's corporeal connection to Christ, this chapter ultimately holds up one question: Who is Jesus Christ for African women? Oduyoye centers African women's voices, experiences, and constructive ideas to provide an answer. She announces her Christology through the standpoint of women, giving most space to the worldview of African women.

Being Understood

African women declare that Jesus knows the conditions of the marginalized. He is cognizant of the suffering caused by social, religious, and political structures. He challenges broken systems and powerful people. And he upends the forces trying to separate the gospel message from its liberating power. African women are, in part, drawn to Jesus' familiarity with hard circumstances. He recognizes those who lead marginalized lives. But African women also are drawn to his liberating potential; he assures the marginalized that there is a way forward with his just, radical, and inclusive vision.

In giving African women the floor, Oduyoye's framing of Jesus Christ imaginatively pushes current conceptions of Christology toward wholeness. African women's Christology is inclusive, holistic, uninterested in leaving any stone unturned. Oduyoye's christological approach burrows into the realities of human sin, centering details that mark the stories of African women—namely, their race and gender. African women, Oduyoye discloses through this contextual move, are critically important to naming Jesus' identity and work in the world through the elements of their existence; why else would Jesus trust "in women sufficiently to reveal himself to them"?[8]

It is significant that Jesus "related to women as human beings, to be respected and to be trusted."[9] He made a conscious effort to interact with women; he trusted them to carry his message. The scriptural accounts of Martha and Mary among others prove as much. Women are part of the christological formation of the Christian church; they are critical to Jesus' telling. We can conclude, then, that women's words, the same words that also curate God-talk, are doing Christology.[10]

African women understand Jesus as extremely close to marginalized bodies—as a *part* of these bodies, even. For Oduyoye, the church's knowing who Christ is *begins* with women, with the words between and exchanged among them. In African culture, where oral tradition and

storytelling compose the foundation of how one knows oneself, the notion of Jesus as Word (of God) resonates closely and keenly.[11] Jesus Christ
is the embodied Word, the story of his body a critical connective point
for African women. Oduyoye helps us realize that words in this way—in
the stories of bodies—do christological work. We see this work unfold in
the excited speech of two women.

Between the Women

Christological markers are found in the company of women. The events
and conversation that ensue from Mary's visit to Elizabeth in Luke 1
demonstrate this firsthand. The simplicity of their interaction is crucial:
the divine is found in ordinary moments, joined to the events of women's
bodies. It is connected to the stories of women who have been narratively
humbled in scripture, women like Mary and Elizabeth.

We witness God's "yes" to the world in the "yes" of a young, engaged
Jewish girl.[12] Oduyoye asserts as much. After meeting Gabriel, Mary
finds someone to share the inconceivable. She goes to Zechariah's home,
greets Elizabeth—their visit pregnant with holy potential. "Together,
they rejoiced at God's salvation which comes through women," Oduyoye
writes.[13] But there is more to this interaction than two pregnant women
sharing excitement to see one another. What we witness in this scriptural
moment is a salvific dimension to women's community. In these women
coming together, the possibility of salvation (soteriology in addition to
Christology) is given flesh. "As unborn speaks to unborn, God's future
as discerned by women is made ready by women to be communicated
among and by women to the whole community," Oduyoye contends.[14]
The moment is small yet immense—these women carry the message of
the world's salvation! In their communing moment, the world is being
prepared to receive Jesus, the Christ figure known to these women before
he was ever known to anyone else in the world.

Oduyoye keeps us here, on this incredible occurrence. Her observations inspire us to pause. Readers of scripture are encouraged not to rush to
the male stars of this beautiful scene, but to wait and sit with its current ac-
tresses. This pause allows us to be privy to some theological reconfiguring.

We stay with these women, grant them the holy recognition that is their due. These women are contributors of christological revelation; this is a theologically critical moment of narrative gender-reversal. Keeping these women in the center reframes the narrative focus from John and Jesus back onto Mary and Elizabeth. In utero, John leaps, rejoicing at Jesus' presence. This is an important confirmation, a conversation of and in the spirit, but if in focusing *only* on the leap we forgo the women *also* present in the conversation, or if we shift focus too quickly, the details of the account and the revelatory potential of this messianic moment are diminished.

The commonplace conversation between these two women houses the declarative moment of the world's total deliverance. Though John's leaping can preach, so, too, does Mary's coming, Elizabeth's meeting, and Elizabeth's prophetic tongue. So, too, must the actions of the women make their way into our theological accounts of Christology. These women's actions constitute an important moment in our canon of christological knowledge.[15]

Jesus Christ lives first in, on, and in between words spoken by women. To think of Christ's beginnings as confined to a different moment, such as John baptizing Jesus, is to miss the chance to honor a metahomiletical moment when the Christ is introduced through women's preached word and prophetic utterance.[16] Oduyoye reminds us that salvation "comes through women."[17] These women are preaching not only through their words but with their bodies. The paradox is theologically telling—God lives, moves, and has being in the communion of women.

This scene offers readers a number of details to explore, for good or bad. Pregnancy bears significant weight in this story. It shapes how women, including African women, know Christology. But it is also the proverbial elephant in the room. Pregnancy is a gendered social expectation often forced onto African women and girls. Many women and girls cannot get pregnant. Too many women and girls lose their sense of identity to maternity; many lose their lives to it. Pregnancy is not a small detail, but a sensitive factor for women. Another complex layer of difficulty—namely, the question of women's value—surrounds pregnancy when it is associated with the world's salvation.

Oduyoye is keenly aware of the controversy around such a physiological connection to God incarnate. The fear of childlessness is a real factor that looms in the background of this account. This has been a social-cultural concern for many women across time. Pregnancy is too often cast as the social means of cementing womanhood. Though pregnancy is a joy for many, childlessness as a social stigma is a global fear, including for African women.[18]

The visitation of Mary and Elizabeth can easily be read in a number of ways, including as an affront to childless women.[19] Concerns about pregnancy in such a holy moment are understandable: Are pregnant bodies the only bodies that play a role in salvation's manifestation in the earth? Are women who can bear children more valuable, purer, or holier beings than others? Oduyoye would argue, "No." Pregnancy is merely a means of uplifting a different message: women's embodied experience is the means by which God bore flesh in the world. Those whose bodies and beings experience the world with difficulty—with tragedy, even—are those best suited to "hold" the Christ. The subversiveness of women's bodies is what holds christological power. Women are crucial to how the world knows Jesus Christ *because* of the *experiences of their bodies*, because of what they carry because they are females in a male-dominated world.

Oduyoye's reflections in "A Coming Home to Myself," in *Liberating Eschatology*, are helpful. She examines in depth the painful realities of women who are unable to conceive or reproduce. The gendered expectations of African women's reproductive capabilities spur intense psychological stress and duress for many women.[20] Her focus, however, is not centered on one's ability to physically reproduce, but rather on the fellowship of women undergoing and experiencing challenge and change in and through their bodies. Women's overarching embodied experience is the x factor; what women experience corporeally is the means through which Christ is known. It is not in women's ability to procreate.[21] Being a woman is the only prerequisite to God's prescription of viable womanhood. Womanhood as prescribed by God is holy enough to carry the holy; womanhood as prescribed by a patriarchal society only engenders the opposite message.

Oduyoye masterfully attends to the problematic patriarchal paradigm with which African women's bodies (and ultimately their sense of being) are forced to align. She states, "Childbearing is central to African women's self-image, and the scene of the two women swapping pregnancy announcements is a precious one for African women. That the younger woman paid a visit to the older one to share her strange experience signifies for them the solidarity that women crave in times of crisis and in other significant moments of their lives."[22] The moment of similitude and solidarity—*of being woman*—is what renders this moment christologically relevant and impactful. The connecting point between Mary's and Elizabeth's stories on the one hand and women's stories all over the world on the other is the experience of *womanhood*. One can, by virtue of being a woman, tell the world something new about Christ.

Oduyoye's own christological sensibility is described as a journey she takes with other women colleagues such as Bette Ekeya, Anne Nasimiyu, Teresia Hinga, and Musimbi Kanyoro. Their communal gatherings parallel "Mary and Elizabeth sharing stories of salvation."[23] These women feel leaps in their spirits when they share accounts of their lives. Christology for African women originates not from traditional doctrine but from personal and communal experience.[24] Where women are *is* the generative space for Christology.

The question of who Christ is closely parallels the inquiry: Who do (the) women say he is?[25] The women know something; they are clued in. They are the first preachers of the Word; they are preachers among themselves. They must be listened to, for they may very well hold the world's announcement of salvation. This should mean something in the scope and shape of Christology writ large.

The nature of Mary's interactions overall inspires feminist readings of Christology and soteriology. The constructive possibilities are inspiring. Her interaction with Elizabeth incites community—in particular, women's togetherness and support—as creating a different view of how the world knows Jesus. Their conversation brings into focus the feminist power of curiosity, inquiry, and community. But Mary's interaction with Gabriel also has feminist potential.

When the divine messenger greeted her, Mary did not remain silent but asked questions; her questioning pressed on when she was informed of the task the divine had assigned to her body. Can we read Mary's asking the angel of the Lord how her pregnancy could "be" as a type of feminist inquiry? For Mary to question Gabriel, for her to question a divine figure much like scriptural male protagonists such as Abram or Moses do, is a demonstration of agency.

Although Oduyoye does not address this specifically in her work, it is helpful to consider the levels of agency in these divine moments. Mary's questions to Gabriel are just as weighty as her interaction with Elizabeth. The conversation with Gabriel is also part of the larger event of these women showing the world who Christ is. Oduyoye does not name Mary's questioning moment as part of the voice, the words, the "conversation" and interaction of the women (though, to be fair, Oduyoye's intentions and analysis are focused on the embodied conversation between Mary and Elizabeth and not on that between Mary and the angel). But vocality as a demonstration of agency brands instances where power occurs—whether in question or conversation—as feminist. A feminist reading of this tangential moment brings women's voices and agency to the forefront of the scriptural account.

Women are critical to a sound Christology and soteriology. If we look closely, the moments that inform Christian doctrine are littered with women-affirming and feminist moments. The gospel does not register without the feminist register. Like Mary's and Elizabeth's words, African women's words are critical in helping the Christian church understand who Jesus Christ is to, in, and for the world. What the women say matters just as much to who Jesus the Christ is as the words of any other.

What the Women Say

Unfortunately, African women have not been given enough room to co-determine who Jesus Christ is to the church. This paints a deceptive picture representing Jesus as not belonging to them. Oduyoye challenges this discrepancy outright, asking a series of poignant questions: "What do women say about Christology? Is there such a thing as women's Christology? Do the traditional statements of Christology take into account women's experiences of life?"[26] Her questioning points to a theological chasm—what women do not get to say about Christ suggests theological self-censorship in the church. How might African women, then, be included in discerning the movement of God incarnate in the world? What role does African women's Christology play in the understanding of human existence, shared life, and cultural and social community as a whole? A more central question lurks underneath, one cognizant of context: From whence does one's Christology come? For African women, one's Christology comes from how they understand their bodies culturally and socially. It comes from where the divine intersects with such realities. Context informs Christology.

To answer the question of who Christ is for African women requires women's shared reflection. Hemming together the experiential narratives of women's lives, Oduyoye outlines African women's christological frame: African women "all talk about Jesus, believe in Jesus, relate closely to Jesus the son of Mary and testify to what Jesus has done."[27] They see Jesus as the one who has lived through and overcome a marginal life. Perhaps it is that simple.

Women's insight *should* bear great weight in contemporary interpretations of Christology. The generative and exciting moment when words are exchanged between Mary and Elizabeth embodies the christological promise of love, hope, and salvation. It also points out a new way to see the church, a church recognizing women's theological imagination. This acknowledges the church in its entirety. "Christology then is the church's word about Christ. The question asked by Jesus does not go away. What do *I* say about The Christ?" Oduyoye asks.[28] African women's involvement in this question and subsequently in Christology's formation incites a prophetic tongue, a calling out of what is and what needs to be. Oduyoye's question both challenges the church to grant women's voices weight and incorporates women into the notion of "church." She gives them permission to also be the "*I.*"

The fact that Oduyoye has to reread christological moments in scripture for women's inclusion points to the historical reality that Christology has not been the church's word about Christ, but the church's *men's* word about Christ. In the dealings of the church—at least in the definition of "church" that Oduyoye teases out here—women are both internal and critical. Her question "What do *I* say about The Christ?" is important *only if* the emphasis placed upon the individual "I" *represents the fullness and completeness* of the collective and communal "I." Thinking the "I" solely individually or personally flags an inclusion problem. Christology should be determined by both women and men of the church. One should not have to fight for women's voices to be included; they are already in the "I."

Inclusion is a promising cultural gesture. In including women's constructive christological claims, Oduyoye privileges the best of African cultural hermeneutics. Although Eurocentric culture still has a hold on African religious imagination in part, Oduyoye offers an alternative theological reckoning.[29] Her turn to inclusion is a cultural turn to African beliefs attuned to the wellness of the community over the individual.[30] This move, privileging African ideology over European practice, grants the African community authority to determine the features of its own Christian identity. In response to the question "What do *I* say about The Christ?" Oduyoye asserts that African Christian women's voices are important to how the African church articulates its respective "I."

Oduyoye is not ignorant of christological ideas that came before her; she instead chooses to outline an approach truest to her reality. She understands "what has been said by the Church,"[31] acknowledging accounts of christological origins in the Hebrew Scriptures as well as the Greek biblical text. Aware of the social, political, and cultural issues of the first five centuries of what she calls "the Christian era," Oduyoye intentionally crafts her own christological approach, one sensitive to postcolonial realities and African feminism. Hers is a Christology "whose concern has been how to make the story of Jesus the context in which African women read their lives."[32] Taking historical frames as well as her own experience into account, her christological position validates the African woman's perspective as informed and insightful.[33] Her position is the result of tracing christological history, seeing where women were missing from the narrative, and returning to texts and tradition to see where women have been present and contributing all along. Oduyoye's Christology is the product of outlining how she, and others like her, are no longer accepting their stories as missing from the Christian canon.

Jesus with Us

African women see potential for their social inclusion in the life and message of Jesus. He embodied communal uplift and bore a different message than the dominant social, political, and religious voices of his day. He saw people the rest of society chose not to. African women appreciate the nuances of Jesus' activity in the community—whom he spoke to, whom he blessed, whom he saw.[34]

Women had a role in the "life and teaching of Jesus."[35] Validating those who have been made invisible is at the heart of African women's Christology. It models the compassion and attentiveness of Christ. Jesus saw the socially marginalized and gave them hope and vision for a different future. He lived into that which African women are still advocating that their men adopt—the recognition of and fighting on behalf of the least in their community. This mode of christological embodiment, African women urge, is discipleship for African women and men alike—to embody Christ's resistance against forces that mistreat their people. Jesus most appeals to African women because his inclusiveness is his witness.

Oduyoye draws our attention to a few notable ways African women experience Jesus: Jesus as sufferer, redeemer, and victor. These experiences move in and out of each other. In them, the overarching themes of race and gender—realities with which African women are forced to contend—are addressed.[36] The hope is for the Christian church to see itself in light of the one who sees into the fullness of the human condition.

Sufferer: Bodies in Christ

Social suffering bore itself into Jesus' salvific mission. Though it is impossible to name to what extent this suffering contributed to God's enfleshment, Oduyoye suggests Jesus was impacted and further brought into the narrative of suffering through his constant and continuous encounters with suffering. Jesus' life among the poor and oppressed "saw suffering, sacrifice and the Cross, as salvific."[37] She continues, "The Christ is the one who suffers so that humanity might have the fullness of life intended for them by God."[38] In order for Jesus to be the bearer of the good news of life in God, suffering featured prominently in his narrative. In order to invert suffering's impact and determination on humanity's future, to save humanity from suffering as death-destination, he had to know it.

While it is understandably risky to think suffering vital to understanding Jesus' impact on constructions of abundant life, this is precisely the position of many African women and other marginalized persons. Jesus is, as Oduyoye noted earlier, "the context in which African women can read their lives."[39] He is the balm to their wounds.

To argue that suffering sharpens salvation's effects is still controversial at best. The implications are many. Can one truly "live" without suffering? Might part of salvation's revelation be in suffering's ebbs and flows? Must one know suffering intensely to feel the power of salvation? Is suffering a step in the full knowing of the true nature and expression of life? This is a tough sell. The suffering African women endure is not a desired requirement but a difficult, inescapable truth. For many, suffering holds meaning in the christological narrative insofar as it makes the impact of salvation all the more poignantly felt. What does one do with this reality[40]—that one must be saved from something? For many women suffering is a universal introduction and plotline, salvation the conclusion.

But "suffering as relief" varies from "suffering as beneficial." Can suffering heighten one's spiritual consciousness? Is it a mode of discipleship? Oduyoye would think not. It is a consequence of sin and evil in the world; it is not humanity's lot to make suffering either effective or purposeful. This would be an improbable construction. Jesus is the only one who can relate to suffering in such a way that its power is diminished. Only Jesus can relate to suffering on both sides of existence, as creation and Creator. Only he can know suffering at unreachable depths. Christ is the one who "suffers so that humanity might have the fullness of life intended for them by God."[41] He does not suffer as an invitation for humanity to suffer as he suffered; they cannot. He does, however, invite humanity to *see* suffering and *engage* its victims with compassion. Jesus is not immune to suffering, but uniquely calls his followers forth to meet it, to recognize its complicated manifestations, and to respond to it as well as is humanly possible.

Jesus is in close proximity to the ills of human existence. He is fully aware of the stresses of a marginal, embodied life. For African women this comes as a great comfort; Jesus knows—in his mind and in his body—not only what suffering is but, most importantly, what suffering *feels* like.[42] But while his embodiment directly connects him to the experience of African women, it is less easy to connect the *particularity* of Jesus' embodiment and that of African women.[43] To overparticularize Jesus' living into his body and African women's embodied life as it relates to suffering brings up questions concerning Jesus' reach and ultimately his relationship to suffering. Is Jesus only for those who suffer? Does he only connect to the least of these? Aligning Jesus with the marginalized alone throws into question to whom else he can belong and connect.[44] At the very least, this would be a potential perception. Jesus belonging *primarily* to the least of these could spread the idea that in his embodiedness he only peripherally belongs to those who hold more power and influence in society.

What is reflected in this potential dilemma where Jesus belongs primarily to marginalized persons? Who owns Jesus? Who gets to "have" Jesus? These questions are fraught with ideas of control but also the possibility of the God-man's *being had* in a fixed way. The audacious proposal of making Jesus property is also at play. Can Jesus belong to someone? African women see this question at the heart of Christian colonial and missional endeavors; Europeans relied upon a polluted logic of gendered ownership and theological truth claims.[45] Leaning too far on either side of the spectrum is cautioned against. To assert Jesus as connected to the marginalized in society alone limits Jesus' amplitude. This logic jeopardizes the principle that Jesus is for all people. To assert one's right to mete out Jesus according to hierarchical decrees also limits the good news. An ideological shift to Jesus' life as a claim on all of humanity, however, is a productive corrective.

The difference between having sole claim on Jesus and Jesus laying claim to humanity can be found in the perspective of the theologian. African women's theology asserts that *humanity has Jesus through Jesus having humanity*. The claim is felt in one's being claimed by Jesus. African women "have" Jesus only insomuch as *they are had* by Christ. But this "having" functions not in a propertied or domineering sense, but in a mode of discipleship joined to the meaning Christ has made for them.

In Christ, human being, which does not preclude human embodiment, is claimed for and moved toward God. Christ moves bodies and embodiment toward wholeness in the Creator. Christology is thus captive and captivating in this way—human life is taken into the Christ and made his. Thus, when African women have to state the obvious in claiming that the body of Christ and their bodies are connected, a problem emerges, not in Christology, but concerning a racialized and gendered hermeneutic of Christ and African women's bodies. To distance women's bodies from the embodiment of the Christ is to assert both ownership over the purpose and function of African women's bodies and the magnitude of what Christ can be and do. It signals the dominance of a Eurocentric theology.[46]

But the problem does not lie with the West alone; African women have struggled for recognition among the men in their societies, too. Gender issues and sexism in African churches are not a Western phenomenon alone, but an age-old issue for many African women dealing with African men shoring up positions of power.[47] African women's writing and thinking themselves into theological relevance touches on their intersectional identity of being both African and female. This is a topic to be further explored as a matter of theological anthropology, but for the moment, we can hold the following as true: African women's theology provides an alternative viewpoint determining Christology and African women's ontology to be a pair that is critical to forward-thinking theology.[48]

Can Jesus be had? Can Jesus be owned? For African women, this is not the question, but the problem—the problem that has a hand in producing their experiences of suffering. Jesus' embodiment is not a means to power, ownership, or theological superiority, but reminds us that he knows human suffering. Jesus knows what embodiment of the most painful sort feels like. His connection to African women's embodiment is not a theft of Jesus' body for African women's theological ends; it is, rather, claiming space for African women to affirm alongside everyone else that Jesus knows how their bodies feel, what they have experienced, and what they have encountered.

The christological implications are massive—Jesus knows our bodies as well as we know our bodies. God enfleshed knows the details of all of our flesh, in and out.[49] In this, African women are not as distant in embodied experience from Christ as colonial and slave history have tried to make them out to be. Jesus knows the embodied experiences of African women, the details of their hardships and obstacles. He is cosufferer. The one who took the sins of the world on his shoulders to the cross knows the weight of sin—sins that ensconce suffering. He names the true nature of suffering for what it is and where it is—it is not the plan of God.[50]

Jesus is suffering kin not only because he experienced suffering in his own body but also because he knows the inner workings of suffering's impact on *all* bodies.

African women understand fully the theological limitations of embodiment—thus they join themselves to the one who experienced embodiment in difficult ways as well, who defied normative respectable embodiment in order to preach the end of suffering and death in and through his own body.

Redeemer: Colonialism and Patriarchy

Colonial encounters color the concept of redemption for many Africans, but not in the ways some may imagine. Many Africans sought to be free from the rigidness of the colonizer's Christianity. Freedom from colonial regulation and from the monitoring of religion and culture is part of the liberative African Christian narrative. Oduyoye finds connections between Africa's and Israel's experiences with colonial rule. She briefly characterizes how God redeems and delivers in the Hebrew scriptures in the following ways: (1) nation from nation; (2) from national sin; (3) individuals from other people; (4) from dehumanization/poverty (that begets slavery); (5) from personal actions that disturb others' relationship with others and with God; and (6) in God orchestrating repentance or a return to right religion.[51] Overall, in Israel's narrative, redemption is characterized by right relationship with another.

In order to be redeemed, one has to know from what or from whom one is being redeemed, restored, and rescued. In *The Open Secret: An Introduction to the Theology of Mission*, Lesslie Newbigin expresses Oduyoye's sentiments well: Africans gave the white man's religion a try, but white men built a false narrative of white dominance and superiority upon it. We must remember that Africans' hearing a message did not equate to blind and total conformity to it. The white man gained religious, political, and social acumen in his religion being "heard" but not necessarily "accepted."[52] The difference between religious exploration and religious residence (or commitment) came to be the sticking point of missional Christianity.

The very existence of disturbing European missions built the case for redemption. For Africans, redemption holds a definition and weight similar to that which it held for the Jewish people in scripture. Oppression and evangelical hierarchy leading to moments such as the slave trade provided perspective for Africans about Jesus' power over and against the colonizers.[53] For African women, the opposition is multifaceted; even if oppression manifests in different forms, it comes from the same origin—patriarchal thinking tethered to flawed understandings of whiteness.

Oduyoye leans toward connecting whiteness with patriarchy, but does not voice the connection as explicitly. Instead, she asserts the broader argument that Western influence as a whole works adversely against African communities. The combination of African culture (patriarchal forces) and foreign culture (European colonial forces) proved itself the craftiest adversary for African women to overthrow. The problems of masculinity and whiteness found in colonialism highlighted both new and entrenched problems in African culture.

In the colonial evangelistic moment, masculinity—an offshoot of whiteness—was arguably evangelized most vigorously. Recall, the messengers—European men—carried the message of Christianity to West Africa. In Ghana, many male British missionaries who were "not fitted for English ordination" wrestled with their own need to be seen as respectable men in their various communities.[54] According to Oduyoye, missional archives convey that "people of dubious intelligence and integrity were launched upon the unsuspecting savages of Africa south of the Sahara."[55] Men who were not the best and brightest of their societies thought themselves the moral authorities and spiritual experts of the Christian message.

The most important aspect of these missionaries' formation gestures in this direction: toward *what* were these men striving, and how did it manifest in their movement in the world, especially in their interaction with African peoples? Francophone cultural theorist Aimé Césaire suggests that this is the detrimental effect of colonialism, that not only are the colonized violated, but the colonizers are also harmed in subscribing to notions of superiority that can only be striven for but never truly obtained.[56] This colonial logic wreaks havoc. Coupled with the underlying activity of masculinity's exemplification through imperialism and conquest, colonialism and competitions of masculinity set the stage for oppressive conditions both African men and women would not only be subjected to, but also evangelized under and through. Masculinist and patriarchal narratives colored colonial missional ambitions. The "scramble for Africa," to which African colonialism would be historically connected, had economic *and* social roots.[57]

But patriarchy is not an import. Where did patriarchy, as Africans now know it, come from? *Against whose* patriarchy is African women's theology resistant? Did patriarchy connect itself to an idea already present in African culture? Oduyoye holds to the latter view, that patriarchy existed in African culture and society, but "colonial rule reinforced these patriarchal systems."[58] In reflecting on the dynamics of Akan matriarchal culture (and Yoruba patriarchal culture), we already know that patriarchal thought is not new to Africans; it would merely be intensified through colonialism's toxic combination of conquest and machismo.

Patriarchy in itself is familiar to African women. The notion of the patriarch is commonplace in many cultural contexts; it is deeply rooted in African culture. In *Daughters of Anowa*, Oduyoye utilizes the medium of African creation storytelling to assert this point. Patriarchal thought is woven into many aspects of African life and thus forms and shapes African culture. It is the foundation of proverbs and creation narratives—patriarchy is found in the culture's wisdom references and how peoples come to understand their origins and beginnings. For Oduyoye, patriarchal thought and worldview had been present in African myth-making and storytelling since before the initial moments of colonial contact. It surrounds African notions of origins and origination.[59] It, however, had not reached its dangerous peak until it made colonial contact. In Africa, colonization did not create patriarchy; it exaggerated it.[60]

The combination of what African men sought to obtain (the benefits of European manhood) and what already secured their position as powerful figures among their own (African manhood) created a culture resistant to traditional African values of community. Colonialism introduced the notion of individualism to the African worldview, corrupting its vision of communal well-being. Individual gain and security became the goal. Individualism, a new way of primarily being for oneself instead of for another or for the collective whole, found footing in Africa through Western Christian discourse.[61]

With theological ideas this imbalanced, one can imagine how Christology followed suit. A colonial Christology did not have room in its framework for African understandings of Christ in general, let alone African women's perspectives. Contrary to what colonialism largely promulgated, Jesus *could* be known in ways and in cultures outside of what the West designated. Africans came to see that what Jesus came to do—to draw people to God—did not run counter to their cultural realities and understandings. But they first had to survive the missionary slander.

Oduyoye notes, "The Western missionary enterprise in Africa inaugurated a Christology that took no account of Africa's realities beyond the existence of numerous divinities and ancestral spirits. The emphasis, therefore, was Jesus as the only way to God."[62] Jesus was narrated as a heroic figure adamantly against the polytheistic Africans. Already religious people—many who accepted the values of Christianity—Africans were under siege. They were commanded to do the impossible task of separating their religious sensibilities from their sense of self in order to welcome a Eurocentric brand of Christianity. Many, instead, made Christianity their own, adding it into their already religion-infused cultural lives.

The European colonizers did not understand that who an African is cannot preclude their religious foundation. Oduyoye puts this in front of us. Christology in its original form is meant "to identify saving acts and to cling in hope of liberation . . . and to celebrate the victories over domination and death and to attribute these to Jesus rather than to any other power."[63] Colonial Christianity did not fit the bill. It slowed the force of the gospel, the impact of the message.

The gospel could not be spread if preached from a problematic starting place and purview. Colonialism tried to teach Africans that they had no history or rightful religious foundation. It justified selling Africans into slavery. Jesus could not be argued to be the Christ of such actions and beliefs.

The message of Christ many Africans were initially exposed to was not accurate. African people were being told *who they were to be* in order for Jesus to be Christ to them. Colonialism positioned the gospel as conditional for Africans. A right Christian life was advertised as a Eurocentric way of life. But one's being cannot be imitated. Though many Africans accepted Western standards of living "as necessary to the religion,"[64] because of their preexisting religious foundations and beliefs, they already had experience with the salvific proclamations Christianity thought it was introducing.

For African women the central issue does not concern whether patriarchal theological thinking doomed Africans and African women to inauthentic theological and christological positions, but rather how to parse the *conditions* that introduced the European Christ from who Christ is for Africans. The distinction between the colonial evangelists and their gospel message must be parsed out in order to gauge christological authenticity. Recall, African women are interested in theological truths reflecting their experiences and including their voices.[65] African women's religious expression, including their Christology, must fit into the understandings of their culture; anything outside of this is an affront to the foundations of who they are.[66] Colonialism's work is not only racial but gendered; and it seeps into ideas about who Jesus Christ came to save and from what.

Has colonial Christian culture wreaked havoc between the sexes? Oduyoye reminds us that women were always a part of the origins of Christology. Both Mary and Elizabeth rejoiced about God's plan to save the world through the child Mary would bear and raise.[67] God's salvation is not only literally born through women, but announced as such. Mary, mother of God, was the first one to preach the Christ to a pregnant woman and an unborn child.[68] Women named Jesus' purpose. They provide the first context in which Jesus was nurtured, educated, and made aware of the world in which he lived. Jesus, in part, learned the conditions of being human from women. If women played such a central role in the world knowing who Jesus was, and in Jesus knowing who he was, why are women's lives and place in society devalued? Why do women struggle as much as they do for recognition in the Christian church?

The divide between men and women speaks not necessarily to theological premise, but social and cultural conditioning. Inequality is learned behavior; it is an instantiation of injustice, the very injustice that Jesus came to upend. As we will see in the next chapter, Oduyoye shows where and how theological anthropology is directly linked to theological understanding of women and men as creatures of God. This is the understanding of human communal existence that comes to bear on the church's account that Christ came to mend the fissures thwarting human community and to uproot the divisions that have caused and fed the turmoil of gender discrimination.

The divide existing in humanity's misunderstanding of the self and "the other" continues to feed gender stratification in the church. This divide is symptomatic of a flawed anthropology, a misunderstanding of what being created by God means to those who live into this reality. It is the result of failed and harmful lessons of relationship.

Victor: Subversive Resistance

The Bible is a collection of contextual encounters with the divine, with the self, and with others. It is particular to certain moments in time. In the present day, it is through one's socioeconomic and cultural lens that one reads scripture.[69] Across time, a theme of Jesus as victorious over foes is quite clear.

The imagery of kingship and power was important in ancient Israelite culture. The hope for a powerful king made sense given the social condition of the Israelites; the king would be the one to restore honor and order upon a pained community overrun by dominant forces.[70] Analogously, African cultures subscribe to certain societal hierarchies where ruling figures, such as kings, are given certain directive responsibilities procuring great respect from their community. The notion of kingship sharpens Africans' case of claiming cultural practices parallel to the cultures of the scriptures; in their similitude to ancient cultures, African cultures render themselves valid. Of course, what is good for most may not be good for all. King imagery is both culturally important and yet harmful to African women, Oduyoye contends. To quote her at length,

> In Hebrew religion and culture, prophets, priests and kings were anointed, as were the sick, the dying and the dead. In their struggle to survive as a culturally and materially insignificant and martially impotent nation among the powerful ones of the Fertile Crescent, the Hebrews hankered after the return of the one illustrious king they produced, David. Buffeted around by more powerful nations, the People of Israel were sustained by the faith that, in due course, Yahweh will send them a Ruler like David,

an anointed one, a Messiah. The hope was very much alive right into the period of the Roman colonization of Palestine.[71]

The emphasis on the power of God to defeat Israel's enemies is a key characterization and marker. Israel's concern involved their experience of the historical moment. They were feeling the pressures of being the colonized with no clear end in sight. Israel believed they needed a saving figure who could resist colonial forces. The Roman Empire was a colonial enemy against which they could not compete. Because they could not beat back colonial supremacy, Israel was made to feel like a lesser people.

Many Africans see a point of connection, for they, too, needed and still seek a savior of this sort: a savior who would resist and even destroy harmful colonial influences.[72] For many, the image of salvation included "the overcoming of external physical enemies"[73] as well as resistance against life-denying forces.[74] This rings true across a continent devastated by European colonial and economic greed.

This imaging of a Christ-figure resistant to powerful external forces is framed within the bounds (and toward the benefit) of a predominantly male-oriented society. Men led the colonizing efforts in West Africa. In tracing this history, Oduyoye identifies a point of connection between ancient Hebrew Messianic understandings and modern African women's conceptualization of the Christ-figure. The two are not mutually exclusive, but issue the same hope: the Christ is expected and trusted to be powerful enough to defeat the enemies of God's people, especially on behalf of the least of these in such societies.[75]

What is illumined here are two pathways to see Christ as victor if African women are equally assumed part of the African community: (1) Christ as victor as a response to colonial evangelism and (2) Christ as victor as a response to gender inequality. The latter imagery acts as a resolution to the first because, in addressing both race and gender, African women find and experience Christ's liberative action amid multiple sites of identity.

The colonial angle illumes Africa's problems with imperial forces. In scripture, violence is meted out upon the Christ figure by an imperial enterprise. The European arm of this same enterprise actively positions Christ against African religious culture in favor of a Eurocentric one. The gendered angle examines the victor imagery as primarily a male-dominated one, but seeks resolution for and reconciliation with the "Christ as victor" image. It questions whether the Christ figure can escape the colonial structures and the patriarchal ideas present in "victor" imagery. It asks, "Can Christ save those from a system in which men gain prominence and power? How might this manifest?" The question remains if salvation can in fact include right recognition of all human beings.

Insisting on Identity: Against Racism

For European Christian missionaries, the victory of Christ would look like the erasure of African religious culture and the implementation of a European-style Christian lifestyle. Kenyan religious scholar Teresa Hinga calls this Christological imagery "Christ the conqueror."[76] This image created a divide between conceptions of the divine that Africans had held for centuries and this new religious approach called Christianity that claimed any and all other gods evil. This religiously spawned racism tethered to European Christianity seeped into the social imagination of some African Christians. African Instituted Churches, also known as African Independent Churches, or "the churches begun de novo on the initiative of Africans" (as Oduyoye names them),[77] were some of the first institutions to take up this mentality against their own.[78] They took up the language and fears of their European predecessors. Faith in a victorious Christ, for many, would come to mean a transmitted faith and fear against African traditional religion and its belief systems. Oduyoye labels this movement a form of alienation. In her 2001 work *Introducing African Women's Theology*, she writes, "Since the 1980s a new form of Christianity that dispenses salvation through the total alienation of Africans from African culture and the instrumentalization of the gospel for material prosperity is taking over the Christian scene."[79] According to Oduyoye's observations, the historical narrative remains that opposition to African traditional religion in African churches points to the slow integrative work of European religious ideas and ideals.[80] Many Africans were taught self-hate through colonial Christianity.

For Europeans the "victorious Christ" was purported to be a Christ positioned against the African polytheistic culture of these "superstitious

barbarians."[81] Europeans who did not understand the religious foundation of various African communities would be the ones to deem African
religious history and its actors irrelevant and evil. This European Christ
was sent to destroy African religious culture, or, as they perceived it, he
was brought to Africa to save it. The Euro-conception of a "victorious
Christ" could defeat the darkness and dark forces of African traditional religion as well as those connected to it. This Messiah was successfully used,
in some cases, to alienate Africans from themselves.[82] Oduyoye reminds
us, however, that christological interpretation and its use are contextual.

God did not take issue with African religious culture; Europeans
did. Africa was held captive to Eurocentric ideas of divinity, but God is a
liberative God, a force of justice and redemption. Jesus Christ lives into
this truth as well. For Africans, especially African women, the weight
of oppression and marginalization is quite familiar. Christ who delivers
through his very enfleshment speaks to the power of this God to return
God's creation back to its life-giving form. For Oduyoye, "the redemption Africa experiences by turning to God through Christ is not only
from 'wrong religion' and 'wrong government,' it is also from the perver-
sions of human nature that make it possible for some to prey on others
and for individuals to trample upon the humanity of others."[83] At its root
the problems with colonial depictions of a victorious Christ come down
to recognizing one's humanity and right to exist in the world freely. Gender disparity exponentially increases the threat of losing one's freedom.

Feminine Resource: Against Sexism

"Christ as victor" language also contains intracommunal power dynamics.
Oduyoye's account of "Christ as victor" argues in two directions. The first
concerns liberation refuting colonial ideas against Africans as a whole.
The second, exponentially more intricate and subsequently more difficult
than the first proposition, is liberation through undercutting patriarchy's
prominence. The first falls short if it does not consider the latter.

Jesus' victory over colonial forces also presents a potential gender issue
for African women. "Liberation into *what*?" becomes a critical question;
into *what conditions* will women and men be liberated? Acknowledging

the range of African life does not equate to equally affirming all persons within it. Historically, African colonial resistance still begets African women and men living in predominantly patriarchal societies. Even if Africans aligned their Christian culture with postcolonial liberation, christological hope still appears most beneficial to African men.

Even after colonialism, patriarchy remains. This begs the question if African women's christological hopes can and should associate with a patriarchal society. Should African women align with a Christ figure who redeems one from one's enemies through patriarchal articulations of power? In other words, what is Christ's victory outside of violent depictions and demonstrations of power that still mirror patriarchal norms? The problem seems vast. African women's liberation relies on equitable cultural and social shifts, but these shifts must do the collective and difficult work of changing the core of many African societies.

Oduyoye and other women forge new and liberating paths in liberating Christ *even from this imagery* toward more accurate depictions and descriptions. Factors such as the gender of Jesus are directly challenged in offering liberation freely to women and men. Jesus' liberation from gendered restrictions also counters colonial perceptions of control; it is a total liberating effort. If African women's voices were heard in the church, this reality would be clearer—liberation for all *is* liberation at its core.

It is made clearly evident "in Africa that Jesus is at work freeing people from the unedifying history of sexism."[84] That he sees the importance of all of humanity is already a sign of Jesus' victory in the world; he does not succumb to tiered notions of human existence. In liberating all peoples, women included, Jesus shatters oppression, subverting and dismantling total systems.

Paying attention to where women are present in the stories of Jesus illustrates this liberating power. Women must be included in Jesus' victorious work in the world. The "subject of women in the life and teaching of Jesus is receiving more and more attention in the church as women ask for recognition."[85] Women are relevant to Jesus' salvific mission and its details. The problem rests in acknowledgment. From whom are women asking for recognition? How the Christian church sees the work of Christ can answer this question for us. At a fundamental level, the church's hermeneutical lenses are being challenged. To best understand the unique life, ministry, and work of Christ, Bible-reading Christians must turn hermeneutically toward seeing Jesus gain victory in surprising, new, and nuanced ways. Though Jesus is understood in a tradition that privileges masculine conceptions of victory, Jesus subverts them; Oduyoye sees this subversion in Jesus' feminine attributes.

In Jesus, African women find a man who took "a revolutionary stance in the patriarchal context in which he had to operate."[86] Though Christ was anticipated through male conceptions of victory and liberation, the ministry of Christ took a different form. Oduyoye and other African women think his victory—his liberative action in the world for all—is best seen through a feminine perspective. Jesus' feminine qualities act as a subversive site of connection and liberation for African women (and ultimately African men).

Jesus is maternal. Oduyoye asserts that the "Christ of the women of Africa upholds not only motherhood, but all who, like Jesus of Nazareth, perform 'mothering' roles of bringing out the best in all around them."[87] Ugandan nun and scholar Anne Nasimiyu goes so far as to describe Jesus as "the mother," making plain African women's claim to and connection with him as giver of life.[88]

Jesus' involvement with women and his message toward women's inclusion and liberation are his victorious work with which the church must align itself. Christ as victor is only so insomuch as Jesus defeats harmful patriarchal standards that are harmful not only to women but also to men. The truth of Christ as victor concerns the proper treatment of women.

Jesus tramples gender boundaries and binaries toward a vision of humanity turned toward God. Since the church too often allows "the silence and invisibility of women in men's stories," refuting gender limitations is how Jesus exercises victory.[89] Oduyoye argues that a christological revolution begins in Jesus' deliberate advocacy for and communal involvement with women. "He rendered them service, teaching them, healing them, waking up their dead, saving them from exploitation and victimization," she argues.[90]

Oduyoye's characterizations of Jesus, interestingly enough, blur the lines of femininity and divinity, and perhaps intentionally so. It is not too far-fetched to imagine Jesus the salvific figure as feminine. Socially, service, and other kinds of action usually relegated to women, joins a list of Jesus' saving work. Of course, men serve and teach and occupy what can controversially be named "feminine roles," but to miss the gender-bending work of associating the feminine with Jesus would be a mistake. Jesus' strongest qualities are often culturally associated with and assigned to women.

To be clear, neither women nor men can heal the sick, wake the dead, and save people from the sins of exploitation and victimization. Finite human beings are not capable of these feats; only Jesus can do these things. But as Oduyoye helps us notice, he is a Savior who echoes the practices of women. The character of women shows up in God's saving work in the world.

Jesus not only advocates for women, but he is also understood as feminine in some key ways. He is known as a "compassionate and caring one who anticipated people's needs. Jesus was a mother par excellence," Oduyoye asserts.[91] This understanding of Jesus has serious implications for the nature of salvation, in terms of from whom salvation comes; it also, in part, contributes to an understanding of salvation and the efficacy of salvation. It reintroduces the question of Jesus as victor in his salvation—if his salvific work is not victorious in masculinist ways, what would it mean to think salvation "feminine," "womanly," or "motherly"?[92]

The inclusiveness of women in the salvific nature of Jesus Christ is empowering and subversive. It creates room for salvation to come forth in ways unbeknownst to humanity or overlooked in ecclesial circles or theological spaces. Jesus Christ as feminine is a sign of salvation for Africans as a whole.

Jesus' decisions to choose the least and most overlooked tasks and positions in society—which can be seen as undertaking "much that was seen as women's roles and attitudes"[93]—push the envelope toward a feminine Christology and soteriology. His willingness to be in the world in a socially feminine manner suggests his power might have a different character—a more conscious one.

There is correlation between the work of Jesus and the work and labor of women in African social contexts. Jesus' salvific works on the earth were mediated through women's socializations, meted out through women's work, and channeled through service typically regarded as feminine.

The Savior embraced the feminine. Salvation can, in fact, come through women.[94] This way it is a mode of liberation.[95]

Women's words about Christ tell salvation, whether the church fully recognizes it as so or not. Women are present in the Lord's salvific work. We see "women's faith and faithfulness" most brilliantly in narratives of the resurrection.[96] The victory of Christ, in colonial resistance and through gender inclusiveness, is a sign of resurrection, for resurrection involves women.

Scripture is helpful in narrating the importance of women in discerning Christ's purpose in the world and for the church. During their visitation to the tomb and not finding him there, the women who received instruction from the angels were given the task of spreading the message of Jesus' resurrection after the third day. Oduyoye calls this message "the burden," as "the tradition was against them."[97] She further points out, "Their witness carried little weight in the courts of the country."[98] Even the account in the book of Matthew, Oduyoye notes, "seems to be an attempt to explain how the stone came to be rolled away."[99] Unfortunately, the women's word of resurrection did not hold much weight on its own. It had to be validated, verified, or explained into existence by male voices. In the Matthean passage, it is Jesus' appearance that confirms his resurrection; a man had to back the words of the women. The women could not, would not, be believed on their own. Gender entrapment in a narrative of liberation is the aspect of Jesus' victory the church would do well to notice and call out.

Jesus disrupts masculinist discourse through just actions. Inclusivity is both a measure of his holy work and a sign of his salvific presence. Jesus can be found among the women. "We observe that African women's Christology derives directly from the Gospels highlighting women's presence in the life and teaching of Jesus. The cultural hermeneutic out of which they reflect enables them to see the ambiguities of the Jesus model as culture-coded and therefore open to transformation."[100] Oduyoye is right: the presence of women in scripture is formative for African women's christological perspective and hermeneutic. Scriptural women provide corrections to christological models that do not serve the entire church.

Christ as victor over colonial oppression and gender discrimination requires women's hermeneutical perspective. They are valuable and necessary in any doctrinal hermeneutic, exercise, or expression. The church would not understand who Christ is, what work he has done, and what work he is doing without women. Women are christological resources, for in and through Jesus' interactions with them, the entire church learns the shape of divine relationship.

Revisiting the Question

What does African women's Christology reach toward? What is its end goal around the depiction of Jesus Christ and of African women?

Jesus Christ is a figure who advocates for the full humanity of every human being. For Oduyoye, "the Christian liberation of African women is necessary if Jesus Christ is to be credible."[101] Thus, instead of asking, "Who is Jesus Christ for the African woman?," as I started off, African feminist Christology subverts the question, asking instead, "Who is the African woman in Christ?" This reversal sets up the contextual claim: one's experiences detail the ways one knows Christ.

Our contexts detail and shape our theological outlooks. It is in asking questions about the human condition and human being that theology unfolds and reveals itself. Thus, in turning to Oduyoye's theological anthropology, African women's theology and Christology become more cemented as foundational precepts to understanding God and the form of human life itself.

CHAPTER SIX

THEOLOGICAL ANTHROPOLOGY

Our stories are precious paths on which we have walked with God, and struggled for a passage to our full humanity.
—Mercy Amba Oduyoye, *Introducing African Women's Theology*

Characters in a Story

Theology tells a story—of Creator and creation—giving voice to theology's various characters. Be they human, material, or spiritual, these characters ultimately advance the plotline of divine relationship. Humans know this well. Creation myths, or origin stories, in particular, narrate the core of the human condition: that our createdness is meaningful only insomuch as it is tied to another—to our Creator and to other created beings. The lens with which we read an account—our hermeneutics—translates this core truth, shaping how we understand proper relationship.[1] Stories holding the range of human experience—"what we feel in our society, how we feel about our children, our families, what enrages us, what makes us laugh, what our lives mean to the next neighbor and how we experience God in all these"[2]—keep us connected to one another and to the divine. They narrate both how and why our lives are so.[3]

Our cultures house stories—stories of how we are supposed to be in the world both with and to one another. Throughout Mercy Oduyoye's life, Akan culture told prescriptive stories of the path to proper womanhood; stories from Akan women, however, gave Oduyoye another sense

117

of self. Both poured meaning into her Akan Christian identity. Both illumined what ideas she would decide most befitted her freedom.

Theological anthropology similarly treads a fine line: if people do not feel ownership of it as *their* narrative, the story of humanity's relationship to God and each other can easily become a weapon, a means to own the stories of everyone. In this state, the story's incomplete form will garner resistance. For African women, at least, theological anthropology has been a delicate and critical area of theological engagement, because they have not had the opportunity to narrate themselves in the story of human existence. Wishing to right this wrong and include their insight in humanity's story, they assert a liberative theological anthropology broad enough to include everyone. Everyone can honorably see themselves in humanity's story, a story that primarily centers the truth of God's role in such a reality.

African women's theological anthropology seeks to wrestle the storytelling power out of the hands of a few and return it to the entire community. Oduyoye, particularly, does this in acknowledging that every aspect of her identity contributes to her story as a human being God has called "good." Akan religious worldview and Akan Christianity, Akan feminism and Christian assertions of personhood all influence Oduyoye's story, and she claims each part as impactful. Although elements of Akan belief critically shape her Christian practice, Oduyoye has also seen both Akan culture and Westernized Christianity capitulate to the worst parts of themselves, namely through patriarchy, sexism, and racism.

African women are not treated on a par with their male counterparts in social or ecclesial settings. Both their culture and the church too easily dismiss their voices. They are not able to tell the story of how African Christianity unfolds in their own lives in the same way or on the same platforms as their African male or white peers. Splintered anthropological vision in Akan and Western (Christian) cultures begets an Akan Christianity with the same mistaken viewpoint. Women's silencing and invisibility leads to their inaccurate depiction. They are not treated on a par with men, but literally are positioned as antagonists in humanity's story.

If, as theologian David H. Kelsey offers, "the root question of Christian anthropology is 'What is implied about human personhood by the claim that God actively relates to us?,'"[4] then African women's theological anthropology asks if we truly understand and honor the details of the "us." Deficient imagination around the notion of the created "us"—of humanity as a whole—breeds anthropology determined by men and assumed onto women. It further welcomes a theological anthropology determined by men, assumed onto God.

Anthropology is the root issue. The world needs to hear how African women theologically conceive it, then join with their conception of anthropology toward a constructive vision of human life together in God. Oduyoye's anthropology works through Akan cultural-religious ideas, calling out the impact of both cultural patriarchy and colonial racism, and, within the chiasm of such indoctrinations, boldly asserts an alternative vision of inclusion, a vision that entails returning to and embracing productive cultural values.

African women's theological anthropology thinks African women's wellness is synonymous with Africa's wellness and thinks that African women's personhood, like the personhood of African men, is connected to the divine. These women do theological anthropology from both the space of African traditional wisdom and the hope of the gospel; they think human-divine connection from a space of constructive imagination, all toward radical inclusiveness.[5] But they must first interrogate the source of exclusionary thought and practices among their own.

Same yet Several

Ironically, African women's perspective is and is not seen as the African perspective as a whole. African men have taken the liberty of telling Africa's stories for the whole. African women, then, have constantly had to fight to name themselves in society and in the Christian church. They work tirelessly to refute harmful narratives put forward by men (and some women) loyal to sexist and colonial frames of African women's personhood. In this reality, these women have to wade through the mire of African men trusting European men's ideas before listening to African women.

Although African men and women agree that context is crucial to doing any theological work, "women's voices often differ from and sometimes come in conflict with" men's interpretation of "African traditional religion and culture."[6] Because of their "socialization as women and experience in life," African women experience African culture differently, are positioned differently with respect to it than men. Their lens allows them to dissect cultural dynamics their men have neither experienced nor have challenged within their religious ideas.[7]

African women etch a different way of thinking of humanity's story, one that includes the nuance of particular personhoods. In this venturous move, African women dare to think themselves part of the African perspective. In standing firmly in their own voices, they model how women can claim themselves to be critical partners in African vocality. African conceptions of theological anthropology must include the fullness of African personhood, especially narratives rooted in women's experiences.

African women's theological anthropology presses into the idea that God is already present in Akan conceptions of divinity *and* in Akan feminist assertions of the self. Africans do not have to choose one position or the other; God is in the essence of men *and* women. The Akan believe God to be the Source-Being within which the human experience begins.[8] This is the idea African women's theological anthropology wants to elevate: the truth of life is already present in core constructive African beliefs, beliefs contending that the Creator knows their creation and destines them to a full, holistic, and communal life—beliefs that African men and women can draw on models of community in their cultures toward communal equality.

African women aim to reform the frameworks they have been handed. When it comes to gender practices, African culture typically employs communal ideas of "collaboration and complementarity." In Akan tradition, specifically, "complementarity and reciprocity" dominate communal frameworks.[9] A constructive eye sees the potential in these frameworks. If African women primarily approach communal wellness with the lens of "collaboration" and "reciprocity," "complementarity" begins to transform. It transforms—envisioned more akin to how Oduyoye imagines it—as "egalitarianism."[10] African culture can shed the questionable aspects of itself if its women are given space to lift up the generative elements of their culture. Beliefs of shared communal wellness must be unearthed and recaptured as the heart of African Christian theological anthropology.

Patriarchy and sexism have planted harmful ideas about men's and women's humanity in the Akan cosmological and Christian imagination, but a different message rests at the core of both traditions: care for all of God's creation. Gender inclusiveness, then, is a part of Akan Christianity's most honest posture. Christian and Akan religious tradition center care and attentiveness in divine and human relationships—these truths must be harkened back to. Communal values embedded at the heart of African and Christian religiosity distinguish a true Akan Christian theological anthropology from a perspective born of human antagonism, a perspective with which African women have constantly been at war.

Relational care is the greatest detail of Christianity's theological anthropology. God cared enough to create humanity and to task all humans with caring for one another and the rest of creation.[11] African women's theological anthropology both uncovers and advocates this posture as reflective of true human being.[12] These women show how it is not a farfetched idea that Akan thought and Christian precepts are rooted in the inclusion, wellness, and thriving of connected beings. We see this possibility in Akan cosmology, where divine and created beings are connected on an ethereal level.

Akan Cosmological Thought

The Akan people think of the self and the world around the self as being in continuous relation. Both spiritual and physical dimensions guide their conception of life. The physical world consists of "the environment and the secular activities that go on in it. The spiritual is the invisible or immaterial dimension of life."[13] Ancestral beings and deities act as personal spirit beings impacting and guiding life events in the spiritual realm. Spiritual and physical dimensions also include other impersonal yet potentially harmful forces such as sorcery, magic, and witchcraft. All spiritual beings have the ability to impact human life but fall in line within the hierarchy that God, the Supreme Being, ultimately creates.[14]

In Akan belief, there is no such thing as the separation of spiritual and secular life—both live within each other. Harmony between the two worlds is critical; it is a moral compass and ethical guide.[15] To someone from the West, the Akan cultural-religious expression might appear polytheistic, but Akan cultural beliefs function no differently than some ideas found in the Christian faith.[16] Categories of spirit beings who impact life's rhythms are one such connective point between the two traditions.

Ghanaian pastoral theologian Esther Acolatse asserts that the religious framework of the Akan is cosmologically tiered; it is full of various classes of spirits. In the spiritual realm, God, the Creator of all things (also known as the Supreme Being), demonstrates their power through the divine pantheon of other gods. The spirits of the inanimate, such as rocks, trees, and charms, as well as the spirits of ancestors, are also players in Akan spirituality, but in a lesser sense than the Supreme Being.[17]

Humans show respect to the Creator God, spiritual beings, and other human and created beings, such as land, particular animals, forests, and bodies of water, known as the "minor deities."[18] Created beings experience life connectively, because life depends on the movement and status of the rest of creation. Just as with patterns in Christianity, one's life is not isolated from the Supreme Being or from other members of creation in any way.[19] At Akan cosmology's core, God—the Creator, the Supreme Being—is the center of existence. Human life is determined by the Creator.[20]

Complex and multilayered, human being (*nipa/Nnipa*) is fourfold, as Acolatse explains.[21] Humans contain blood (*mogya*), body (*nnipadua/hunam*), soul (*kra*),[22] and spirit (*sunsum*) (62, 65). God-granted, the soul—the *kra*—is "a vital part of the human being" (62, 64). An entity considered both male and female, the *kra* fuels one's lifeblood. It impacts one's ability to lead a good life (62). Each person's *kra* is both sacred energy and "the real essence of man, his vital force." It is "divine spirit and carrier of inspirations, dreams, and fantasies," Acolatse notes (63). Deeply intertwined with an individual, the *kra* (soul) is impacted by humanity's discipline and temperance, for good or bad. Impacted as much by humanity as humanity is impacted by it, the *kra* is the instinctual part of the self, one's "protector and guardian" (63).

The body and the soul are interconnected to the point where "what happens to the body also affects the *kra*" (64), but the body is still only that "which includes the *mogya*, 'blood,' and *kra* and *sunsum*" (65). Aco-latse notes that "the Akan place great emphasis on the *kra* and *sunsum* and very little on the *hunam*" (65). Though impacted by the events of the soul and spirit, the body is not humanity's most significant marker.

In building a framework of African women's conception of the human, we can take a few lessons from Akan cosmology. One's *kra*, their essence and life-force, constitutes the heart of human being. Neither physical sex nor gender assigned to such sexes is the truest identity marker of a human being. What makes personhood is honoring one's soul. What also marks a person is their connection to the Supreme Being. If "the soul is a gift from God" and the source of "the human being's relationship with the creator," then it should be the starting point of theological anthro-pology, especially for Akan peoples. This essence, sourced from God, that guides human existence should have the strongest pull on how humans know and identify each other. Connecting creation to each other, other spirit beings, and God's self, the Supreme Being is the connective tissue to all forms of life.

Humanity is incredibly small in the grand scheme of God's creation. It is critical, then, for humanity to understand the details of its life first and foremost in God. We find details of how the Akan relate to God and each other in further exploring Akan conceptions of the humanity and the divine.

Relation to the Divine in Akan Worldview

African religion "plays a significant role in culture, and thus in world-view," Acolatse argues (32). African religious life *is* African culture. How Acolatse employs the word "worldview" borrows from the anthropolo-gist Michael Kearney's claim that "worldviews classify the reality with which they are presented" (34). Worldview codifies reality, tells the story of the order of things. Kearney specifies, "Above all a worldview deals with causality, answering fundamental questions regarding origins and power" (34). Worldview explores the connections between events involv-ing and impacting people and assigns them function and meaning. How the Akan see the world is based simultaneously on the flow of life events and a common understanding of what *should be* according to cultural beliefs. Kearney further states, "A people's worldview, especially their understanding of the relationship of the cosmos to themselves, is so ingrained and inheres at such a subconscious level of the psyche that it is difficult to change. At best, it may be modified from time to time, but only by the people themselves" (34). In this statement Kearney leaves the door ajar for cultural modifications. In suggesting that people have the ability to rewrite their story, he seems to allow space for the evolution of cultural thought. But this possibility exists only insomuch as people are willing to adjust their cultural ideas and subsequently their worldview. Cultural modification is less an impossible task than a massive undertaking. Shifting cultural ideas invites and involves shifting worldview.

One's worldview is tied to cultural imagination. Worldview roots itself in the patterns of life and cultural foundation, of what is expected and what should be (34). It is arguably a belief system itself. Worldview and cosmology are thus intertwined to the point where they need each other to hold meaning. One knows God through one's corporeal body and cultural system. These experiences fuse worldview and cosmological stance. In relation to the divine, the story of people groups is not only internalized but also "eternalized," fixed, and almost made permanent.

Religion is arguably a cultural manifestation in itself, the cultural-religious connection an artifact of African identity.[23] The interlocking of culture and religion illustrates how the religious faculties of the Akan are extensions of social worldview. Religion is the evidence, the working out, of culture. Africans trust the interconnectedness of ordinary and divine life and expression; they do not compartmentalize each into their own area of life. What happens culturally signifies the cosmos.

Even with this seeming permanence and the grand structure of cultural worldview, African women believe there is room for revision. They mine their respective cultures for gems; and shifting African cultural focus back to inclusive ideals can be one such treasure. The "collaboration and complementarity" and "complementarity and reciprocity" approaches to gender in African communities hold great potential. I mentioned earlier how African women home in on cultural aspects of "collaboration" and "reciprocity" to make a case for a culture concerned with an "egalitarian" community. This adjustment of African values is, in some ways, their constructive practice of including themselves in the thought life of the African community.

But these frames are also pushed against because of their contradictory message. African women deserve better from their cultural systems, so they challenge and transform the ideas that do not include them. Complementarianism's religio-cultural use seems antithetical to notions of collaboration and reciprocity. The gendered communal frameworks read as diametrically opposed. "Coming alongside" or "supplementing" does not carry the same weight as "working equally with" or "working mutually with" another. African women, thus, revise the gendered cultural ideas to reflect a more parallel reality. They assert that when one is constructing an inclusive theological anthropology true to God's intent for humanity and true to Akan cultural values, the latter two terms are more suitable for defining "complementarity": "working mutually and equally with one another." Human beings are best positioned to join together with each other and to God's self with cultural ideas that herald equality. For the Akan, the notion of equal humanity can be traced, in part, to one of their popular creation accounts.

Calling Culture to Account

One of the Akan's most popular origin stories is the story of Ananse Kokroko (lit., "Great Spider," referring to Nyame/God), who mediates the problem of fighting between "Half and Half" (assumed to be some manner of human being) by slamming them together to make one human being.[24] God's "direct involvement in order to transform a situation of disharmony"[25] is a key component of humanity's story. A few things stand out from the details of this account: first, humanity's origins are literally attributed to God; second, humanity's origins are literally rooted in joining. But what is also narrated in this origin story is a subtle third point: the many-sided nature of human being. This must not be brushed over.

Humans are of two halves. Recall, stories narrate how and why our lives are so—how humans understand and relate to God but also how they understand and relate to one another. How God is introduced into Akan cultural consciousness also introduces *the manner of human being as a combined being*, made of different parts. Human being is the expression not only of God's desire and power to form a particular kind of life but also of the multiplicity of beings. Unfulfilled when alone, but harmonious when together, true humanity has a complex and joined narrative. Humanity is composed of two halves and a divine clash.

While the two halves of this story are not specified as male or female, this dichotomy is useful when thinking about gender and theological anthropology. If we map notions of gender onto these two beings, Akan cosmological thought helps us consider that one is not simply male or female, but a product of God's combining many modes of being into one expression called person.[26] Personhood, then, at its core is multiplicitous. Separately, both beings exist incompletely. It is only when they are connected that their maximum potential is truly known, that they are seen as a person. This African cultural principle is interrupted once humanity forgets the story of its beginning, of its two-now-one self. A patriarchal anthropological perspective taints this reality; it is impossible for one manner of being (male) to decide the fate of the other (female), for, by himself, he is not whole.

Akan Cosmology from a Woman's Point of View

The problem with the Akan cosmological worldview is also its potential: creation stories have a direct hand in forming cultural ideas and practices. Myths and folktales condition people toward certain social worlds. Women are most aware of this reality. How they are imaged, how they are "told" in stories, have major effects.[27] Fragmented storytelling provides "the justification for their [women's] ascribed roles."[28] Unfortunately, the Akan fall into this pattern, as a number of their folktales scapegoat women as the original sinner and thus the "lesser" human being.

In Akan folklore tradition women have often been blamed as the cause of humanity's ill fate.[29] One popular account suggests that division and separation between the sky (God/Nyame) and humans were the consequence of a woman's insolence and greed, her taking too much from God, and thus causing God to move further and further away from humanity.[30]

The gendered pattern in African storytelling is incessant. Out of five Akan folktales summarized by literary critic Samuel Kwesi Nkansah, three of them place the blame of humanity's downfall solely on women. The consequences of these five accounts are numerous. In one story, an old woman takes and stores too much food, and eventually it rots, offending God's nostrils. In another, an old woman kept bumping into God while cooking, hurting and offending God. In a third tale, while God was covering the Akan people like a towel, they kept cleaning their hands on him, offending and soiling God. Still another myth asserts that an old woman took a piece of God every time she cooked soup, hurting him. In the fifth story, God—living with man and lying atop Mother Earth (Asaase Yaa)—got annoyed at the spatial arrangement. There was not enough room for him and man to move about comfortably.[31]

These offenses resulted in God moving higher up and away from humanity. Four things are crucial to note as troubling gender themes in the five Akan folklore accounts. First, the troublemaker is cast as an older woman. This harkens to African taboo beliefs about a woman's old age. An old woman doing anything often sends the sexist signal that she participates in witchcraft; why else would she be alone?[32] "Women, especially when they are old, constitute a mysterious—if not sinister—phenomenon," Oduyoye reminds.[33] Without her purpose and life tied to a spouse or children, an elderly woman is cast as inciting trouble; she is imaged as socially inferior. In three of the five accounts the old woman is made a caricature whose "evil" repelled the Creator from humanity. The leap to associate her with evil is not far-fetched, since, as Oduyoye contends, "many African folktales describe old women as demons."[34]

Second, the women in these accounts act individually. This solo action can be read as a direct violation of Akan communal values. Her individual, selfish action both repels God and shames her culture. She violates not only divinity but her people's dignity as well. The blame falls squarely on her shoulders. Unlike the Genesis account of the Christian tradition, where Adam is summoned to participate in sinful and disruptive action,[35] men are largely absolved of any major infraction. In Akan folklore, men are often positioned as moral superiors to (old) women.[36]

Third, in all three accounts, the female antagonist is physically harming God by taking too much from or asking too much of God. God's impassibility is not a factor, as it is in most of the Christian tradition. God is close enough to humanity that God can be impacted, harmed even, by the actions of God's creation. God's immanence proves to be the privilege humanity was unable to handle. This, combined with the lack of domestic prowess of these women, drives God away. Through menial tasks, these accounts provide narrative pretext for women's devaluation.

Lastly, a smaller detail concerns the domestic situations within which these women are narrated. It seems these women ruin humanity's relationship with God through the domestic tasks of cooking or feeding. The lesson is subtle yet significant. Even in the gendered domestic tasks assigned them, women still "get it wrong." This sends the message that these women could not even *be Akan women* in the right way! When they live poorly into this cultural portrait of womanhood, God is offended or harmed. To put it plainly, the mythos of women's "natural" inclinations within certain gender roles is narrated as not only fundamentally against God but also against the Akan community. From all angles, their practice of womanhood reflects a fractured human-divine relationship and a basic failure to be rightly human.

This idea becomes cemented in Akan cultural imagination: Akan women's existence runs counterintuitively to God's intention for humanity. The root of humanity's displacement from God is women's fault.[37] In this train of thought, patriarchal cultural assumptions and practices become a means of justifying gender divides. Read in this light, patriarchal suppression is not some type of evil consigning women to submission, but an expression of relational correction and concern.

African women disagree with this foundationally sexist mythical framework. A right theological anthropology requires more than a male perspective: "The meaning of full humanity cannot be defined by only one sector of humanity."[38] A theological anthropology attentive to the gendered dynamics of cultural stories—often created and told by men— names and addresses these very discrepancies. One-sided storytelling is bound to be biased and rooted in a displaced understanding of God, self, and others. Tragically, some men misunderstand themselves to be powerful, able, and authorized to label God's creation—to label women—sinful, ontological failures.[39]

If the core of women's existence is stereotyped as fundamentally evil and lapsarian in Akan folklore, destructive patterns of gendered, hierarchical relationships will only continue to be further fortified in an Akan *Christian* framework. The contrived, narrative source of this division fundamentally grounds harmful ideas into a theological culture. Instead of teaching that humanity exists on a different plane than God, it believes that men and women are the ones who exist on different planes.

Some cultures cannot imagine women's roles exceeding marriage and motherhood, and even then, there are parameters around whether they are even living into *these* identities properly! Oduyoye observes a different truth. Finding connection with a Bemba creation myth, a story from Bantu-speaking peoples from parts of Zambia, Congo, and Zimbabwe, Oduyoye argues that women were "created neuter with the possibility of differentiation."[40] Difference here means distinctive potential. It is not an invitation to demean. The possibility of difference invites new theological ideas about gender. The Creator expects human beings to "learn to appreciate, respect and value one another as primarily human," not to harp on biological distinctions.[41] Female and male differentiation was never intended to be a point of discord between humanity. Rather, the option for difference serves as a reminder of God's creative decision. If difference in any capacity, but especially in sex or gender, can be seen as a detail of God's action, how much richer can Christian theological anthropology become?

African women's theology resists demonizing differences between males and females. "Male-humanity is a partner with female-humanity, and . . . both expressions of humanity are needed to shape a balanced community within which each will experience a fullness of Be-ing,"[42] Oduyoye poignantly writes. African women's theology resists sexist action, not the male sex. Thinking of human difference as signaling affable distinction rather than virulent opposition grounds African women's theological anthropology in a communal understanding of relationship. Mutuality between the sexes can still exist even amid their experiential and biological differences. Difference was never a barrier to mutuality, but a pathway toward it. It should illumine the lives of variant, yet interdependent created beings.

Akan wisdom assumes all persons to be children of God desired by God.[43] Traces of the divine are present in each person. This is to be celebrated in its fullness. Yet the way theological rationale is used to position and treat women shows a misunderstanding of divine sharedness and recognition of the divine nature present in all.

In African Christian circles, women's identity is often used against them—no doubt punishment justified as traceable back to the actions of Eve.[44] "What is described as feminine and masculine are culture-coded and should not be allowed to circumscribe our humanness," Oduyoye asserts.[45] Skewed theological anthropology only clears the ground for a partisan "doctrine of man." If African Christians want to address the tensions and problems in the cultural traditions inherent to them and inherited from Western Christianity, they must heed African women's insights.

An Akan Christian Overview

For the Akan, one's relationship with God influences one's relationship with oneself, with another, and with creation as a whole.[46] For one to conceive of life apart from a divine center is to abandon life itself, to not know the essence of life. To this extent, Christianity and Akan cosmology hold similar foundations. They share the centrality of God as a permanent fixture in their belief systems. Similar core values, different contextual homes.

As an Akan Christian woman, Oduyoye is in a prime position to argue Akan cosmological and Christian traditional connectedness because of contextual diversity. Christian theology is not tied to one culturally interpretive direction; it is global and has many expressions. If it is to include Akan Christians, Christian theology *needs to recognize* Akan cosmology as a valid viewpoint in order to live into its fullness. Thinking Christianity within and alongside Akan cosmological thought, or any other cultural religious identification for that matter, creates a theological faith tradition to which particular peoples can lay claim. Christianity's hybrid and syncretic nature are seen not only in its European expressions—as history has unsuccessfully tried to frame it—but also in its African ones.

For Akan Christians, theological anthropology is an exercise in making Akan cosmology and Christian belief speak to one another. This move to include Akan cosmology in, rather than remove it from, Akan Christianity claims African religious culture as critical to Christianity's expression in the world. For Oduyoye, Akan cosmology (a mode of theology in itself) does not fade behind the presence of Christian theology but joins it; both frameworks ultimately mark a distinct and deeply important expression of Christianity.

It should then be considered a problem when African women like Oduyoye are discouraged from applying this same hermeneutical flexibility and freedom to gender ideas and practices in Akan cosmology, Christianity at large, and Akan Christianity, specifically. Confronting ideas of social power creates possibilities for a more inclusive theology, one rooted in communal care, one rooted in African communal values and ideas—as co-determined by African women.

We witness a radical failure of theological imagination when African Christians do not confront religious-backed power structures. Acceptance of narrow hermeneutics mimics European colonial theology quite closely. Colonial theology believes theological assimilation to be its goal instead of theological growth and inclusion. It thinks theo-geographical conquest the ultimate victory for Christ (and Europe) and finds Western culture to be "a favorite tool of domination."[47] Again, this is a failure of imagination, because Christianity, contextual across space and time, is supposed to serve as a reminder of "God's presence in [the] day-to-day life" of everyone.[48] For Oduyoye this imaginative failure and lack of awareness are animated by a human-centered standpoint. Colonial Christianity rejects God's centeredness, a notion essential to Christian, traditional Akan, and Akan Christian religious customs alike. This human-centered standpoint instead coronates certain populations of humanity as the deciding head of humanity's relationship with God—quite an impossible task without the voice of the full community. Forgoing African cultural values of holistic, communal wellness in order to practice sexism and patriarchy only intensifies African women's claims that Africa is losing itself.

Naming Imbalance

By scapegoating Eve, Oduyoye offers, a Christian "doctrine of man" justifies women's experiences of suffering and discriminatory practices.[49] It emboldens the confidence of some to negate the divine and good createdness of another being, to tell stories about and place labels upon them. But ideas and convictions of this sort attempt to dictate divine order instead of allowing room for God's creative intention in Christ—for Jesus to reconcile humanity back to God's self. By widening the gulf between genders, a "doctrine of man" broadens the chasm between humanity and God.

A "doctrine of man" thus suggests the Messiah cannot save humanity, but that man must try to do it himself. Women's maltreatment, in the name of biased hermeneutics, reflects a soteriological misconstrual.[50] Man wants to rescue and save, but does not admit that he, too, needs saving. This admission would expose his inability to save himself and others. It would insist on the necessity and value of all humanity. For the Akan, certain ideas of gendered value and humanness were already present within the cultural baseline.

Western Christian patriarchal values typically assert that man "includes" the woman; therefore, "maleness has been made to stand for humanness, and femaleness means either to be supportive of or to tamper with the male norm."[51] But is it not a mistake to assume that humanity knows what "the norm" entails or means? How might a fractured humanity know God's divine intent for God's creation? Men have speciously positioned themselves as "the Supreme Being of human being,"[52] but the God label has wide implications. How do men have the authority to claim the same power as *their own Creator?* While our focus has been on human ability and deduction, a deeper question resides: What does a "doctrine of man" approach to theological anthropology disclose about God, the Creator? It may disclose that in creating them male and female God did not make an error, but a rather remarkable decision.

If we harken back to the Christian creation narrative at its core, we see where the "re-marking" happens. The female's creation is only slightly different than the male's, for to be female means to be created by God in a unique moment similar to the male—from preexisting material (dust). This woman is "the express will of God."[53]

The human differences of the created beings are slight. But taken the wrong way, this creative distinction interprets women's existence as a response to the man. Being a woman comes to mean being a nonman, or rather a non-human-being. It means not having humanity. Oduyoye calls this being a "non-anything."[54] Being a non-anything mimics the "zone of non-being" that Antillean psychoanalyst Frantz Fanon so poignantly names as indicative of the colonial problem of assigning value to human being.[55] That anyone can be a "non-anything/non-being" illumines the central problem of patriarchal Christian values: human beings cannot assign value to one another; only God can. They can, however, affirm the worth *God has already declared* over God's creation. A man cannot reverse God's declarations.

But to assert itself as relevant, maleness tries to gather significance unto itself, tries to position man as the corrective to the error of woman. Maleness is lifted up as the model of right, embodied life. Sadly, those who practice sexism and patriarchy *choose* to believe in fragmented understandings of human existence. Whether in Akan cosmological culture or Christianity, when it comes to gender discrepancy, too many begin with an asymmetrical anthropology. Left unchecked, this narrow and incomplete view has many ramifications lamentably rooted in fixating on bodily difference.

Bodies and Difference

The fear of women's bodies "has made it difficult to accept the integrity of our being and led to the separation of our make up into material and spiritual, body and soul/spirit/mind," Oduyoye notes.[56] Bias against bodies taints how the world, but especially how those in the church, understands another's essence, another's soul. Narratives and interpretations about the body—a body that is deemed the most visible marker of one's value—interfere with humanity's ability to relate in a healthy manner.

Skewed perception spawns a biased narrative. How someone *perceives* another's body should not comprise the story told about that person. Those in power conflate how *they* receive a woman's body with that of her essence, with her soul. Akan cosmology is a helpful theological conversation partner here.

Recall, a human being has a body (*hunam*) that carries the soul, the *kra* (along with blood [*mogya*] and spirit [*sunsum*]). If the soul (*kra*) is the most important aspect of being human, what does it signal if another aspect of the self, the body (*hunam*), is wrongly elevated—judged as the total essence of one's personhood? Even further, how much deeper does the transgression reach if the part of a person being judged is only the *perception* of them—the *projected image* of what the body (*hunam*) *might* be or *might* mean? Is the person truly known if they are skeptically judged? Punishing women based on a perception of their bodies is less a matter of distrust in women's bodies and more a problem of projection.

Which is unacceptable—the *hunam* (body) of a judged woman or the *kra* (soul) of a judging man? Deliberating a woman's worth by her body only signals man's unfitness to sit in the judgment seat. It reinforces the need for the Supreme Being's presence in all relationships.

Homes to souls, women's bodies are integral to expressing humanity's fullness, as are men's bodies. Adhering to a male-centered anthropology is choosing stagnation over the dynamism of both male and female perspectives.[57] Too often maleness creates narratives of contrast rather than community when it comes to the gifts of gender difference.[58] African women's work returns us to the heart of the matter—recognizing humanity's created nature. Ontological diversity is one of God's creative details. Gender diversity encourages us to read being human through various genres of existence. It literally reflects God's creative intention: human existence is dynamic, not static.

God at the Center

From whom, then, should Christian theological anthropology take its dogmatic cues? Should the desires of the socially powerful be trusted as its authors? If so, God would not be needed; if such certainty could come from outside of God's self, from cloistered members of God's creation, of what importance is the Creator?

African women's theological anthropology contends that the interpretive lens of a culture should come from the collective, not solely from one sector of society. One gender, sexual caste, or class segment cannot know the needs of all; everyone, in communion with the divine, must be a part. A monolithic anthropology is not the Christian way, and most certainly not the African way. As Oduyoye has reminded us, in Akan culture, "God is experienced as the very foundation of existence."[59] God cannot be missing from humanity's theological declaration; if this is the case, it is not theology.

"Anthropology should aim at our being human together," Oduyoye offers. Being human requires the hand of the Creator.[60] Human relationship creates the possibility for communal life in God.[61] One cannot, must not, understand oneself without the other. One must not think oneself superior to another.[62] For men and women, the other gender must be a critical part to understanding oneself. In turning to each other, they turn to God. A faulty theological anthropology tries to dictate life without turning to God, without communal input about the sense of this holy direction. Oduyoye argues, "We do make a mess of our world when we ignore God's voice and mis-use both the natural order and our human companions in the process of seeking our interests. The earth is the Lord's, not ours, and hence there is a limit to how far we can bend it to suit ourselves. Contravening the laws that hold it together cannot but result in a return to the chaos from which it was created."[63] Human beings, *creatures themselves*, are not removed from the rest of creation. Our redemption is connected to the redemption of all created things. A holistic theological anthropology connects the scope of human life with creation and the Creator.

An Akan Woman's Anthropology

African women are tasked with undoing the "stereotypical views of the African woman and her spirituality" buttressed by African culture and Christianity.[64] Oduyoye's solution is to be inventive. She builds her position on a key principle in both: communal wholeness. Though Akan tradition and Christianity are both in dire need of correction, she deserts neither Akan tradition nor Christianity but examines them for an alternative solution. She understands the "need to return to . . . religious underpinnings to unearth the resources necessary for dialogue."[65]

In delving deeper into the constructive elements of both cultures, Oduyoye remains true to her identity as Akan *and* Christian while reforming their foundational pillars. When confronted with the problems of home, you do not leave, but stay and resolve the issue.[66] African women interrogate the foundations of their religious-cultural identity to source a liberative way forward. This re-sourcing and resourcefulness require truth telling.

If God expects human beings "to learn to appreciate, respect and value one another as primarily human,"[67] the African cultural cornerstone of communal well-being might be the antidote to unchecked patriarchal practices.[68] Through her work Oduyoye creates space for African women to claim space in their culture and the Christian faith. She proves women important to conversations on African communal wellness. For Oduyoye, it is possible to balance progress and tradition, to advocate for gender equality through highlighting and amending ideas of one's respective culture. Claiming her own theological voice honors the fullness of *her* African personhood. With theology that is feminist in nature and Akan in origin,[69] Oduyoye shows the world how all theology is devoutly communal.

How We Need Each Other

Theological anthropology requiring or expecting women's silence is a fractured form of theological anthropology.[70] Human beings were created to need each other. African women emphatically advocate for an anthropology inclusive of all persons. This holistic understanding of humanity yields a holistic understanding of God.

Human beings' need of each other is suggestive of the relational complexity they have with God. Human beings were created by God's choice and doing, not by their own volition. "God knows what we need," Oduyoye reminds us.[71] Humans were created for relationship with each other, creation, and God.

A theological anthropology that centers God requires reverential imagination; it requires a vision of the self and of others emphasizing "justice, caring, sharing and compassion," for this "is the expression of the divine image all human beings are expected to reflect."[72] God can be seen in the apertures of connectedness. A communal-focused approach begets a more complete theological anthropology. African women's theological anthropology wants to "build a human community whose obligations arise from within ourselves rather than from outside pressure."[73] Community is crucial to a right theological anthropology.

A True Theological Anthropology

A sound theological anthropology professes that "all originate from the express will of God, be they male or female"; insists on "the equal value of all human beings"; claims "that there is something of the divine in the human"; affirms "the dignity and integrity of humanity"; and contends that each human "is to reflect the divine and be related to God the source of human being," reminding us that "all humans are created in the image of God."[74] Profess, insist, claim, affirm, contend, remind.

African women's theological anthropology helps humanity remember that life is good because of "relationship with God."[75] It calls humanity to approximate "God's creativity, justice, and compassion and exhibit the holiness to which they are called by God."[76] Theological anthropology guides humanity back to God, revealing God's creative intention for human beings as companionship—with God and with each other.

Oduyoye argues that the first three chapters of Genesis can be read as a reminder of humanity's createdness.[77] Centering God should counter any hierarchical thinking among creatures. The "head" of humanity is not man or woman, but God; not creature, but Creator. Together humans constitute community, but they only do so in collective communion with God. Understanding community as the product of God's creative imagination is germane to a fruitful human life. To further the premise of male superiority rattles the foundation of God's creative action. The man's (the *adam*'s) being created first is insufficient grounds to tier humanity, especially along the lines of gender. Human being was created to be in relationship and community, not to rank itself as superior or inferior based on factors outside of its control. For Oduyoye, then, *koinonia* in Christian community is critical to remember; it is human community with and in *God*.[78]

Human beings' createdness is their shared core identity. This universal truth allows for Christians to culturally express their theology in a generative manner. Oduyoye's theological anthropology rightly centers constructive elements of both Akan traditions and Christianity to form her Akan Christian voice. With this proper footing and approach, it is easier for her, and for African women like her, to sift through and keep the most innovative and life-giving aspects from both traditions.

A Way Forward

Oduyoye calls for "an inclusive theological response to the spiritual needs of African Christians."[79] For the Akan, inclusion is a culturally ardent practice. The whole community must consistently work to reimagine themselves, especially if they want to honor their women.[80]

Like the image of newly woven tapestry, Oduyoye's theological anthropology imagines mutual dependence and reciprocity between African men and women.[81] Galatians 3:28 echoes in the background of her approach. Just as there is no "male and female" in Christ, for Oduyoye, "we can all say that neither the male nor the female is greater than the community, for the community transcends the joint existence and contribution of women and men who compose it."[82] The community is a living, breathing entity—only complete when inclusive. Women must be lifted up as equals for the ultimate good of the entire community.[83]

African women have innovative theological ideas. If given space to do theology, women can convince the patriarchal church to relinquish its desire to be Creator and own its status as creature, as created being.[84] For Oduyoye, to delimit women is a serious spiritual offense, akin to sinning against the movement of the Holy Spirit;[85] but to count women's voices as part of the African theological voice is to affirm wholeness and unity under the Supreme Being. This unity in createdness is reflected most profoundly in the function of the Christian church. Turning to Oduyoye's ecclesiology, we recognize the benefits of a theological anthropology that extends recognition and respect to all human beings; in this, we receive the vision of a holistic church such as God intended.

CHAPTER SEVEN

ECCLESIOLOGY

We must be careful as we work on tasks of self-definition.
—Mercy Amba Oduyoye, *Introducing African Women's Theology*

Claiming Each Other

In 1967, the World Council of Churches (WCC) released an ecclesial report entitled *The Church for Others.* In it they proposed reordering the sequence of God's relationship to the world from "God-Church-world" to "God-world-church." Their point in doing so was to reemphasize God's relationship to God's creation as a whole: "God's primary relationship is to the world, and it is the world and not the Church that is the focus of God's plan," the report offers.[1] The radical notion that the WCC report put forth—that it is "the whole cosmos that occupies [God's] attention"—struck a chord with one of its members. She would hold this very notion in front of them over twenty years later when it came to the inclusion of African women in the vision for the Christian church.

Since the 1960s, Mercy Oduyoye's ecumenical work has taken ecclesiology into account from an African women's theological perspective. African women advocate for a theological vision with nuanced African God-talk, an embodied christological hermeneutic, and renarrated accounts of human-divine relationship, all toward an inclusive and connected "community that claims special relationship with Jesus of Nazareth who was named the Christ."[2] They understand that theology is never without an opening for inclusion and liberation.

African women's ecclesiology, much like their overarching theological position, is liberationist. At the core, African women believe the Christian church is a communal space for inclusiveness and collective freedom. Unfortunately for many African women, this liberation only comes after they fight for their own inclusion in the African and universal Christian church. But for the Christian church to live into its authentic identity, African women contend, women must be present participants in its events, affairs, and decision-making.

The beauty and challenge of the Christian church is its diversity. For Oduyoye and other African women, the church is like a family—its various members, "communities of Christ-believers,"[3] seeking God together. The hearth-hold imagery in African women's theology comes back to mind, its subversiveness a means to ground their ecclesiology. "The church is indeed a hearth-hold with God as mother, the whole earth is the hearth and all human beings as the children of God," Oduyoye notes.[4] This implies that the church is a "domestic" space where women must be treated as foundational, for how the people know God parallels how the community knows and treats its women. African women's ecclesiology invites the people—invites the church—to revisit how it treats its women, for this treatment is a quintessential reflection of its theological beliefs.

At first glance, the hearth-hold ecclesial imagery seems hopeful; different people coming together as a sign of God's love in the world invokes a sense of unified purpose. But we run into a dilemma, given African women's experiences with interpretations of difference in the Christian church—in terms of how racial and gender matters have been dealt with in the history of Christianity in Africa. European colonialism has left a historical mark on African Christian conceptions of God. Jesus Christ has been argued away from the community of women who assert they know his pain most closely. Fractured relationships in humanity fueled by gender misconceptions have led to rifts in understanding God. These doctrinal problems all have homes in the notion of difference; one party lords it over another with difference as a weapon of authority, deeming the other unworthy of full inclusion. In the church, difference has become the lynchpin of inequality.

Although the Christian church was never a "unitary structure" but rather the unanimity of diverse people, language of diversity may not solve problems birthed from difference. What are we to make of the historical reality of a church whose "differing views and emphases struggled for ascendancy"?[5] The Christian church has long been a place where different parties have tried to assert their power; hierarchy has long been a Christian reality and tradition. For those with vulnerable identities, the risk of maltreatment is exponentially higher.

Where might African women fit in the Christian ecclesiological conversation, given their double marginal status of being both African and women? Oduyoye has a radically simple proposal that attends to the problem of African women's doctrinal invisibility: *all* Christians must assume that African women are a crucial part of the Christian church. In doing so, the church will be exposed to new and constructive ways of exploring the Christian life.

What makes Oduyoye's proposal radical is not her claim of African women's importance to the church: African women *already* know themselves to be critical characters in the Christian story. The radicality is in the force with which these women shock the system of patriarchy. Women already regard themselves the fulcrum of the church; the church cannot function well without their presence and labor. Oduyoye, in concert with other African and third-world women, desires decision-making power as well. She develops an ecclesiology, a way of explaining the identity and rhythms of the Christian church, that is attentive to experiences on the underside of that church.

African women's ecclesiology illumines the church's relationship with God, church members' relationships each other, and the church's relationship with the world through a deep sense of awareness, radical inclusion, and expansive imagination. It repurposes domestic imagery and traditional hermeneutical ideas toward a discourse that honors the depth of human and divine connection. Through local and global ecumenical efforts, African women decided their ecclesiology would be one subverting space—taking up plenty of it, entering into it, and reimagining what the church has the capacity to hold. They have always considered themselves members of the Christian church; it is the rest of the church who needs to catch up to this fact.

Akin

For Oduyoye, "family"—not the Eurocentric nuclear family model, but the kinship frameworks found in African culture—can work as a metaphor to describe the Christian church. African notions of family and kinship allow for an expansive understanding of how people in different stages of life and with different identities can still belong to and be responsible for one another. "The traditional African family is an ever-expanding, outward-looking community structured as concentric circles," Oduyoye offers.[6] In Akan culture specifically, although there are "nuclear" families, the members of one do not represent the total family unit. Multiple nuclear units compose a household (an *abusua*),[7] a concept of family referencing living and spiritual beings, including the dead and unborn.[8] This is important, because one does not act individually but with the entire *abusua* in mind. One thinks of oneself *as* the household, not apart from it.[9]

The church, the literal embodiment of collective difference, can learn from this model of life. If church includes the culmination of living and spirit beings and functions as a complex communal organism of holy connection and intention, then all of its members are critical to its wellness. But the biological barrier still stands in the way of a Christian iteration of an *abusua*; women are not treated as full-fledged members of the ecclesial household. We see a crack in the *abusua* foundation (both culturally and ecclesially sourced). The household unit is not prioritized, but individuals within it are privileged over one another. The household unit does not work for the wellness of the whole but hierarchizes the desires of the designated "head" of the household, typically male.[10]

Even with the conundrum of male headship in the church, if an *abusua* is an "organ committed to group welfare" and "its members are brought up to be committed to the group and to one another," how does the church account for the dismissal of women's voices?[11] When it does not honor women's voices like it does the voices of men, the church is functioning "opposite to what it claims to be."[12]

This kinship contradiction is the place from which Oduyoye's ecclesiology is born. Can the church know and honor the fullness of itself if it excludes women? In embodying difference in some ways but not in others, is the church embodying God's will of inclusion? Patriarchy's firm grasp on the affairs of the church suggests not.

Oduyoye's work in organizations such as the World Council of Churches, the Ecumenical Association of Third World Theologians, and the Circle of Concerned African Women Theologians illumines the problematic rationale behind a Christian church that refuses to appropriately acknowledge all of its members across both racial and gender lines. Although they are part of the church's makeup, African women have fallen on the wrong side of the church's neglect and misrecognition. That African women have to fight for the same visibility that Africans as a whole had to wrestle from Europeans proves that the vision of the church is biased and in need of hefty imaginative reform.

In a holistic African woman's ecclesiology, the church sees itself first as belonging to God and then sees its members as belonging to each other. It demonstrates welcome and care reflective of life in God.[13] Harmful gender dynamics and myopic ecclesial vision hinder progress toward such an ecclesiology. In the same way that African theology recognizes the fullness of African personhood, African women's ecclesiology challenges the church both to confront unjust systems and ideas and to advocate for justice and inclusion.

African women's voices rightly trouble the waters of the ecclesial institution.[14] They assert the need for what Oduyoye calls a "two-winged theology," where both men's and women's viewpoints are needed for a sound ecclesiology.[15] A one-winged approach cannot work. In order for the church to soar, one gender must not think itself superior to the other, but *in need of the other*.

Calling for a Welcoming Church

Like the African saying goes, "A bird with one wing does not fly."[16] The church cannot be one-sided, cannot excel as half of itself. Insisting on this illusion brings up questions of fitness. Unsurprisingly, patriarchy insists on this one-sidedness with fervor. It breeds sexism and discriminatory attitudes and practices directed toward women, all in the hopes of half-flying. Those in the church who think patriarchal practices are holy principles do not recognize women's invisibility as derisive. Oduyoye brands this disassociated belief self-division—the church literally divided against itself.[17] This division skews rationality, disparaging women's humanity.[18] It dismisses players crucial in Africa's life and the life of the Christian church. This is a grave mistake. A two-winged theology, Oduyoye asserts, where both men and women are a part of theology's future in Africa, most represents the future of the Christian church. This, however, can feel somewhat impossible in a church that insists on marginalizing its members because of perceived differences.

For many Africans, the presence of European colonial Christianity introduced the racial and ethnic devaluation of African culture. Many Africans resisted. They insisted on their humanity, the validity of their culture, and the sacredness of their religio-social practices. They fought for their inclusion. Ironically, where African men feel racial scarring from a force external to their cultural community, women feel scarring internally. In addition to responding to colonial insults against their culture, African women do theology against injurious systems of thought from the men in their own cultures.

While many African men in the third world focus their attention on stopping their people's erasure on a global scale, Oduyoye notes how the treatment of third-world communities runs parallel to gendered treatments *within* third-world cultures. If colonialism taught Africans that they were overlooked and ignored, the irony must be explored that, in the same breath, African women are culturally treated as imperceptible. We must revisit the difficult truth that African women's theological oppression already had a home base in African cultural practices. Oduyoye reminds, "The pyramids of power that exist in African culture have found companions in Christianity."[19]

African women's oppression, then, is, in part, intracultural. Their oppression comes from home. The domestic and the cultural structures exist simultaneously: "The structural violence against women is only matched by the familial one," Oduyoye reminds.[20] African women are often caught in the crosshairs of multiples sites of oppression, of destruction and harm—from military to economic to racial injustices.[21] Women's perceived inferiority is a by-product of cultural norms that structurally benefit men, African and otherwise.

A one-sided hermeneutical position that exclusively benefits men, even within African social life, is not the means to either a healthy or whole vision of the hearth-hold of Christ.[22] For Oduyoye, someone whose theological position dishonors the fullness of creation, male and female, is resistant to—and even stands in opposition to—what Christ represents. The Christian church fully cognizant of and fully honoring its members belongs to Christ; the church acting otherwise does not function as Christ's body.[23] Oduyoye advocates for a theological vision fully inclusive of women; the church would not be able to realize its whole self otherwise.[24]

African women must find a way to take their voices back from patriarchal culture.[25] For Oduyoye, eruption is the answer. Women must advocate for the freedom to *be* the church, and they must do so by troubling patriarchy's core. In the thralls of women's fighting for their freedom, the patriarchal calm, as Oduyoye calls it—like a volcano—is troubled. It erupts, overpowered by the rumblings for liberation. Surprisingly, what emerges from the patriarchal wellspring *is* liberation. Diverse voices bubble up, scorching the ground on which the world previously thought it stood.[26] Liberationist efforts, led by women, conjure up movement and a fiery cleansing. The soil of the old ground, now scorched, is ripe for new, inclusive initiatives. African women happily disrupt the patriarchal calm in order to bring about a new way of being community and being church in the world.

Biblical Solidarity in the Christian Church

African women consider Christian scripture to be soil ripe for liberation. New life can spring forth from the witness community that scripture offers, but this insight requires the right interpretive lens. Typically "read in ways that oppose traditional African beliefs and practices"[27] or in a way "that subordinates women to men, silences women, and alienates them from dynamic agency in home, church, and society,"[28] the Bible provides imagery and language for a new ecclesial framework—if read subversively. The hermeneutical imagination *toward* the text is important. If the church were to read the Bible toward ecclesial communal vision, it would find that Scripture provides an image of communion in Christ.[29] How African women employ scripture is important to note here. Scripture's contents are not material for philosophical reflection or theological debate, but an illustration of the pathway toward symbiotic life. Scripture is the story of how a "community gathered by God through Christ"[30] should be in the world. Scripture's core lesson is the communal charge to the church: that as long as it exists in the world, it must point toward God.

While many women have experienced scripture as a "patriarchal and ethnocentric" tool,[31] Oduyoye constructively decides to interpret scripture inclusively.[32] Her hermeneutical lens looks at the bigger picture of the church's communal life in Christ instead of parsing microdetails and ideational frills. "The biblical picture of the church is . . . that of an assembly of believers, gathered in the name of Jesus to acknowledge the sovereignty of God. . . . It is an assembly in the making as the Holy Spirit continues to . . . lead it into all truth, and to purge it of unnecessary accessions," she asserts.[33] Oduyoye frames her ecclesiology around the Creator-creation dynamic. The church is the assembly of God's creation reflecting God's will in the earth in Christ.

Oduyoye's hermeneutical approach highlights two characteristics about the church: (1) the church is focused on life in God; and (2) the church thinks of itself as a collective toward this mission. The latter detail is most important. The church is a collective, one in which women are automatically and equally included. African women's ecclesiology wears this inclusive hermeneutical lens *because of* scripture. The Bible's overarching message empowers African women to assume themselves to be already part of the Christian church and to boldly participate in its purpose. It is not a radical detail for women to be included, but rather a given.

Oduyoye tells a story of how when she was a girl in Mmofraturo, a Methodist girls' boarding school in Kumasi, Ghana, she and her classmates felt empowered to make scripture their own, so they took interpretive liberty. Since the proverbs from the bible were so close to Akan proverbs, the girls would recite Akan proverbs in place of the proverbs of the Hebrew Bible. They confidently lived into their hybrid religious identity. Why not translate their own cultural wisdom into biblical language?[34] For these girls, the sentiment behind these proverbs already lived deeply in Akan culture. Oduyoye and her classmates could already hear themselves in the lessons of scripture. What's more, they already counted themselves equal members of the church, interpreting scripture in such a way as to include themselves in the affairs of the church.[35] Moments like these invite the wisdom of scripture into dialogue with African culture. They also invite girls and women to practice their inclusion!

In honor of this liberative memory, Oduyoye calls for biblical solidarity that acknowledges the condition of all of humanity. Biblical solidarity occurs "when people act with God to end oppression and to build new communities of freedom in partnership with God."[36] It has less to do with biblical inerrancy and more to do with the inclusive message at the heart of scripture. For Oduyoye, biblical solidarity creates an ecclesial household where no one is made to feel as if they are on the "outside of the church."[37] Biblical solidarity assumes African women *to be* the church.

African women's ecclesiology proposes that men and women need each other in order for the Christian church to fully be itself. Only in living into its communal purpose can the church "discern the signs of God's life-giving presence in church, community, and nation."[38]

Rolling Stones

The Christian church could be in solidarity with its women if it simply decided to choose itself. Oduyoye pushes this sentiment in her seminal ecumenical work, *Who Will Roll the Stone Away?* At its core is the question for the World Council of Churches: "What does sexism have to do with what we consider churches to be?"[39] What does the church consider itself to be? Who does the church consider itself to be? If the experiences of women are "part and parcel of the church's experiences," then the church should have no problem extending equal recognition to them.[40] Despite the council's push for greater inclusion, women's recognition and inclusion are, unfortunately, not the reality in the wider Christian church.

Oduyoye's questions and assertions to the World Council of Churches identify a chasm between the church's verbal claims and its actual practice. The church has still not learned how to be itself.

Like Mary asking, "Who will roll the stone away?," African women in the church are asking who will remove the obstacles hindering women's meeting Christ. Like the stone, male-favoring interpretations and claims to power stand in the way. Who will move them? The women alone do not have the ability to budge such a massive obstacle. Movement requires everyone's strength; men and women alike must volunteer to do shifting work.[41] But such a major shift requires that the base desire include women in the affairs of the church.[42]

Ecclesial inclusion means creating "a network of mutual support."[43] The whole body of the church—not only the women—must be involved in the fulfillment of this inclusion. It implies a sharing of power previously set aside for one group alone. For Africans, it requires an awareness and recognition of the dynamic that if power imbalance was unwelcome in colonial racial encounters, gendered injustice in the church must be equally unwelcome.

Honoring women as God's creation mirrors a sound theological anthropology. Anything outside of women's equal recognition in the church replicates sin, for it suggests humanity "has reduced stewardship to domination, husbanding to control, and complementarity to the paternal determining the scope of being for the maternal."[44] Women are complete beings in themselves; they do not need men to assign them value or visibility. Patriarchal thought tries to cement a different logic in the ecclesial imagination. It distorts and destroys human beings' ability to truly see and thus partner with one another. It hinders the church's efforts to be in step with the message of Christ.

For Oduyoye, the church should demonstrate the faith work of its people—it should witness Christ.[45] She is clear with her hope for the future of the African church: "The vision I have of the church is quite simply this: It should be a community that demonstrates to Africa how variety and diversity may become a blessing."[46] The church should bring a rightly lensed African cultural practice to the forefront, emphasizing love and care for the entire community, to "enhance them with the good news and Jesus Christ."[47]

The objective of bringing the proper lens to Christian ecclesiology is communal development and thriving. For African women, the mission of the church is to be "a community able to be salvific and present to the least of the sisters and brothers of Jesus the Christ."[48] In the right and equal treatment of women and men, the essence of the gospel will be received as an agent of healing.[49] Equality rolls the stone away, but it takes the collective strength of the entire church for any movement to be possible. Once women are recognized, the church can recognize the extent of God's reach; God is the Creator of all, and the Christian church would do well to recognize that its followers are not the only ones for whom God cares. For Oduyoye and other women, this inclusive recognition is part and parcel of a healthy ecclesiology.

On Many Faith Traditions

African women's ecclesiology honors all human beings as God's children. Though Christian, this understanding of religious human community is not reserved for Christianity alone. Oduyoye's hearth-hold imagery works well here. For Oduyoye, the hearth-hold—the central gathering place of many—describes the centrality of God's presence in the life of persons of various faith traditions. God is the center of the "house" whether its inhabitants are Christian or not.

The Christian church asserts that all creation belongs to God, and the church holds to a more particular message that calls for believing in "Jesus Christ as the Wisdom and Word of creation."[50] But the two beliefs are not mutually exclusive. The church should know that the whole world is sacred—the world and all who live in it are God's.[51] Like the 1967 World Council of Churches report, African women's ecclesiology asserts that it is critical to Christianity's voice to know God and God's creation as good and sacred. Africans understand this, since the way African Christianity came to be was through a level of openness to a new religious frame. Oduyoye comments at length:

At the beginning of the modern missionary enterprise, Africans converted to Christianity because they saw an affinity between the gospel of Jesus

Christ and the African worldview of the sacredness of life and the human attachment to life, fullness of life. They were drawn to the gospel's inclusiveness and wholeness, its care for the vulnerable and its affirmation of humanity's dependence on God. . . . The sacredness of life, and specifically human life, was reinforced by Christianity through its humanitarian stance and its concern for the individual and for the quality of life of the whole community.[52]

Christianity as a religious framework is concentrated on God's care for God's creation. For Christians, God's knowing and caring for all creation renders everyone and everything sacred. The church's ecclesiology, then, should function similarly. "A desacralized world that makes human beings into objects to be exploited does damage to religion as a whole but in particular to Christianity," Oduyoye reminds.[53] Care about and for God's creation is a central cornerstone of the faith. The Christian church should lovingly and inclusively lay claim on humanity as a whole. It calls forth disciples to live into a new form of freedom void of separatist structures.[54] Christianity should proclaim God's delight in all creation. The entire world is critical to Christianity's claims of love, life, and wellness.[55] African women's ecclesiology centers *God's* proclamations about creation, rather than elevating humanity's own judgments about its fellow created beings. African women position God as the head of the house.

God, not man, must be the center of how the Christian church understands itself. "We human beings, with all created things, participate in the life whose source is the One God," Oduyoye asserts.[56] In seeing another, the Christian church sees itself. This radically inclusive position undergirds how African women theologize. The elementary principles are most telling: God created all; therefore, all are important to God's movement in the earth.

The communal focus is key for African women's theology. African women's experiences are not separate from the church's reality but a critical part of it. The experiences of African women *are* the experiences of the Christian church; women and church are not separate entities. The flesh of the church is dense with the stories of African women just as much as with those of any other people group.

Thus, the calls for justice, participation, and ministry that African women are claiming for themselves are not merely vested points of interest; they are the crux of a holistic Christian ecclesial life. These called-forth truths are the full revelation of the church. If the church does not embody these realities for itself, it fails to be itself.

How African Women See the Church

Oduyoye, in calling for the equality of women and men in the church, is calling the church back to itself. *Koinonia*, or the sharing of common life, is the Christian church's original intention, but the church must be attentive to its members. Oduyoye's work asks: Who are positioned as "church" and who are the bodies the "church" must step on in order to procure its greatness? Can the church be great if it does not know or value its entire self? Does the church know itself?

Her work prophetically interrogates the limited imagination of a Christian church that does not recognize itself (or another). The church, Oduyoye argues, must relearn not only what it was intended to be in the world but also what it was intended to look like. When finally able to look at itself, the church will be troubled by "its own self-inflicted divisions, by the multiplication of division, by the failure to recognize the Church in the 'other,' by internal divides between clergy and lay, women and men, adults and minors, Black and White, rich and poor."[57] When it *sees* itself, the Christian church will see Africa's humanity as a whole; it will see itself respecting the full humanity of its women. If the church is to be a reflection of—to use *mujerista* theologian Isasi-Díaz's terminology—the kindom of God, "an inclusive community of women and men of all races and tongues,"[58] the church must understand and honor itself in its entirety.

If Oduyoye's theological anthropology teaches us of God's true intention for the creation of humanity, her ecclesiology shows us God's expression through such joined creation. Oduyoye invites us to call the church incomplete if it is not rooted in its creaturely identity. Even further, she and other African women theologians challenge us to birth and practice new ways of being church if the current iteration falls short.

The Christian church is how God can be recognized in the world, but it must first learn and know itself in order to live into its promise. It must first open its eyes and ears to those it has marginalized and turned away.[59] God's creation is privy to God's goodness, love, and life. African women's theology, and Oduyoye's standpoint in particular, reminds the Christian church of God's plan of abundant life for and in God's creation—but only if it wants to know itself.

CHAPTER EIGHT

WHAT REMAINS

Women's theology comes as words that are lived.
—Mercy Amba Oduyoye, *Introducing African Women's Theology*

Furthering the Conversation

Mercy Oduyoye has created room for herself in worlds not necessarily built for her; her cultural, educational, and ecumenical experiences no doubt contribute to her theological prowess. True to herself, Oduyoye's commitment to African Christianity is an incredible model for African women theologians; she has shown that women can contribute to and highlight cultural truths. African women's voices can be heard, but they must be resolute in their vocality. Without question, Oduyoye's work has tilled the ground for future theologians to push the agenda of African women's theology forward, not as a niche area but as one critical to the theological discipline as a whole. Her work has successfully highlighted Christian theology's various gaps and blind spots and has championed revised thinking around issues of gender and race in the African context. However groundbreaking it is, we must note that the effects of her work are only partial: the magnitude of the issues at the heart of racist and pa-triarchal theologies are that numerous.

Oduyoye's work begins the conversation that others will carry on. It is unwise to assume that her work, while extensive, will cover every issue African women's religious or theological experiences spotlight. She overviews and explores what she knows; she tackles issues in which she believes her voice can create a difference. This inevitably means that she, too, will have a few gaps in her work. This signals not a deficit on her part but the invitation for the next generation of African women theologians to continue the work that needs to be done.

Occupied with overturning ill-founded assumptions about African women's cultural and theological place, Oduyoye's work is based in rebuttal. Primarily in a position of refuting biased positions, she can only take African women's constructive theological possibilities so far. Her work richly examines and counterargues theological and cultural aggressions. These are the parameters of her work; nevertheless, there are areas still in need of significant engagement. A few areas I lift up are conceptual gaps around sexuality, the character of African men's theological accountability, and a push to engage further with the African diaspora. These areas of Oduyoye's work remain in need of further interrogation and conversation.

Sexuality is a tough topic to broach. Oduyoye's reflections on issues of gender and sex—that which she considers "sexuality" in the breadth of her work—rest in particular contextual and conceptual parameters. She is working in a certain ideological terrain and with vocabulary of a certain time frame and cultural context. "Sexuality" is not theorized for Oduyoye, but frames sociocultural ideas tied to biology and anatomy. Throughout the breadth of her work, Oduyoye faces the same problems concerning gender and sex; she primarily argues against sexism. This cyclical engagement is a fixed problem. She has not had much opportunity to venture beyond her initial analysis and resolutions, only to repeat them. Her engaging the same issues creates a gap in constructive feminist theological responses. What might new theological gestures toward African women's full sexual liberation look like?

While Oduyoye's life's work identifies the pitfalls of patriarchy and sexism, what is missing is a clear call for men not only to include women in theological decision-making but also for *men* to head theological restitution efforts. What might African women's theology look like if it directly called African men to take theological responsibility for African women's marginalization? How much more room would African women have to constructively do theology if their men spent the life of *their* theological careers in a position of penance?

Oduyoye has mothered countless African women impacted by and interested in doing Christian theology.[1] Women all over the world are gaining visibility and traction to do theology with fervor and courage. What would more attention to these voices mean for the evolution of African women's theology inside and outside of the continent? In conversation with the liberationist and the Black theological traditions, the reach of African women's theology is significant; it extends beyond Africa well into the African diaspora. More intentional collaboration with such voices could expand the reach of African women's theology even further. But would African women theologians be comfortable seeing the face of their theological movement shifting shape and broadening in name, method, and tactic? What might Oduyoye's engagement with second- and third-generation African women's theology mean for the future of African women's theology?

Oduyoye has a tremendous theological legacy. Her work has not only helped African women feel seen but has also generated conversations that would not otherwise have happened among men and women all over the world. Even in the areas where her work can be pushed further, readers still gain tremendous insight. We still receive wisdom on how to propel justice further.

On Sexuality

An elephant in the metaphorical room must be addressed when it comes to Oduyoye's notion of sexuality: the bulk of her work does not employ the term theoretically, as it is thought of today. In her writings she is not working with the modern conceptions of the term. For Oduyoye, "sexuality" implies the imbricating burdens of biological sex and gender roles. This is important to note so as not to place the wrong expectations on her articulations of sexuality.[2] When reading Oduyoye's work, we must enter and think within the framework of the experience from which *she* writes. Her use of "sexuality," as she knows it through her

experiences of being an African woman of a certain age, references social attentiveness around anatomical bias. Oduyoye wants to free women
from the pressures and trappings of sociocultural gender roles. She advocates for women's liberation on that front.

But even with her liberative ideas around sex and gender, sexuality
(in this way) is still confined to limited cultural parameters. This is seen in
three areas. Instead of speaking constructively to African women's sexuality,
Oduyoye's approach (1) highlights what African women's sexuality *is not*;
thus, it (2) asserts a focus on gender roles as substitutive for speaking to the
range of sexuality, sexuality that is often (3) understood primarily within
heterosexual marriage. Marriage seems to be the primary site—if not the
only site—within which African women's sexual relevance is discussed
in Oduyoye's work. Her conception of sexuality is more about undoing
harmful narratives around sex and gender and freeing sexuality from restrictive frames instead of crafting new definitions of what African wom-
en's sexuality could be if authored by said women.

Currently, African women's sexuality is fighting to determine itself.
Too many women spend the bulk of their work trying to undo and refute the theological rationale that has tried to silence or dismiss their
voices and bodies. Oduyoye has spent her life addressing concerns of
women's visibility, yet she has not ventured to create her own framework
of African women's sexuality in her work.

Oduyoye's approach seems more reparative than constructive. The
grounds for women's social and sexual limitation stem from men's incessant misuse of Christian scripture and abuse of cultural ideas, not from
women's vocalization of themselves. This sends a message about African women's sexuality; it is not posed as a constructive being on its own,
but rather it is a male-authored idea to be deconstructed—one where
women do not determine themselves but end up spending energy defending themselves and their bodies from misconstruals.

African women's sexuality, a chief characteristic of African women's
embodied being in the world, is described by Oduyoye primarily through
negation. The breadth of her work points out what it is not (over and
against false patriarchal imagery) but does not strongly assert what it actually *is*. As Oduyoye engages it, African women's sexuality, then, becomes
an argument against male-favoring religious logic, not the self-determined

reality of African women themselves. This positions African women's sexuality as, first and foremost, a response to men. The sexuality conversation still tethers women to men.

In the scope of her work Oduyoye speaks against the problematic aspects of gender roles but also offers few alternatives to imagining African women differently in the world. Refuting gender taboos and limitation is one thing—and often a time-consuming thing; offering constructive discourse on African women's sexual expression is another. The lack of constructive conversation around African women's sexuality resurfaces questions of why African women's sexuality is such a "nonissue" in the Christian church outside of notions of morality[3] and, further, why African women have not had the space to name the form of their own sexuality.

As I noted earlier, in Oduyoye's analyses she does not parse gendered social assumptions (sexuality as gender and sex) from the freedom of sexual expression (sexuality as known on the spectrum). Sexuality, as Oduyoye presents it in her work, appears to be most important in critiquing male-authored marriage and procreative expectations for women. African women's sexuality is *only* spoken of in relation to men and the categories they create for it; this is a problem. With the "Christian fear of the 'flesh,'" notions of purity and taboo remind us that biological marginalization, women's sexual expression, and faith values are inextricably linked.[4]

Oduyoye tries to liberate women from male-authored sexuality but is ultimately caught by the same trap of reading sexuality's importance through the lens of heterosexual marriage. She does not explore women's sexuality outside the bounds of traditional, oppressive kinship structures. It seems that for many African women, sexuality is mainly a hetero-reality.

Outside of a brief mention and critique of a limited Pauline interpretive logic on same-sex love, conversations around nonheterosexual relationships are scarce in Oduyoye's theological work. She does name the interpretive boundaries around same-sex relationality as directly tied to "women's freedom in Christ," but it is unclear whether this freedom translates into speaking about women's conditions socially (gender and sex) or sexually (sexual identity).[5] How does African women's sexuality manifest? What does its liberated form look like? Oduyoye's work gives us hints, but only within heterosexual relationships. Although African women historically and currently wrestle with sexual freedoms within heterosexual marriage,[6] the cultural reins on the sexuality conversation are tight. Holding them too tightly limits the possibility of further theological exploration.

Oduyoye glimpses the constructive possibility of women's sexual freedom in *Beads and Strands*. Over and against the argument of heterosexual marriage she asserts that attention to sexuality can be a liberating force for women. "Men and women are sexually distinct beings who do not necessarily have to be identified with the opposite sex in marriage or in other forms of complementarity. Women are persons in communion, not persons who 'complete' the other," she claims.[7] Human sexuality is a concern of theological anthropology, since sexuality expresses proper communion between human beings.

Sexuality is more than something to be performed within the confines of marriage. For Oduyoye, "Sexuality is a central factor of being human and not a peripheral luxury for intellectual explication."[8] It must be taken seriously as a communal factor that determines relationality. But it must first be recalibrated to exist in ways that unburden women.[9] Everyone's full humanity must be honored in order for there to be a constructive conversation about sex and gender. But for some women it is difficult to get out from under patriarchal ideas and relational systems.

Accountability and African Men

Some African women theologians, already burdened with other social hurdles, find issues such as sexuality hard to address. Because of the overwhelming reality of the multiple oppressions she addresses, Oduyoye's work in particular does not create new avenues to talk about sex and gender.

Oduyoye has spent her entire career trying to reverse the damage colonialism and patriarchy have inflicted upon African women. She has had to carry burdens she did not create, her voice prevalent primarily in debunking theological falsities about women. While this reality is ultimately positive, it is also burdensome. The excessive work stalls the possibility of her exploring constructive routes in African women's theology.

This is reflective of a larger problem in theology. Because they are often responding to African male misinterpretations of scripture and culture that are wrongly pressed upon their bodies, African women have little space to create alternative ways of framing their own theological lives.

Herein lies the problem of theological responsibility: while calling men to account, Oduyoye does not fully give women's theological issues *back* to African men; she believes men should take up the case of women but does not clearly or altogether state that men must take *full* responsibility to clean up their own theological messes before they can promote their own ideas. She does not state outright that men's voices will only regain validity if they admit their wrongdoing and dedicate *their* work to overturning the myths from which *they* have benefited. This is a radical desire, but a fair one.

Oduyoye does not push African men—despite all the bias from which African men have benefited—far enough to fix theological problems reliant on sexism (nor does she push white men and white women, I would add); she does not name how African men need to redo *their* theology in order to theologize radically and justly in the modern moment.[10] Instead, her work demonstrates that women must do the theological cleanup of problematic stances from which their male counterparts profit. She invites men to join in with the work African women are doing, but is this enough?

An example lies in some of her claims about the Circle of Concerned African Women Theologians. Though powerful in purpose and origin, the Circle still holds some questionable ideas, namely around the desire for male approval (in the form of participation). It seems that true community requires male participation.

While proclaiming their mission to help "cure Africa of wanton sexism and gender insensitivity, by keeping in focus the role of culture and religion,"[11] the Circle states that male theological voices are necessary to ensure the fulfillment of its mission. Oduyoye firmly advocates for a communal theological foundation inclusive of women *and* men, a positive and Afro-centric move, to be sure. But this move also has problematic elements. In this narration, the notion of communal influence can be utilized unfairly: by stating that African men's involvement is necessary as a sign that the movement is working, the Circle endows men with even more power and influence than they had before—even though communal collaboration is championed as a means to empower African *women*. Though the intention is understandable, this view can feel regressive because it comes at the expense of African women.

Oduyoye claims that the Circle knows "*we are being heard when our brothers in theology take up these issues, and join us in this effort.*"[12] While this statement is true and the sentiment behind it is understood, it does not fully attend to where accountability lay for the work the Circle was created to address in the first place. Is the Circle's theological efficacy only confirmed when men join in?[13] What about the women? Can women hearing each other be enough to confer "being heard"? Are women empowering enough on their own? If not, can communal empowerment include theological responsibility from those actively holding power—namely, the men? Here, Oduyoye's inclusive and communal moves can feel counterproductive if not clarified and pushed further. It seems that little to no corrective responsibility lies with the men; instead, they are proffered new levels of importance through women's reparative efforts, efforts designed to refute the very theo-logics men created and affirmed and about which they remain silent.

Women and men working together does not mean that men can just pick up where the intellectual progressive work of African women began. They do not get to join a cause and continue on without taking responsibility in tangible ways—through revising *their* theologies and practices. Collaboration must require that men be the *most* active agents in theological repair. Saddling women with the job of fixing the oppressive logics that have tried to render them socially, culturally, and theologically lesser does not seem to align with the message of women's empowerment that Oduyoye's theological position promotes. Responsibility needs to be picked up and carried forward by the men.

Empowering African women could mean unburdening them from being forced to defend themselves and their theological presence. This defense work should be men's work. In the name of communal good, realigning responsibility returns the impetus back onto men to make major reforms. Men should begin and *stay* in the reform until it comes to pass. If both genders take on this responsibility, there is a good chance African women will carry the bulk of the work—as the genesis of a lot of their work has been defending their place in their cultures and in Christianity.

A communal or collaborative approach with no male accountability will continue the tradition of African women's theological burdening. African women doing theological apologetics is not the same as having equal weight in theological conversations. If Oduyoye pushed harder for men not only to admit their errors but also to fix them, the scope of African women's theology could take on an entirely different tone and have a potentially larger global impact.

Other Voices in the Diaspora

It bears repeating: Oduyoye has *already* done a lot of theological heavy lifting over the course of her career. She has paved and continues to pave the way for African women to do theology with authority. The problems around sexuality and theological responsibility are not necessarily *her* problems, but issues that arise because of her field. Over time Oduyoye has taken on the great causes, including women's health, stigma narratives, and intercultural valuation;[14] she has paved the way for African women all over the world to do African women's theology from and for their particular contexts. As a result, African women are rightly considering themselves important voices in the African community.

Through her work alone African women's theological vision has gained significant continental and global visibility. African women's voices and theologies are being recognized as impactful beyond the African continent. African women all over the globe are expressing how they have theological contributions to make; inspired by Oduyoye's determination and by the scope of African women's theology, they will now have precedent to do so.[15]

A movement of global importance and promise, African women's theology "springs from a conviction that a theology of relationships might contribute to bring us closer to human life as God desires it."[16] Women all over the world are connecting with Oduyoye's liberative and life-giving theology.[17] Its emphases on right relationship with God, self, and others resonate deeply with women in the African diaspora especially.

Grounded in physical, economic, and spiritual well-being, African women's theology is more and more becoming recognizable in international discourse. In her ecumenical work, for example, Oduyoye has conversed with Black theologians and womanist theologians and ethicists in the United States for decades.[18] African women's theology is no stranger to the theological liberationist movement. It is already inspiring the next generation of African women in the diaspora wrestling with the legacies that colonialism, racism, sexism, class, and ethnocentrism have built. Oduyoye mentions where and whom else her theological premise can reach; she does not, however, spend a great deal of time imagining how African women's theology can evolve based on the experiences of African women in the diaspora. Where else might African women's voices be heard beyond the experiences forged on the continent?

The impact of Oduyoye's theological reflections and offerings can reach farther still. Oduyoye's ambition to inspire women to take their place in "global woman-centered theology" is being realized in the present day.[19] As long as the need exists to uplift women into proper life and human dignity,[20] African women's theological work is never done. Groundbreaking possibilities and generative sites for African women's continued theological presence exist in the next generation and outside of the continent. Their voices and work will create stronger foundations for life not only in Africa but all over the world. Because Oduyoye has directed more attention to these voices and efforts, the world can know that African women are doing theology from the space of their ethnic and geographical experiences. The women doing this work can be affirmed as part of the evolving life of African women's theology, whether they are members of initiatives such as the Circle or not. If Oduyoye were compelled to look in these directions, these diasporic branches of African women's theology would confirm her staying power and influence.

African Feminist Theology and Christian Ethics

Racial and gender bias are undergirded by particular moral frames. Oduyoye counters such systems with wisdom and fortitude. Though chiefly known as an African women's theologian, by virtue of the nature of her work, it can be argued that Oduyoye does both theology *and* ethics. Not deliberately calling it such may be problematic for those firmly planted in the ethics camp, but her impact is undeniable. Her theological responses to notions of "right" and "wrong" and "good" and "bad" frameworks and practices, especially as they are mapped upon women's bodies and notions of moral credibility, render her work ethical. If ethics attends to the effects of practices or decisions upon others, Oduyoye's work fits within the frame of ethical work.

Oduyoye's ethics are already present in her theological reflection. "The African women's theological reflections intertwine theology, ethics, and spirituality," she argues; such reflection "therefore does not stop at theory but moves to commitment, advocacy, and a transforming praxis."[21] Oduyoye's theology *is* her ethic. For some, especially those who require categorical brackets for their comprehension, the question becomes "Within which category?"

Because of her focus on community and the social implications of one's actions, I associate Oduyoye's work most closely with social ethics. Theology attentive to voice, communal impact, social practices and their effect on the world and those in it is the mission of social ethics.[22] Though Oduyoye makes no formal claim on the discourse of ethics either in her work or in commenting upon her work (as this categorical debate is unimportant to her), her place in the conversation of ethics is a rightful and natural one. The turn to social ethics makes the most sense. Hers is an intrinsic African cultural ethos articulated through an Akan feminist Christian social ethic.

Oduyoye's feminist theological tongue grounds her moral thought, moral thought rooted in her culture. Her voice ultimately argues, and subsequently centers, African ways of knowing and ways of being—African particularized cultural living and moving about in the world—as ethically discoursed in itself.[23]

Oduyoye frames African social ethics through the lens of gender in African culture. She asks how women and men of the *same* culture might be attuned to their own people's conceptual wellness. For Oduyoye, the task is in sharing responsibility for the entire community's thriving. Along with other African women, she calls out culturally divisive ideas and calls forth practices mindful of the communal whole.[24] In this Oduyoye reminds Africans of their own cultural value systems. Africans value community and strive for the thriving of the collective.

Oduyoye, however, does not rest the fate of the African peoples on the shoulders of its women alone. Her ethic demonstrates that cultural, social, and religious egalitarianism is a matter of cultural cooperation, the ethical feet on which communal convictions stand. African women's theology and ethics concern "relations, replacing hierarchies with mutuality."[25] Justice language gets closest to Oduyoye's sentiment. Her reflections on dealing justly with African women from a Christian perspective are helpful here: "Dealing justly with African women must begin with taking seriously women's questions and concerns about their status. Trivializing women's concerns . . . does far more harm than good. Women's voices should be listened to when they speak about the God-ordained dignity of every human person and the consequent need of each person for respect."[26] To reiterate Oduyoye's aim, African women's social ethics is a means to return African cultural praxis to its true form, to its actual self.[27] Oduyoye hinges her ethic on the principle that all persons are created beings desired by God.[28] On a practical level, the inclusion of everyone in the community expresses Africanness at its best. Oduyoye's ethical stance, then, is African centered, because in it, *all* Africans are esteemed.

The Christian church must catch up to and learn from Oduyoye's theological journey and ecumenical life. Minimized at every turn yet present at every turn, Oduyoye's voice not only teaches African theology valuable lessons about itself but teaches Christianity as a whole—especially Western Christianity—that for its values to resonate with people all over the world, it must be honest and open to correction. By reading Oduyoye, one is informed of her distinctive perspective and also learns the truth about the practices and value systems of dominant communities. In reading Oduyoye, we are reading about ourselves.

CONCLUSION

Adjusting Lenses, Correcting Perspective

The Burden of Western Interpretation, or How to Read Oduyoye Properly

The Theology of Mercy Amba Oduyoye underscores a fraction of the incredible insights and charges Mercy Amba Oduyoye has issued in and to Christian theology over the course of her career. Her attentiveness to those made invisible by faith and culture reflects the core of Christian values and African communalism. The nature of her work—caring for and honoring the overlooked—*should* be the gauge by which the Christian church measures its theological efficacy. Oduyoye's truth telling holds oppressive and universalized categories of belief accountable to persons impacted by them, mainly African women. The church can no longer pretend not to see its areas where improvement is sorely needed.

Oduyoye's remedy for injustice is inclusivity and liberation. African women theologians as a whole promote the same ideology. In anchoring itself in inclusive approaches to social and ecclesial life, African women's theology asserts that African women deserve to be co-determiners of cultural ideas and ecclesial values. But it has only had this impact because of Oduyoye's acumen. She has, over the course of numerous decades, fought against antiquated and injurious ideas about Africans, about women, and about those who occupy both of these identities and more.

At best, this book only offers a glimpse of how feminism, Christian theology, and African studies fit and connect within Oduyoye's story and the women who find solace in it. Through interrogating African women's interpretations of feminism, she challenges those of us with feminist leanings to broaden our scope of inclusion and understanding. In addressing the pernicious effects of colonialism on the message and practice of Christianity in West Africa, she challenges those of us who assume we have a grasp on Christian theology to remember and tell its entire history—good and bad. Forgetting is a privilege only Europeans seem able to afford.[1] Oduyoye challenges those who think themselves familiar with African studies to honor women and other marginalized persons by interrogating how religious life has had a hand in determining the social life of many African peoples.

Oduyoye does feminism, Christian theology, and African culture a service by identifying their deficiencies. She does not leave them in a state of disarray, however. Instead, her life gestures toward their constructive possibilities. Feminism, Christian theology, and African culture are all places of promise, but each area must seriously listen to and include those who live at the intersection of each. African women theologians have a world of wealth to offer the worlds from which they come; but these worlds must be open to understanding not only their shortcomings but also their own strengths. These worlds must listen to their marginalized.

Oduyoye finds a way to make feminism, Christian theology, and aspects of African culture her own; she crafts them into a religious position. African women's theology rattles the seemingly solid foundations of feminism, Christian theology, and African culture—cracking them open to reveal hollow bases. If void of African women's contributions, these areas are bound to crumble in upon themselves. But when African women's contributions are included, African women reveal the richness of these areas of life and interrogation. They rightfully consider feminism, Christian theology, and African culture critical parts of their identity—African women's theology claims that African women's experience *is* women's experience, *is* Christian experience, *is* African experience—*is* human experience.

Oduyoye's work nuances the stories the world assumes it already knows and on behalf of which it errantly speaks. Her presence in

Christian theology is her refusal for this reality to continue to be true; by virtue of being present in theological and ecumenical conversations and events, she has not allowed and does not allow African women's agency to be wrested from them. Her work wonders, "What challenges does the Third World pose to Christian theology and Christian witness to the Gospel of Jesus Christ?"[2] And further, "What challenges do women in the Third World face in their own contexts?" These wonderings, in turn, draw the reader's attention to *their own* theological locales in relation to the conceived, contrived, and perceived theological locations of others.

Oduyoye forces us to grapple with where we are theologically located. Her message is clear: we who think our lives unaffected by the factors that impact African women are unable to see not only the truth of African women's lives but also, and primarily, the truth of *our own lives*. African women's theology calls African culture to account: abandoning its women reflects an abandonment of African culture's greatest virtues. African women's theology also, however, debunks the falsehood that Western religious imagination is the most prominent voice in Christian thought. It proves untrue the notion that theologies are not impacted by the culture of another. It forces the West to recognize where it exercises colonial privilege and advantage in its own theological house. How the West "reads" Oduyoye should have a reflective effect. What is she showing the Western reader about their theological imagination, their theological *abusua*, their theological priorities? The burden of Western interpretation rests on the Western reader, especially if they are not accustomed to seeing African women as a critical part of theological processes and conversations.

Oduyoye's work then, through African women's theology, restores African women's agency on many fronts. In utilizing African feminist, liberationist, and systematic theological registers, Oduyoye's theological and ecumenical work frees African women up to be their truest theological selves. In this, she firmly places African women in the center of many theological conversations. Oduyoye has, in many ways, become "all things to all people";[3] her work traverses the thematic landscapes of African feminism, liberation, and systematics and is precisely what Christian theology needs. Those in dominant communities learn from Oduyoye's work how important women who identify as African and Christian are to the universal theological landscape.

African Feminism

What does it mean to live a life where one does not have to explain why one is important and necessary to the larger whole?

Oduyoye's work points to the absurdity of this questioning. No one should have to claim their importance as a human being. By virtue of being human, of being God's creation, every person has inherent purpose and divine intent. Oduyoye's work and struggle to articulate African women's worth illumines the androcentric and patriarchal problems of theological discourse; if unchecked, they threaten the image of the divine in everyone.

Oduyoye's theology is the result of a wrestling—against violent messages of colonial Christianity, Western culture, and even her own Akan culture.[4] This wrestling is important, for it has opened the door for African women to continue resisting the diminishing of their own stories. It has given them permission to challenge theological and cultural ideas deemed the status quo but harmful to their personhood. Many follow her example. The theology of countless African women is characterized by a righteous refutation; they combat the narratives others try to press into their identities by elevating their voices and claiming truth in a liberative way.

The feminist tinge of African women's theology honors the foundational belief in Christian theology by asserting the importance of God's full creation. "Feminism in theology springs from a conviction that a theology of relationships might contribute to bring us closer to human life as God desires it," Oduyoye proclaims.[5] African women's task is not one of securing the particular interests of a few but of celebrating the full humanity of all, and they start with themselves.

For over six decades Oduyoye has contributed to the conversation of Christian theology in African and global contexts. In placing African women's experiences at the center of her work, she has created a movement of African women's theological vocality critical to the continual growth of the Christian theological canon.[6] Oduyoye's ideas push the Christian church and African sensibility to recognize themselves.

The church must name the parts of itself that have failed its own. The same goes for African culture. Women are the church, too. Women are Africans. It is a travesty that African women have to assert the obvious. African women's theology, again, is reflective work. It holds a mirror up to the Christian church and to the African continent and reflects back both what they need to do and how they need to change in order to live into their true identities—identities enriched by flourishing together.

The task of African women's theology is a liberative task.

Liberation

According to Oduyoye's former thought partner and the Latinx father of liberation theology, Gustavo Gutiérrez, the task of liberation is to create a way for all human beings to live well with one another, for everyone to have agency.[7] African women's theology aims to free African women from misogyny and racism, to grant African women voice in spaces that have intentionally and unintentionally silenced them. Liberation announces that African women have the right to question cultural and ecclesial ideologies and paradigms that have tried to bridle them.

Oduyoye's work identifies Western Christianity's blind spots and African culture and theology's missed opportunities in order to make room for African women. African women's theology unashamedly puts its confluence of womanhood and African identity in full view through its own theological language and emphases. It claims that African women are able to illumine the contours of their oppressions, including but not limited to those they experience in economic, political, and religio-cultural affairs. This is the material out of which their liberative stance emerges.[8]

With emphases in Christian theology as traditionally considered (i.e., doctrine), ecumenical movement and reform, and a rootedness in Africa culture, Oduyoye's theological stance is one of synthesis and a creative vision that is forward-looking.[9] The breadth and depth of her theological work demonstrate that she is a pioneer in creating space for African women in the world. African women's liberation includes creating room where there is none.

African women's theology, as Oduyoye has modeled, emphasizes the power of speech. Women liberate themselves by telling the truth. They also articulate a different path forward. In telling their stories in light of

who they know themselves to be in God, African women are doing theology. They are uncovering reality and proclaiming what is not yet.

How African women do theology means something for theology's
efficacy. It exposes colonial religious ideas and social practices and gendered tradition and values and challenges them to become something
different. Oduyoye's voice leads the charge on this, especially in her
imaginative reframing of Christian doctrines. Her doctrinal imagination
places her in the conversation as a systematic theologian, one of the few
attentive to and vocal about how context is ushered in not only by culture, geography, or gender but also by theological voice and rationale.

Systematics

Oduyoye has dedicated her life to interrogating the complexity of theological concepts, language, and practice with both African and Western
cultural nuances in view. Her body of work suggests that Christian practice is unstable if missing the perspective of *all* the church's members.
Oduyoye shines a light on broken interpretations of African relationality
and Christian theology. One way she combats these deficits is by identifying the core doctrinal messages African women have received from
Christian theology; she then reimagines their true nature. Across her body
of work she has taken on four major doctrinal positions—the doctrine
of God, Christology, theological anthropology, and ecclesiology—shed-
ding light on how African women might approach and reframe systematic theology.

African women know God in historical and gendered registers. God
asserts that African women are God's good creation. God calls all human
beings to God's self through right interaction with each other and creation. African women's theology of God encourages the church to remember God's intention, that all members of creation are entangled with
one another in God, who is the center of life.[10]

God lived among humanity enfleshed. Women were the first to recognize this. African women's Christology reminds the church to resist
overlooking its women in favor of its men, for Jesus was a man who exercised a holistic vision of God's creation. African women are drawn to

Jesus because of his inclusive ministry; he sought to draw all of creation back to God's self. He knew imperial resistance, subverted gendered ideologies, and elevated those typically overlooked in their communities and societies. To African women, Jesus sounded more like an African woman than anyone else.

The question of right relationship is critical to African women's theology and Oduyoye's theological stance. Because humanity is God's creation, human beings' relationship to one another must be determined by their relationship with God. African women's theological anthropology affirms God's declaration that all creation is good. It allows African women the opportunity to echo their worth through their Creator's words and reject any ideology that says otherwise. It is this mentality that sustains the Christian church.

For African women, the Christian church is an instantiation of God's movement on earth. African women's ecclesiology, their understanding of the function and narrative of the Christian church, is inclusive. It also frees those who are trapped by the weight of a different message. The church's power is not in its ability to dominate, but rather its power is in its ability to reflect God's care for creation. The gift of the church is its multiplicity; it is diverse in nature, and God affirms it as such. African women's theology reflects these ideas and more.

Oduyoye's doctrinal insights illumine that the values with which the Christian church and African culture think themselves aligned are often different than they are purported to be and different from how they are practiced. In this vein, Oduyoye's voice and African women's theology as a whole divulge the truth about good intentions: they are meaningless and even malignant if oblivious to the world around them.

A Significant Contributor: Oduyoye's Legacy in Christian Theology

What makes Oduyoye's voice so critical to Christian discourse is the dynamism of her approach. She is truthful in every facet of her scholarship. She both centers and criticizes African culture. She challenges universal racial and gender biases in Christianity and appeals to its humane values. Her work holds both African culture and Christian ideology accountable to African women. She charges both to live amicably. She does not abandon her foundations but works to strengthen them.

Oduyoye fashions her own Christianity—a faith uniquely her own—and gives African women permission to do the same. She models for African women how to be complete beings in themselves. She encourages African women to critique the harmful parts of their own culture but to hold on to its places of possibility and empowerment.[11] In this she signals how African women are valuable contributors to their community's ideologies. She reminds them never to shy away from the complexity of their identities, for it is theirs.

African women deserve what the rest of the world has access to. These women have questions, desires, differences of opinion, and assertions all their own. African women are deserving of both liberation and the pursuit of a full life. Oduyoye encourages women to own their worth—cultural, theological, and otherwise. Any theological platform that rations God's love and power to a select few does not convey Christian theology, but rather a distorted articulation of it.

Oduyoye has spent her life illumining how theology should empower, free, and move its participants toward thriving. African women's theology unapologetically counts its voice as critical to Christian theology's efficacy. Their theological perspective tells theology what it must become in order to live its purpose.

Rooted in inclusivity and right relationship, Oduyoye's theological work is a necessity in a world of thought that desperately tries to tether theological correctness to whiteness and maleness. This improper theological foundation—her life's work shows—lacks God at the center.

African women's theology, and particularly Oduyoye's work for and in it, counters women's marginalization by asserting God's interaction with and in the world, Christ's saving work in being human, humanity's proper understanding of itself, and a fuller understanding of a loving, inclusive Christian church.

Oduyoye's experiences with family brought her to these conclusions—the righteous resistance of the women in her life and of her ancestors courses through the pages of her work. Teaching stints in local grade schools and internationally known universities grew her theological vision. Her work in churches and communities of faith all helped sharpen her theological acumen.

Mercy Amba Oduyoye is a product of her own genius, but also the genius of the communities around her; each life lesson informed a theological idea. Oduyoye's dedication to African women and her theological commitment to truth telling model a life well lived and a voice forever endowed with religious authority. There is no doubt: the world is much better because of Mercy Amba Ewudziwa Oduyoye.

NOTES

Introduction

1. Mercy Amba Oduyoye, "Christianity and African Culture," *International Review of Mission* 84, no. 332/333 (1995): 85. Oduyoye reminisces that Idowu "saw the need for the participation of women in the theological enterprise and in the ministry of the church, and took steps towards its realization."

2. Oduyoye notes that her "African" perspective is Akan (Ghanaian) and/or Yoruba (Nigerian). Oduyoye works with and learns from the perspectives of African women of various ethnicities and backgrounds all over the continent; her work, however, primarily references the experience of Akan and Yoruba culture.

3. Rachel NyaGondwe Fiedler, *A History of the Circle of Concerned African Women Theologians (1989–2007)* (Mzuzu, Malawi: Mzuni Press, 2017), 10.

4. Sources that Oduyoye has inspired that lend voice to African women's tangible lives include but are not limited to Isabel Apawo Phiri and Sarojini Nadar, eds., *African Women, Religion, and Health: Essay in Honor of Mercy Amba Ewudziwa Oduyoye* (Maryknoll, NY: Orbis Books, 2006); Mercy Oduyoye and Musimbi R. A. Kanyoro, eds., *The Will to Arise: Women, Tradition, and the Church in Africa* (Eugene, OR: Wipf and Stock, 1992).

5. Fiedler, *History of the Circle,* 10–11.

6. It is important to note, however, that several issues have not been addressed in African theology, including the invisibility of nonheteronormative African gender and sexual theological perspectives and, as within the larger discourse, issues such as anti-Semitism. See Amy-Jill Levine et al., "Roundtable Discussion: Anti-Judaism and Postcolonial Biblical Interpretation," *Journal of Feminist Studies in Religion* 20, no. 1 (Spring 2004): 106–11.

7. For a detailed and rich treatment of Oduyoye's doctrinal positions from her own voice, see Mercy Amba Oduyoye, *Introducing African Women's Theology* (Sheffield: Sheffield Academic, 2001).

Chapter One

1. Oduyoye was born near Kumasi, Ghana, a rural area approximately 250 kilometers northwest of the southeastern capital, Accra.

2. Mercy Amba Oduyoye, "Say Her Name! Africana Women as Interpreters, Healers, and Revolutionaries," keynote address, Spelman College, Atlanta, July 2016.

3. Mercy Amba Oduyoye, *Beads and Strands: Reflections of an African Woman on Christianity in Africa* (Maryknoll, NY: Orbis Books, 2004), xi; Christina Landman, "Mercy Amba Ewudziwa Oduyoye: Mother of Our Stories," *Studia Historiae Ecclesiasticae* 33, no. 2, http://www.christina-landman.co.za /mercy.htm. The accounts of Mercy Oduyoye's birth are multiple. Some, such as religious scholar Bartholomew Chidili, claim she was born in October 1934, whereas others, such as South African theological research director Christina Landman, offer October 1933. I went with Landman's account for two reasons: first, she states that when she spoke personally with Oduyoye, the latter clarified her birth date as October 1933, and second, in *Beads and Strands* (xi) Oduyoye speaks of being baptized as a baby in April 1934. This would corroborate the 1933 date as the most accurate.

4. Mercy Amba Oduyoye, "Be a Woman, and Africa Will Be Strong," in *Inheriting Our Mothers' Gardens: Feminist Theology in Third World Perspective*, ed. Letty M. Russell et al. (Louisville: Westminster, 1988), 38.

5. Elizabeth Amoah, preface to Phiri and Nadar, *African Women, Religion, and Health*, xviii.

6. Oduyoye, *Beads and Strands*, xii; Oduyoye, "Be a Woman," 37. Oduyoye and her family lived in Sunyani, Wenchi, Winneba, and Akroprong (near Kumasi).

7. Mercy Amba Oduyoye, "God Alone Gives and Distributes Gifts," in *Mystics, Visionaries, and Prophets: A Historical Anthology of Women's Spiritual Writings*, ed. Shawn Madigan (Minneapolis: Fortress, 1998), 454.

8. Oduyoye, "Be a Woman," 46.

9. Ibid., 45–46.

10. Fiedler, *History of the Circle*, 14–16.

11. Oduyoye, "Be a Woman," 37, 45–46, and 159 (endnotes for the chapter). Interestingly, Oduyoye described her mother's ecclesial involvement as an attempt to Westernize in order to become liberated from *African* sexism. This represents the dual struggle of many African women against both Western patriarchy and African patriarchy.

12. Mercy Amba Oduyoye, *Daughters of Anowa: African Women and Patriarchy* (Maryknoll, NY: Orbis Books, 1995), 104–5. Oduyoye's story of

educational success is an anomaly. Her level of success and access was not common for women. Education was not as available to Ghanaian women as it could have been, although, as Oduyoye notes, education exploded in Ghana in the late 1950s. Economic disparity caused division between rich, decision-making northern Ghana and the poorer, southern region. Women were included in education reform, but their involvement was considered "informal," and their progress, outside of literacy, was little. The future for women with education was not as promising as it had promised to be.

13. Oduyoye, "Be a Woman," 47.

14. Mercy Amba Oduyoye, "Interview with Mercy Amba Oduyoye: Mercy Amba Oduyoye in Her Own Words," interview by Oluwatomisin Oredein, *Journal of Feminist Studies in Religion* 32, no. 2 (Fall 2016): 155.

15. Fiedler, *History of the Circle*, 14.

16. Mercy Amba Oduyoye, "The African Family as Symbol of Ecumenism," *Ecumenical Review* 43, no. 3 (1991): 467. Oduyoye notes that the Asante (a variant form of Ashanti), Akuapem, Akyem, Brong, Fante, and Kwahu are all "very large groups belonging to the Akan family."

17. Yolanda Smith, "Mercy Amba Oduyoye," Biola University, http://www.talbot.edu/ce20/educators/protestant/mercy_oduyoye/.

18. Oduyoye, "God Alone Gives and Distributes Gifts," 454.

19. Amoah, preface, xx.

20. Oduyoye, *Beads and Strands*, xii; Oduyoye, "God Alone Gives and Distributes Gifts," 454; Smith, "Mercy Amba Oduyoye."

21. Amoah, preface, xx; Smith, "Mercy Amba Oduyoye."

22. Smith, "Mercy Amba Oduyoye."

23. Ibid.

24. Keri Day, "Daughters, Arise," *Journal of Africana Religions* 2, no. 3 (2013): 386.

25. Amoah, preface, xxi; Smith, "Mercy Amba Oduyoye." Among her professors were Alec Vidler and Maurice Wiles.

26. Oduyoye, *Beads and Strands*, xii.

27. Ibid.

28. Oduyoye, *Beads and Strands*, xii; Meredith Coleman-Tobias, "Dr. Mercy Amba Oduyoye: A Brief Bio," speech introducing Mercy Amba Oduyoye before she spoke at Say Her Name! Africana Women as Interpreters, Healers, and Revolutionaries, Daughters of African Atlantic Fund, Atlanta, GA, July 12, 2016; Oduyoye, "Say Her Name!"

29. Mercy Amba Oduyoye, "Culture and Religion as Factors in Promoting Justice for Women," in *Women in Religion and Culture: Essays in Honour of Constance Buchanan*, ed. Mercy Amba Oduyoye and Constance H. Buchanan

(Ibadan, Nigeria: Sefer Books, 2007), 1. Oduyoye's time at Harvard may have been as early in 1983. In her chapter "Culture and Religion as Factors in Promoting Justice for Women," Oduyoye names the collaborative publication *Women in Religion and Culture* as having come from "the course . . . offered in Harvard Divinity School's Women in Religion Programme in 1983."

30. See "Dr. Mercy Amba Oduyoye: A Brief Bio"; Oduyoye, "Say Her Name!"; Oduyoye, "God Alone Gives and Distributes Gifts," 455. All of these honors are either DDs or DTh degrees. One Ghanaian theological institution has awarded her both the DD and the DTh.

31. Oduyoye, "God Alone Gives and Distributes Gifts," 454.

32. Ibid., 455.

33. Oduyoye, *Beads and Strands*, xii.

34. Oduyoye, *Daughters of Anowa*, 2.

35. Smith, "Mercy Amba Oduyoye"; Emmanuel Akyeampong and Ama de-Graft Aikins, "Ghana at Fifty: Reflections on Independence and After," *Transition* 98 (2008): 24, 26; Ken Kwaku, "Tradition, Colonialism and Politics in Rural Ghana: Local Politics in Have, Volta Region," *Canadian Journal of African Studies/Revue Canadienne des Études Africaines* 10, no. 1 (1976): 84. See also David E. Apter, "Ghana's Independence: Triumph and Paradox," *Transition* 98 (2008): 6–22. Dr. Kwame Nkrumah was a political figure and Ghana's first president (prime minister, 1952–60; president, 1960–66), known best as one of the "Big Six" of the United Gold Coast Convention, the first political party of the liberation-seeking Gold Coast (and Ghana as a whole). He was known for his dedication to Pan-Africanism—so much so that "people of African descent around the world were ecstatic about this beacon of 'black pride'" (Akyeampong and de-Graft Aikins, "Ghana at Fifty," 26). He formed the first African government in Ghana when the Convention People's Party (CPP), which he helped form, won the February 1951 election. His impact was felt years prior to the official liberation and independence of Ghana; he created a foundation from which Ghana's voice and liberation would emerge. He attended to the interests of the Ghanaian people and used his voice to affirm the voices of the residents rather than those of the ruling colonial powers in the public discourse concerning the interests and welfare of the people. Nkrumah's success shows that political unrest and the desire for autonomy can lead to political reform. In 1960 Ghana officially became a one-party state under Nkrumah. His desire to free Ghana of colonial rule came to pass. There is debate whether the party had socialist or communist leanings; it claimed itself as socialist, promoting what was called "Nkrumahism, a form of socialism with African characteristics paralleling Mao's socialism with Chinese characteristics" (Apter, "Ghana's Independence," 17). Nkrumah's desire for the liberation of the African continent as a whole

spoke to his thirst for power. All countries would follow Ghana's model of liberation, because Ghana was the first to secure its emancipation in this way. Thus, Nkrumah's desire to expand his influence and rule became his downfall when multiple other parties came into power in Ghana by coup and election (even though the CPP remained and tried to make a resurgence) (18).

36. Oredein, "Interview with Mercy Amba Oduyoye," 157.

37. Oduyoye, "God Alone Gives and Distributes Gifts," 455.

38. Smith, "Mercy Amba Oduyoye"; Oduyoye, *Beads and Strands*, xiii. Oduyoye's home life and educational path set the stage for her ecumenical interests and pursuits of equality and justice for women.

39. David E. Apter, *Ghana in Transition* (Princeton: Princeton University Press, 1972), 12.

40. Apter, *Ghana in Transition*, 12. See also Jon Kraus, "On the Politics of Nationalism and Social Change in Ghana," *Journal of Modern African Studies* 7, no. 1 (1969): 108. Kraus, a political scientist, does not see the correlation quite this way: "While there is a respectable range of sociological/anthropological studies available on traditional systems in Ghana, it has often been difficult to derive accurately the relationship political systems [have] to modern political change." He is unconvinced that Ghanaian attitudes toward particular modes of authority changed significantly enough to motivate Ghanaians to accede to colonial systems of rule. For Kraus something else was at play in the transition of governmental approaches in Ghana.

41. Abena P. A. Busia, "Achimota: From the Story My Mother Taught Me," in *The Ghana Reader: History, Culture and Politics*, ed. Kwasi Konadu and Clifford C. Campbell (Durham, NC: Duke University Press, 2016), 283. Abena P. A. Busia informs us that in the language of the Gã peoples, who had a spiritual affiliation with the land on which the school was first built in the early twentieth-century, "Achimota" means, loosely, "We do not mention people." The British-named school invokes the idea that those who lived there before are forgotten and that people today are walking in this legacy of nonmemory. Busia recounts in a poem, "We too have been taught forgetting. / We are schooled in another language now / and names lose their meanings, except / as labels" ("Achimota," 283–84).

42. Apter, *Ghana in Transition*, 12.

43. David Kimble, *A Political History of Ghana: The Rise of Gold Coast Nationalism, 1850–1928* (Oxford: Clarendon, 1963), 128.

44. Kimble, *Political History of Ghana*, 128.

45. Kwame Nkrumah, "Independence Speech," in Konadu and Campbell, *Ghana Reader*, 301.

46. Ibid., 302.

47. Oduyoye, *Beads and Strands*, 9.

48. Nkrumah, "Independence Speech," 302.

49. Janet Berry Hess, "Imagining Architecture: The Structure of Nationalism in Accra, Ghana," *Africa Today* 47, no. 2 (2000): 35.

50. John S. Pobee, *Religion and Politics in Ghana* (Accra, Ghana: Asempa Publishers, 1991), 8, 117–18; Carola Lentz, "Ghanaian 'Monument Wars': The Contested History of the Nkrumah Statues," *Cahiers d'Études Africaines* 52, no. 3 (2017): 551. According to Lentz, a German social anthropologist, the original statue "had been created by the Italian sculptor Nicola Cataudella and inaugurated in front of the Old Parliament House in Accra at the eve of the first independence anniversary in 1958." The inscription on the statue alludes to, and alters, Matthew 6:33 in the King James Version of the Bible: "But seek ye first the kingdom of God, and his righteousness; and all these things shall be added unto you." It expressed "that as long as the affairs of the Gold Coast were directed by expatriates, it would be difficult to ensure that everything was done in the best interests of the Africans," Pobee asserts. He further explains that "the inscription was asserting that political power was the prerequisite of progress for the Africans." This is so because Nkrumah identified as a "nondenominational Christian and Marxian socialist" who found "no contradiction" between his faith and his position on social issues, often joining them together in his political messaging.

51. Oduyoye, *Beads and Strands*, 9.

52. Ousman Kobo, "'We Are Citizens Too': The Politics of Citizenship in Independent Ghana," *Journal of Modern African Studies* 48, no. 1 (2010): 72.

53. Pobee, *Religion and Politics in Ghana*, 8.

54. Kwasi Konadu and Clifford C. Campbell, "Independence, Coups, and the Republic, 1957–Present," in Konadu and Campbell, *Ghana Reader*, 299. Konadu and Campbell also note that indigenous leaders and the educated elite, who often felt left out of Nkrumah's efforts, "banded together to form . . . the Danquah-Busia tradition, a noteworthy counterbalance to Nkrumah's populist and inclusive politics" (ibid.).

55. Kathleen M. Fallon, "Transforming Women's Citizenship Rights within an Emerging Democratic State: The Case of Ghana," *Gender and Society* 17, no. 4 (2003): 529–30.

56. Takyiwaa Manuh, "Women and Their Organizations during the Convention People's Party Period," in Konadu and Campbell, *Ghana Reader*, 285.

57. Ibid., 286.

58. Ibid., 286–87.

59. Ibid., 288.

60. Ibid., 289.

61. Pobee, *Religion and Politics in Ghana*, 9. Accusations of "corruption in and of the government" would lead to a coup d'état.

62. Ibid.; Konadu and Campbell, "Independence, Coups, and the Republic," in Konadu and Campbell, *Ghana Reader*, 300. Konadu and Campbell fill in the timeline of Ghana's rule from 1966 to the present: Military coups by the National Liberation Council (military and police forces) overthrew Nkrumah's government and ruled until 1969, when the civilian government would be restored. In 1972, the National Redemption Council (made of police and military as well) took control. They ruled from 1975 to 1979 under the new name "the Supreme Military Council." The Armed Forces Revolutionary Council would overthrow them in 1979 and return the government to civilians. The 1981 military coup by the Provisional National Defense Council would give them control until 1992. From 1992 to the present "the country has enjoyed a stable period of civilian democratic rule."

63. I make this assessment precisely because Nkrumah's actions seemed revolutionary. Women in politics and in government seemed an anomaly. His radical actions of inclusion denoted social configurations that did not operate with the measures of equality that many came to associate with his regime. Yet Nkrumah's language of Africa's triumph still holds traces of patriarchy's hold in Ghanaian culture. The self-governing man's ability to prove himself to the world (or a corresponding ability of the men of Ghanaian society, in general) seemed to evidence a logic that prioritized Ghanaian men (despite the fanatical political support of many Ghanaian women, as Manuh reminds us).

Chapter Two

1. Mercy Amba Oduyoye [Amba Ewudziwa], "A Coming Home to Myself: The Childless Woman in the West African Space," in *Liberating Eschatology: Essays in Honor of Letty M. Russell*, ed. Margaret A. Farley and Serene Jones (Louisville: Westminster John Knox, 1999), 105–20: 113.

2. Musa Wenkosi Dube, "Introduction: 'Little Girl, Get Up!,'" in *Talitha Cum! Theologies of African Women*, ed. Nyambura J. Njoroge and Musa Wenkosi Dube (Pietermaritzburg, South Africa: Cluster Publications, 2001), 5.

3. Christine Okali, *Cocoa and Kinship in Ghana: The Matrilineal Akan of Ghana* (London: Kegan Paul International, 1983), 12.

4. Laura Fortunato, "The Evolution of Matrilineal Kinship Organization," *Proceedings: Biological Sciences* 279, no. 1749 (2012): 4939.

5. Okali, *Cocoa and Kinship in Ghana*, 13.

6. Oduyoye, *Beads and Strands*, 58.

7. Okali, *Cocoa and Kinship in Ghana*, 13.

8. Oduyoye, "Coming Home to Myself," 110. Oduyoye's maternal grand-uncle reminded her that "an Asante woman must get married and be the vehicle for the reincarnation of her ancestors."

9. Fortunato, "Evolution of Matrilineal Kinship Organization," 4939.

10. Ifi Amadiume, "Let My Work Not Be in Vain: Doing Matriarchy, Thinking 'Matriarchitarian' with Africa in the Twenty-First Century," in *Africa and the Challenges of the Twenty-First Century: Keynote Addresses Delivered at the 13th General Assembly of CODESRIA*, ed. Ebrima Sall (Dakar, Senegal: Council for the Development of Social Science Research in Africa, 2015), 59.

11. Tabitha Otieno and Alberta Yeboah, "Gender and Cultural Practices: The Akan of Ghana and the Gushi of Kenya," *Journal of Intercultural Disciplines* 5 (2004): 109. Otieno and Yeboah make a case for a different perspective as they call the Akan "a matriarchal group." This implies that women in Akan culture inherently have an ability and power that exceeds that which many currently exercise.

12. The importance of the queen mother will be addressed later in this chapter.

13. Fortunato, "Evolution of Matrilineal Kinship Organization," 4939.

14. Baffour K. Takyi and Stephen Obeng Gyimah, "Matrilineal Ties and Marital Dissolution in Ghana," *Journal of Family Issues* 28, no. 5 (2007): 686–87.

15. Oduyoye, *Daughters of Anowa*, 7.

16. Otieno and Yeboah, "Gender and Cultural Practices," 113.

17. Mercy Amba Oduyoye, "Caught in a Whirlwind," *The Other Side* 36, no. 5 (2000): 51.

18. Oduyoye, *Daughters of Anowa*, 6. See also Oduyoye, *Beads and Strands*, 97.

19. Oduyoye, "Coming Home to Myself," 110.

20. Amoah, preface, xx.

21. Oduyoye, "Culture and Religion as Factors," 4. Ironically, Oduyoye had glimpses of the damage that can be caused by an unhealthy marriage or the obsession with marriage in Ghanaian culture. "In parts of Ghana the idolization of marriage grips women to the extent that they thank their husbands for beating them," she describes. Later, she argues, "In patriarchal families in Africa a wife is absorbed into her husband's family as a means of production and reproduction." Oduyoye clearly sees the problem of idolizing marriage in both matrilineal and patriarchal cultures.

22. Oduyoye, "Caught in a Whirlwind," 51.

23. Oduyoye, *Daughters of Anowa*, 5–6, 90; Oduyoye, *Beads and Strands*, 6. In *Daughters of Anowa*, Oduyoye explains the difference between the Akan (or matrilineal) household and the Yoruba (or patrilineal) household. For Akan women, "a

wife's companions and colleagues are the other wives. In patrilineal groups, these domestic establishments can become small-scale industries and trading coopera-tives." In other words, the juxtaposition of communal living and mechanized liv-ing is brought to the fore and illumines the difference between how Akan culture approaches life and productivity and how Yoruba culture approaches them.

24. George Kwame Kumi, "Good Father-Mother God: The Theology of God from the Perspective of the Akan Matrilineal Society in Ghana" (PhD diss., Fordham University, 1996), 8.

25. Oduyoye, *Daughters of Anowa*, 79.

26. Ibid., 8.

27. Smith, "Mercy Amba Oduyoye."

28. Oduyoye, *Beads and Strands*, xi.

29. Amoah, preface, xviii–xix; Oduyoye, "Coming Home to Myself," 106. Asamankese is a town in the eastern part of Southern Ghana.

30. Mercy Amba Oduyoye, *African Women's Theologies, Spirituality, and Healing: Theological Perspectives from the Circle of Concerned African Women Theologians* (New York: Paulist Press, 2019), 11.

31. Oduyoye, *Beads and Strands*, xi. Oduyoye describes her maternal grand-parents as Presbyterian. See below in the text, under "What Mother(s) Taught."

32. Ibid.

33. Ibid.

34. Ibid.

35. Oduyoye, "Be a Woman," 50. Oduyoye lets on that performing certain church tasks, such as "announcing the word of God," is a conflicting reality for her: "The only limit I recognize in myself is how well I can perform. But it is a limit that the patriarchally organized church discounts, having set up limits based on gender; it also decrees that one has to be commissioned, appointed by the community, and designated to perform specific church tasks."

36. I offer this analytical observation to complexify the genealogy of Odu-yoye's Christian tongue in light of her awareness of her "performance." This training and formation would soon find its own intonation and arc of pronun-ciation and announce spiritual objectives most in line with honoring African women of the Christian faith instead of asserting that they must "sound like their male counterparts."

37. Oduyoye, "Be a Woman," 37.

38. Ibid., 46.

39. Oduyoye, *Daughters of Anowa*, 119. I do not have space to explore this in depth here, but the irony of blood as both sacred and taboo is something for further consideration, especially as it parallels Akan women's movement about and within their culture and society.

40. Amoah, preface, xviii–xix.

41. Ibid., xix.

42. Ibid.

43. Ibid.

44. Fiedler, *History of the Circle*, 12. Fiedler argues that the educational background of Oduyoye's mother, Mercy Dakwaa Yamoah, in Methodist institutions gave her mother "a long Methodist heritage" as well.

45. Amoah, preface, xix.

46. Oduyoye, "Christianity and African Culture," 79.

47. Oduyoye, "Be a Woman," 36.

48. Fiedler, *History of the Circle*, 18–19. Interestingly, although Oduyoye did not know it, her mother wanted to study theology. Oduyoye comes from a line of inquisitive and critically thinking women.

49. Oduyoye, "Be a Woman," 46.

50. Ibid., 47–48.

51. Ibid., 50.

52. Ibid., 50.

53. Fiedler, *History of the Circle*, 15.

54. Oduyoye, *Daughters of Anowa*, 85. Quoting Ama Ata Aidoo, Oduyoye attends to the complexity of African women's agency amid restrictive cultural practice. For many Western women looking from the outside in, African women's questions of agency or lack thereof are more a working-out of Western identity issues. African women hold agency in various forms even amid the strictures of marital and maternal expectations. Western perception of the African woman's (African) life does not examine or address the nuances of her agency, but merely ensures her position as beneath the Western woman in the hierarchical scheme of things.

55. Oduyoye, "Be a Woman," 36.

56. Oduyoye, *Beads and Strands*, xi.

57. Oduyoye, "Coming Home to Myself," 108.

58. Ibid., 106. Oduyoye notes that social mothering is a reality for many African women in general.

59. Ibid., 109. Oduyoye recognizes the problem of biological motherhood for many women, married and unmarried, and urges conversations around the consequences that numerous African women face in their desire for biological motherhood, including "the breakup of marriages, schizophrenia, suicidal quests for pregnancy, and sterile sublimation."

60. Oduyoye, *Daughters of Anowa*, 72. The queen mother is a historical symbol of Akan women's impactful governmental prowess in their society. Oduyoye aims to, in a sense, revive the political importance of the queen mother figure

as she concludes that often, for an African woman, "political decisions are made behind her back, because she is busy keeping the lineage alive, both biologically and domestically."

61. Otieno and Yeboah, "Gender and Cultural Practices," 111–13. This expectation of women is one that systematizes polygyny, so that a man can have as many wives as he wants, but shuns polyandry, the ability for a woman to have many husbands. Polygyny appears to be more socially acceptable because of the cultural emphasis on women's responsibility to bear children *for* a man. Furthering this notion of the importance of marriage is the practice of betrothal, where a girl is paired off to a man, who is sometimes of her same age group but sometimes not. The impetus driving this practice is to "assure the betrothed girl child of a perfect future." The hope is that "she will have many children and thereby gain the respect of members of the ethnic group because among the Akan, the more children a woman has, the more respect and prestige she commands." It is her means of contributing to the continuation of the Akan as a people. This unfairly positions a girl as indebted to her community for her life; the message comes across that she "pays" for her life by continuing the cycle of life. She is allowed to live because she can continue the population of the people.

62. Oduyoye, "Coming Home to Myself," 107.

63. Oduyoye, *Daughters of Anowa*, 6. See also Oduyoye, "Caught in a Whirlwind," 51; Oduyoye, "Coming Home to Myself," 111. It is important to note that she did practice the Akan custom of being at the ready to mother other children as circumstances required, but biological mothering still hovered over her marriage and life.

64. Oduyoye, "Coming Home to Myself," 110–11.

65. Ibid., 111. Oduyoye honestly speaks to the religio-cultural expectations of women and how those expectations impact their choices. Women in scripture often did "their duty as dictated by their culture."

66. Ibid., 116–18.

67. Ibid., 119.

68. Oduyoye, *Daughters of Anowa*, 70.

69. Oduyoye, *Daughters of Anowa*, 100–108. Akan women are further saddled with economic responsibilities to provide and care for their families and communities.

70. Oduyoye, "Caught in a Whirlwind," 51.

71. Oduyoye, "Coming Home to Myself," 119.

72. Oduyoye, "Be a Woman," 38.

73. Ibid., 36–41. Oduyoye's mother was always hesitant to fully trust this Christianity that announced itself and European-ness as the same entity.

74. Beverly J. Stoeltje, "Asante Queen Mothers: A Study in Female Authority," *Annals of the New York Academy of Sciences* 810, no. 1 (1997): 43.

75. Ibid.

76. Ibid.

77. Agnes Akosua Aidoo, "Asante Queen Mothers in Government and Politics in the Nineteenth Century," *Journal of the Historical Society of Nigeria* 9, no. 1 (1977): 1.

78. Oduyoye, *Daughters of Anowa*, 7.

79. Aidoo, "Asante Queen Mothers in Government and Politics," 2.

80. Ibid., 2.

81. Stoeltje, "Asante Queen Mothers: A Study," 43.

82. Ibid., 44.

83. Beverly J. Stoeltje, "Asante Queen Mothers: Precolonial Authority in a Postcolonial Society," *Research Review*, n.s., 19, no. 2 (2003): 3.

84. Isaac Owusu-Mensah, "Promoting Local Governance in Ghana: The Role of Akan Queen Mothers," *Journal of Pan African Studies* 8, no. 9 (2015): 98–114.

85. Aidoo argues that the queen mother has significant political power in her own right, and Aidoo rejects language of complementarity to a male ruler, but even she, whether intentional or not, describes the queen mother as one who would fit well in a particular kind of complementary relational framing where Akan women are seen as prerequisite alongside their men (see Aidoo, "Asante Queen Mothers in Government and Politics," 2). Note that in recognizing that the complementarity model is used, I am not condoning such a model but observing how previous relational formats join with political opportunities forming new modes of political reckoning under old social banners.

86. Stoeltje, "Asante Queen Mothers: A Study," 52.

87. Ibid., 58.

88. I. Owusu-Mensah, W. Asante, and W. K. Osew, "Queen Mothers: The Unseen Hands in Chieftaincy Conflicts among the Akan in Ghana; Myth or Reality?" *Journal of Pan African Studies* 8, no. 6 (2015): 11.

89. Stoeltje, "Asante Queen Mothers: A Study," 43.

90. Ibid.

91. Ibid.

92. Stoeltje notes the various ways non-Western systems of kinship, relationality, and political rule function. Anthropologically, by understanding the systems through which persons relate to and understand each other, we can explain the definitional differences in what might constitute right or helpful practice or rule. Non-Western systems of relationship primarily emphasize practicing

sociality within the bounds of one's distinct gender identity (termed "gender parallelism") (see Stoeltje, "Asante Queen Mothers: A Study," 45).

93. Aidoo, "Asante Queen Mothers in Government and Politics," 4.

94. Stoeltje's observations of women breaking into patriarchal practices with both the Igbo and Yoruba women in Nigeria disarm the argument that in precolonial African cultures men and women were equal. Patriarchal ideations existed long before colonial influence. Stoetlje writes, "Simi Afonja, for example, recognizes that even in preclass situations and precolonial time female autonomy and gender inequality could be found together among the Yoruba (1990)." This makes Oduyoye most valuable. The objective of women's vocality is clear: the point is not to argue for a return to a time that did not exist, but to create something new in the current moment and time (see Stoeltje, "Asante Queen Mothers: A Study").

95. Aidoo, "Asante Queen Mothers in Government and Politics," 2.

96. Oduyoye, *African Women's Theologies*, 7.

Chapter Three

1. Mercy Amba Oduyoye, interview by author, July 13, 2016.

2. Oduyoye, *Beads and Strands*, xii.

3. Smith, "Mercy Amba Oduyoye." Oduyoye lived in Cambridge from 1963 to 1965. The Student Christian Movement describes itself as "a movement of students, past and present, responding to the call of Jesus to follow him and show the love of God on campus, in our communities and in the world. We come together as an ecumenical and inclusive community, fostering unity in diversity and exploring faith through worship, discussion and action." See "Who We Are," Student Christian Movement, https://www.movement.org.uk /about-us/who-we-are. The Christian Union at Cambridge University is currently known as the Cambridge Inter-Collegiate Christian Union. Formerly part of the Student Christian Movement, the CICCU describes itself as "a group made up of students from across the Cambridge colleges who believe the good news found in the Bible about Jesus' life, death and resurrection, and the promise of new life he offers us, is too good not to share." Although the group says it was founded in 1877, the description of its prayer ministry that appears on its website—a ministry Oduyoye speaks of having cofounded—does not mention her or attribute her name to it. See "Who Are We?," Cambridge Inter-Collegiate Christian Union, https://ciccu.org.uk/whoarewe/.

4. Oduyoye, *Beads and Strands*, xii.

5. Ibid.

6. Ibid., 78.

7. Ibid.

8. Katie Cannon, "Going Back before the Beginning," *Focus, the Magazine of Union Presbyterian Seminary*, Spring 2016, 9. Oduyoye would become heavily involved in the World Council of Churches from 1987 to 1994.

9. Oduyoye, *Beads and Strands*, xiii. The World Council of Christian Education merged with the World Sunday Schools Association.

10. Musimbi R. A. Kanyoro, "Beads and Strands: Threading More Beads in the Story of the Circle," in Phiri and Nadar, *African Women, Religion, and Health*, 22; Smith, "Mercy Amba Oduyoye."

11. Tore Samuelsson, "'Behold, I Make All Things New': WCC's Fourth Assembly in Uppsala, 4–20 July, 1968," World Council of Churches, July 4, 2018, https://www.oikoumene.org/en/press-centre/news/behold-i-make-all-things-new-wccs-fourth-assembly-in-uppsala-4-20-july-1968. Martin Luther King Jr. was supposed to speak at this conference but was assassinated three months before. Instead, writer James Baldwin spoke to the gathering.

12. Smith, "Mercy Amba Oduyoye"; Mercy Amba Oduyoye, "Spirituality of Resistance and Reconstruction," in *Women Resisting Violence: Spirituality for Life*, ed. Mary John Mananzan et al. (Maryknoll, NY: Orbis Books, 1996), 161.

13. Landman, "Mercy Amba Ewudziwa Oduyoye"; Coleman-Tobias, "Dr. Mercy Amba Oduyoye: A Brief Bio."

14. Oduyoye, "God Alone Gives," 455.

15. Smith, "Mercy Amba Oduyoye."

16. Mercy Amba Oduyoye, "Women's Presence in the Life and Teaching of Jesus with Particular Emphasis on His Passion," *Ecumenical Review* 60, no. 1–2 (1970): 82; Smith, "Mercy Amba Oduyoye." A note of discrepancy: Yolanda Smith states that Oduyoye joined the World Council of Churches staff in a different capacity in 1987, as deputy general secretary. Smith documents how the gender dynamics at work in Oduyoye's applying for this position in Geneva, Switzerland, were in full display. Oduyoye was discouraged from applying for the position because it would jeopardize her role as wife to her husband. To alleviate the pressure, she obtained permission from her husband, who was reluctant to allow her to ask him for his permission, because he found the WCC's attempt to dissuade his wife from applying to be ridiculously sexist. She recounted that her husband physically delivered to the Methodist Church office in Lagos a sarcastic note stating that he gave his permission.

17. Oduyoye, "Women's Presence," 82.

18. Smith, "Mercy Amba Oduyoye." I follow Yolanda Smith's organization and lead on naming these ecumenical areas.

19. Landman, "Mercy Amba Ewudziwa Oduyoye." Landman asserts that in 1986 Oduyoye experienced a shift in her feminist convictions. Landman suggests that Oduyoye was not highly attuned to the impact of feminism in her work, basing her assertions on Oduyoye's publication of *Hearing and Knowing: Theological Reflections on Christianity in Africa* (Eugene, OR: Wipf and Stock, 1986), a text largely concerned with church history. Only upon teaching stints in the United States at Harvard Divinity School and Union Theological Seminary were her eyes awakened and her feminist critical voice sharpened. By the end of the year, the tone of her work would have a stronger feminist timbre. Landman suggests that Oduyoye gained a keener feminist position upon exposure to the Western education system and Western conceptions of feminist critical analysis. While there might be truth in this on some levels, we would be remiss if we forgot the feminist underpinnings Oduyoye gained from her culture—and, more specifically, from her mother, grandmother, and other women in her life who served as a foundation for the evolution of her voice. For more on Oduyoye's Akan feminist formation, see chapter 2 of this work. Landman states that *Hearing and Knowing* only had minimal feminist engagement; thus Oduyoye's work after its publication signals her Western experience as the stimulus of her "transformation." But in order to accurately understand the development of her leanings, it would be best to learn from Oduyoye's own telling of her emergence. *Hearing and Knowing* had its own pedagogical intention. She explains, "I wrote *Hearing and Knowing* for students so that they would be able to link theology and church history" (Oduyoye, "Interview with Mercy Amba Oduyoye," 162). Overall, Oduyoye describes her work as not formally labeled "feminism" but rather as "African women's theology," since the term "feminism" was not utilized by African women in the 1960s and 1970s when she was asserting herself on the theological scene. Yet to say that she and other women did not have the terminology made so popular in and by the West is not to suggest that she did not hold feminist leanings and values early on in her career.

20. Oduyoye, *Beads and Strands*, xiii.

21. See Mercy Amba Oduyoye, "A Decade and a Half of Ecumenism in Africa: Problems, Programmes, Hopes," in *Voices of Unity: Essays in Honour of Willem Adolf Visser 't Hooft on the Occasion of His 80th Birthday*, ed. Ans J. van Bent (Geneva: World Council of Churches, 1981), 77; Oduyoye, *Beads and Strands*, 49. Oduyoye briefly explains portions of Akan belief: "The Akan abhor murder, suicide, stealing, insincerity and hypocrisy. They frown upon pride and ostentatiousness. Ingratitude, selfishness, laziness, filthy habits, lasciviousness and sorcery are all things that break or undermine community and therefore are to be avoided."

22. Oduyoye, *Beads and Strands*, xiii.

23. Oduyoye, *Daughters of Anowa*, 2.

24. Ibid., 3.

25. Ibid., 2.

26. Ibid., 3.

27. Mercy Amba Oduyoye, in conversation with the author, July 12, 2016. One figure Oduyoye personally names as exemplifying this white colonial feminism is Carrie Pemberton. Oduyoye has described Pemberton's approach to engaging the Circle of Concerned African Women Theologians as colonial. According to Oduyoye, in the 1990s Pemberton attended a Circle meeting and proceeded to request the attendees to fill out surveys so she could document and continue her study of the Circle. She injected her social and religious study into the aura of the meeting with her ethnographic ambitions and attitudes toward the spirit of the event. The Circle was not for Pemberton, though she was welcomed in. Unfortunately, she took advantage of the women's hospitality and treated them like objects of study. Oduyoye found Pemberton's interruption to complete her study rife with power dynamics and colonial traces. She warns against the information presented on her in Pemberton's text *Circle Thinking: African Women Theologians in Dialogue with the West* (Leiden: Brill, 2003). She insists it is inaccurate and based, overall, on skewed analysis and reflection.

28. "As Decade of the Churches in Solidarity with Women 'Ends,' Participants Point the Way Forward for Continuing to Work: Letter to WCC's 8th Assembly Addresses Priorities, Divisive Issues of Human Sexuality," NCC News Archives, 1998, http://www.ncccusa.org/news/news107.html. On this online platform, Mercy Amba Oduyoye is not explicitly mentioned as a founding member of this decade-long initiative.

29. On the basis of the study, the WCC issued a report in its journal: see "The Community of Women and Men," *Ecumenical Review* 33, no. 4 (October 1981): 346–53, cited in Smith, "Mercy Amba Oduyoye."

30. Oduyoye, *Beads and Strands*, xiii; Oduyoye, *Who Will Roll the Stone Away? The Ecumenical Decade of the Churches in Solidarity with Women* (Geneva: WCC Publications, 1990).

31. Oduyoye, "God Alone Gives and Distributes Gifts," 456.

32. Rosemary Radford Ruether, "Liberation Theology and African Women's Theologies," in *Black Faith and Public Talk: Critical Essays on James H. Cone's "Black Theology and Black Power,"* ed. Dwight Hopkins (Maryknoll, NY: Orbis Books, 1999), 168.

33. Ibid.

34. Oduyoye, "God Alone Gives and Distributes Gifts," 455.

35. Oduyoye, *Beads and Strands*, 38.

36. Oduyoye, "God Alone Gives and Distributes Gifts," 456.

37. Virginia Fabella and Mercy Amba Oduyoye, introduction to *With Passion and Compassion: Third World Women Doing Theology*, ed. Virginia Fabella and Mercy Amba Oduyoye (Maryknoll, NY: Orbis Books, 1988), ix–x.

38. Ibid.

39. Ibid.; Yolanda Smith, "Mercy Amba Oduyoye"; Ruether, "Liberation Theology and African Women's Theologies," 168. Such an effort would lead to the first Intercontinental Women's Conference in Oaxtepec, Mexico, December 1–6, 1986.

40. Ruether, "Liberation Theology and African Women's Theologies," 168.

41. Oduyoye, "Interview with Mercy Amba Oduyoye," 159.

42. Mercy Amba Oduyoye, interview by author, July 13, 2016.

43. Mercy Amba Oduyoye, "The Story of a Circle," *Ecumenical Review* 53, no. 1 (2001): 99.

44. Ibid., 100; Kanyoro, "Beads and Strands," 20. Kanyoro notes the historic nature of Oduyoye's presence: she "was almost the only woman from Africa who wrote theology for publication" for years (ibid.).

45. Oduyoye, *African Women's Theologies*, 7.

46. Ibid.

47. Oduyoye, "Culture and Religion as Factors," 1. Oduyoye cites her time at Harvard Divinity School in 1983 as instrumental to the Circle's conception as well.

48. Julius Gathogo, "Mercy Oduyoye as the Mother of African Women's Theology," *Theologia Viatorum: Journal of Theology and Religion in Africa* 34, no. 1 (2010): 3; Kanyoro, "Beads and Strands," 19–20, 21, 22. Kanyoro notes that the Circle started in 1988 but that Oduyoye was already gathering women as early as 1978. She also names the first international planning committee and provides short biographies for the following members of the committee: Dr. Mercy Oduyoye (Ghana); Dr. Betty Ekeya (Kenya); Dr. Sr. Rosemary Edet (Nigeria); Dr. Sr. Bernadette Mbuy Beya (Zaire); Dr. Elizabeth Amoah (Ghana); Dr. Brigalia Bam (South Africa); Ms. Rose Zoe Obianga (Cameroon); and Dr. Musimbi Kanyoro (Kenya).

49. Ruether, "Liberation Theology and African Women's Theologies," 169.

50. Teresia M. Hinga, "African Feminist Theologies, the Global Village, and the Imperative of Solidarity across Borders: The Case of the Circle of Concerned African Women Theologians," *Journal of Feminist Studies in Religion* 18, no. 1 (Spring 2002): 80.

51. Oduyoye, "Story of a Circle," 99.

52. Kanyoro, "Beads and Strands," 21.

53. Ibid., 23, 31–33, 34–36. It is also important to note that a Pan-African committee tried to establish structures of operation, including "electing an

International Coordinating Committee[,] . . . a coordinator and two secretaries." They wanted to move away from the grassroots origin of the Circle, largely bolstered by the life's work of Mercy Oduyoye (and her placement in Geneva, Switzerland). This would succeed only in part, as the elected coordinator, Dr. Musimbi Kanyoro, realized quickly how much the Circle needed Oduyoye's presence and wisdom to continue. Oduyoye was brought back on to the coordinating team to head research.

54. Dube, "Introduction: 'Little Girl, Get Up!,'" 11. The book *Talitha Cum!*, edited by Njoroge and Dube, is structured under this tripart structure.

55. Oduyoye, "Story of a Circle," 99; Kanyoro, "Beads and Strands," 27–28, 31. Kanyoro notes that the original plan was to meet biennially in what were called "the Biennial Institutes," but the seven-year cycle worked best, because women could continue to meet and publish during the cycle.

56. Kanyoro, "Beads and Strands," 20.

57. Mpyana Fulgence Nyengele, *African Women's Theology, Gender Relations, and Family Systems Theory: Pastoral Theological Considerations and Guidelines for Care and Counseling* (New York: Lang, 2004), 29.

58. Nyambura J. Njoroge, "The Missing Voice: African Women Doing Theology," *Journal of Theology for Southern Africa* 99 (1997): 79.

59. Oduyoye, "Story of a Circle," 99.

60. Musimbi R. A. Kanyoro, "Engendered Communal Theology: African Women's Contribution to Theology in the 21st Century," in Njoroge and Dube, *Talitha Cum!*, 170. These four commissions are described as (1) cultural and biblical hermeneutics, (2) women in culture and religion (3) history of women, and (4) ministry and theological education and formation.

61. Oduyoye, *African Women's Theologies*, 18.

62. Hinga, "African Feminist Theologies," 80–81.

63. Kanyoro, "Engendered Communal Theology," 171.

64. Ibid.

65. Njoroge, "Missing Voice," 78.

66. Oduyoye, *African Women's Theologies*, 8–9.

67. Ibid., 9.

68. Dube, "Introduction: 'Little Girl, Get Up!,'" 11.

69. Ibid.

70. Kanyoro, "Beads and Strands," 19–21, 24. Kanyoro, part of the Circle and friend of Mercy Oduyoye, notes its beginnings in 1988, its initial planning stages occurring in 1978, and its official inauguration in 1989.

71. Smith, "Mercy Amba Oduyoye"; Hinga, "African Feminist Theologies," 79.

72. Dube, "Introduction: 'Little Girl, Get Up!,'" 5.

73. Ibid.

74. Hinga, "African Feminist Theologies," 80.

75. Njoroge, "Missing Voice," 77–78.

76. Hinga, "African Feminist Theologies," 84–85.

77. Ibid.

78. Oduyoye, "Story of a Circle," 97; Smith, "Mercy Amba Oduyoye."

79. Oduyoye, "Story of a Circle," 97.

80. Oduyoye, *Beads and Strands*, xiii.

81. Oduyoye, "Story of a Circle," 98.

82. Kanyoro, "Beads and Strands," 23.

83. Oduyoye, "Story of a Circle," 99.

84. Kanyoro, "Engendered Communal Theology," 171.

85. Oduyoye, "Story of a Circle," 99.

86. Kanyoro, "Beads and Strands," 39.

Chapter Four

1. A note of reference: when referring to "Africa" or "African(s)," I am primarily referring to the voice from which Oduyoye writes—namely, black West African, though she has also had contact and has worked with women and men from all over the African continent.

2. Mercy Amba Oduyoye, "Alive to What God Is Doing," *Ecumenical Review* 41, no. 2 (1989): 195.

3. Ibid.

4. Ibid.

5. Oduyoye, *Introducing African Women's Theology*, 45.

6. Ibid., 44. Oduyoye asserts, "That God is the source of life and being is a factor that all religious people avow."

7. Mercy Amba Oduyoye, "The African Experience of God," *Cross Currents* 47, no. 4 (1997): 494.

8. Ibid., 494.

9. Oduyoye, *Introducing African Women's Theology*, 41.

10. See Dietrich Bonhoeffer, "The Image of God on Earth," in *Creation and Fall: A Theological Exposition of Genesis 1–3*, ed. John W. de Gruchy, trans. Douglas Stephen Bax, vol. 3 of *Dietrich Bonhoeffer Works*, ed. Wayne Whitson Floyd Jr. (Minneapolis: Fortress: 2004), 60–67, for more on the notion of limit within creaturely gendered identity.

11. Oduyoye, "Alive to What God Is Doing," 194.

12. Oduyoye, *Introducing African Women's Theology*, 45.

13. Oduyoye, "Christianity and African Culture," 88.

14. Oduyoye, "Alive to What God Is Doing," 194.

15. Oduyoye, *Introducing African Women's Theology*, 39.

16. Oduyoye, *Hearing and Knowing*, 29.

17. Mercy Amba Oduyoye, "The Church of the Future, Its Mission and Theology: A View from Africa," *Theology Today* 52, no. 4 (1996): 497. Oduyoye identifies five types of churches that emerge from within the African context: (1) the originary first-century church in Ethiopian Orthodox and Coptic settings; (2) African Western churches brought by missionaries; (3) the Roman Catholic Church; (4) African Instituted Churches and its inculturation of Christianity; and (5) churches emerging from a new wave of evangelization. For the purposes of this chapter, "church" as I speak of it as of/in the African context refers primarily to the second and fourth church types (the second being the type that serves as a model according to which most ecumenical structures in Africa are made, according to Oduyoye). See also Oduyoye, *Hearing and Knowing*, 15.

18. Oduyoye, *Hearing and Knowing*, 16.

19. Ibid., 31.

20. Ibid., 32.

21. Ibid., 36.

22. Ibid., 31.

23. Ibid., 32–33.

24. Mercy Amba Oduyoye, "Calling the Church to Account," *Ecumenical Review* 47, no. 4 (1995): 479. Oduyoye interestingly calls missionary-churches "mother churches" in order to describe their generational impact in the thought-life and ecclesial practice of African Christianity. It is often recounted, however, that some missionary-inspired churches held a paternalistic attitude toward the Africans they were trying to convert.

25. Russell et al., *Inheriting Our Mothers' Gardens*, 41.

26. Oduyoye, *Introducing African Women's Theology*, 43; Oduyoye, "African Experience of God," 498. Oduyoye fleshes this out more in her analysis of "God in the apartheid system" of South Africa.

27. Oduyoye, *Hearing and Knowing*, 33.

28. Ibid., 33.

29. Oduyoye, "Alive to What God Is Doing," 197.

30. I qualify my statement with "fully" in order to address the reality that for many Africans, Christianity was well received, so much so that it took on an assimilative quality. Some aligned with the belief that their traditional religious foundations were flawed and in need of saving. Oduyoye laments this turning against traditional faith culture. In her 1997 keynote plenary address, "Troubled but Not Destroyed," at the All African Conference of Churches meeting in

Addis Abba, Ethiopia, she argues that blind religious assimilation in Africa has yielded global economic, political, and social consequences. She passionately asks, "When did we learn so much hatred towards ourselves?," and additionally proclaims, "We are alienated from our roots." She asserts that both Christianity and Islam have "launched an assault on African religion in ways that undermine other aspects of traditional culture such as health care and statecraft and the understanding of community." Oduyoye views these consequential positions against the traditional faith culture as problematic and as an assault on African ways of being and worldview. The threat is not in the addition of Christianity but in the invalidation of all of what was *before* the Christian faith took root in West Africa.

31. Oduyoye, "Church of the Future," 501. Though great, African resistance was not total. Oduyoye does note that the colonizing efforts left a painful legacy around notions of ruling, a legacy of patriarchal reinforcement through the "benevolent dictatorships of self-seeking men."

32. Oduyoye, *Hearing and Knowing*, 33–34.

33. Ibid., 41. Oduyoye writes, "Western standards of living were paid for by the West, so Africa, puzzled and awed, accepted them as necessary to the religion."

34. Ibid., 35.

35. Ibid., 36.

36. Ibid.

37. Oduyoye, *Daughters of Anowa*, 32–33. This is also seen in the new Christian names people acquired through baptism. Oduyoye notes, "African Christians became incorporated into the church and into Christ without giving up their incorporation into their human family." Africans kept their names but now had to think through what both of their names meant in concert with each other—what those names were naming about each person. This syncretic reality demonstrated one instance in which Africans theologized from their context.

38. Mercy Amba Oduyoye, "Standing on Both Feet: Education and Leadership Training of Women in the Methodist Church, Nigeria," *Ecumenical Review* 33, no. 1 (1980): 65–66. My use of "syncretism" suggests that Africans include elements of their culture to make Christianity their own, so to speak. E. Bolaji Idowu would call this "enculturation," as it seems to signal the gradual acceptance of one culture into a previously existing one. "Syncretism" and "enculturation" express similar sentiments, for sure. In my opinion, the terminology of syncretism slightly edges that of enculturation, because embedded within the swift acceptance of Christianity, for some, were direct links to African cultural practice. In other words, syncretism allows space for the immediacy of conversion as well as the points of difference in the religious expression. Though

she utilizes "syncretism" to describe the religious shifts and reworkings in African Christianity, Oduyoye also considers enculturation very much a part of the narrative of African Christianity (see Mercy Amba Oduyoye "Unity and Mission: The Emerging Ecumenical Vision," *Ecumenical Review* 39, no. 3 (1987): 336–45).

39. Oduyoye, *Hearing and Knowing*, 36–37.

40. Landman, "Mercy Amba Ewudziwa Oduyoye." See also, Oduyoye, "Standing on Both Feet," 65–66.

41. Oduyoye, "Christianity and African Culture," 85.

42. Ibid.

43. Oduyoye, "Church of the Future," 501.

44. Oduyoye, *Daughters of Anowa*, 2.

45. Oduyoye, "Calling the Church to Account," 482.

46. Ibid., 483.

47. Oduyoye, "Christianity and African Culture," 87.

48. Oduyoye, "Calling the Church to Account," 480.

49. Ibid., 479.

50. Oduyoye, *Introducing African Women's Theology*, 42. Ultimately, Oduyoye would argue that it does not matter. According to her, numerous Africans have no gender specification for God. God is supragender. God exceeds gender.

51. Oduyoye, "Church of the Future," 500.

52. Oduyoye, "Calling the Church to Account," 486.

53. Oduyoye, "Christianity and African Culture," 80.

54. Oduyoye, *Introducing African Women's Theology*, 42.

55. Oduyoye, "Calling the Church to Account," 483.

56. Ibid., 482.

57. Oduyoye, "African Experience of God," 497.

58. Oduyoye, *Introducing African Women's Theology*, 48. Some African women ascribe the title of "Mother" to God in order to illumine God's nurturing attributes. What is also apparent in this practice is an affirmation of African women in the expectation that they fulfill the role of being mothers themselves. It asserts the interrelationship of God's creatures toward one another.

59. Oduyoye, "Calling the Church to Account," 482.

60. Ibid., 483.

61. Ibid.

62. Oduyoye, *Beads and Strands*, 95.

63. In explaining this logic, I want to make clear that I in no way support these labels as the best way to conceive of how humanity ought to name itself. I recognize that the labeling of "father" and "mother," even with human designation, can act harmfully. It assumes many things, including the fertility of women

and men and that they come from a culture with that bodily understanding. Oduyoye's use of "fatherhood" and "motherhood" is solely a means to express how God is referred to in various West African cultures.

64. Oduyoye, "Calling the Church to Account," 482.

65. Ibid.

66. "Final Statement of the Fifth EATWOT Conference, New Delhi, August 17–29, 1981," in *Irruption of the Third World: Challenge to Theology*, ed. Virginia Fabella and Sergio Torres, (Maryknoll, NY: Orbis Books, 1983), 195.

67. Oduyoye, "Church of the Future," 501.

68. Oduyoye, "Calling the Church to Account," 484.

69. Oduyoye, "Alive to What God Is Doing," 195.

70. Oduyoye, *Introducing African Women's Theology*, 78; Mercy Amba Oduyoye, "African Family," 467–69. The familial unit can also be considered through the culturally specific imagery of the *abusua*, the clan within one's people group. Belonging to the people of God is not the only thing it expresses. Oduyoye names the Christian church as one *abusua* and refers to denominations as individual households within the *abusua*.

71. Oduyoye, *Introducing African Women's Theology*, 79. Oduyoye's phonetic and ideational alteration is similar in many ways to the epistemological and liberationist move of the "kin-dom" of God asserted by Oduyoye's colleague, Ada María Isasi-Díaz.

72. Oduyoye, *Introducing African Women's Theology*, 78.

73. Ibid., 78–79.

74. The problem that arises in this structure concerns whether responsibility for care, for sustenance, and for the wellness of all (of the community) is feminized or not. In this structure, that responsibility is made the primary responsibility of females. Would this not further the trajectory of imbalance and assumptive role-playing for African women to be positioned in this Trinitarian paradigm? Are women then expected to model and mirror God, Christ, and the Spirit in self-giving, selflessness, sacrifice, and rectifying work for the whole of humanity (or even their particular community)? Is this parallel healthy for bringing about proper balance between the sexes?

75. Oduyoye, "African Family," 472.

76. Oduyoye, *Introducing African Women's Theology*, 79. Oduyoye asserts that the claim that all in the household of God are Christian is false.

77. Oduyoye, "Church of the Future," 497.

78. Oduyoye, *Introducing African Women's Theology*, 81–82.

79. Oduyoye, "African Experience of God," 495.

80. Oduyoye, "Church of the Future," 501.

81. Oduyoye, "Calling the Church to Account," 483.

82. Oduyoye, *Introducing African Women's Theology*, 44.

83. Oduyoye, "Alive to What God Is Doing," 195.

84. Oduyoye, *Hearing and Knowing*, 91.

85. Oduyoye, "African Experience of God," 495. Oduyoye briefly describes the naming work that particular symbols in Akan culture do. One such example she uses is that of Adinkra symbols, whose star detail "says," "Like the star, I depend on God and not on myself." This symbolism "speaks" of God as reliable and dependable.

86. Oduyoye, "African Experience of God," 495. Oduyoye suggests that African religion researchers, such as G. Parrinder, E. B. Idowu, and J. S. Mbiti, offer a more extensive look into African names for God.

87. Oduyoye, *Introducing African Women's Theology*, 44.

88. Oduyoye, "African Experience of God," 496.

89. Ibid., 497.

90. James Cone, *A Black Theology of Liberation* (Maryknoll, NY: Orbis Books, 2010), 3–6.

91. Oduyoye, "African Experience of God," 502. Oduyoye is realistic in her doctrinal assertion. God being for humanity does not automatically preclude hardship. Oduyoye is clear that sometimes evil does "win." She does offer, however, that for Africans, if evil wins, it suggests the absence of God.

92. Ibid., 499.

93. Ibid.

94. Oduyoye, *Introducing African Women's Theology*, 42.

95. "Final Statement of the Fifth EATWOT Conference," 203.

96. Oduyoye, "African Experience of God," 501.

Chapter Five

1. Landman, "Mercy Amba Ewudziwa Oduyoye."

2. When referring to "Africa/n(s)" in the perspective of Oduyoye's work, I am speaking specifically to Akan (Ghanaian) and/or Yoruba (Nigerian) identities.

3. Day, "Daughters, Arise," 389; Oduyoye, *Introducing African Women's Theology*, 51.

4. Mercy Amba Oduyoye, "Jesus Christ," in *The Cambridge Companion to Feminist Theology*, ed. Susan Frank Parsons (Cambridge: Cambridge University Press, 2002), 155, 157; Teresia M. Hinga, "Jesus Christ and the Liberation of Women in Africa," in *The Will to Arise: Women, Tradition, and the Church in Africa*, ed. Mercy Amba Oduyoye and Musimbi R. A. Kanyoro (Eugene,

OR: Wipf and Stock, 1992), 191. Though Oduyoye clearly states that African women refer to and know him as "Jesus" and not "Jesus the Christ" or "Christ" or "Christ Jesus," I use these terms interchangeably throughout this chapter to designate how the more personal and relational figure "Jesus" is not distinct from the salvific and messianic "the Christ." In using "Jesus" and "the/Christ" synonymously, I am arguing that the salvific is happening within the intimate and vice versa. For African women and their articulations of Jesus Christ, both are working within one another: the personal figure is the salvific in his relationality and relational emphases. The messianic figure is deeply personal and intimately known in his ability to provide relief, redemption, and liberation whether on an institutional or personal scale. In *Feminist Theology from the Third World*, Kenyan theologian Teresia M. Hinga also argues for a "pneumatic Christology" that sees Christ as deeply intertwined with how the church knows the Holy Spirit; given the impact of African traditional religion on Africans, this proves unsurprising. Therefore, Jesus Christ working in all these ways—in the interpersonal, in the salvific, and in spiritual movement—is who I refer to in my interchangeable language.

5. Landman, "Mercy Amba Ewudziwa Oduyoye."

6. Oduyoye, *Introducing African Women's Theology*, 55.

7. Ibid., 52.

8. Oduyoye, "Women's Presence," 83.

9. Ibid.

10. In "Women and Ritual in Africa," in Oduyoye and Kanyoro, *Will to Arise*, 11, Oduyoye argues that "Christian feminists undertaking 'God-talk' must work for the liberation of women from an image of God created for women by men. When examining the roles of women in religion in Africa—whether speaking of Christianity, Islam, or African traditional religions—we must face two fundamental questions: What responsibilities do women have in the structures of religion? How does religion serve or obstruct women's development?" Oduyoye warns against a Christian feminist position (African or otherwise) that universalizes women's Christian experience, especially when handed down from men. She argues for representation, rightly questioning whether the theological voices of men can hold—and, frankly, if they know—the experiences of African women. African women are thus critical agents in determining the shape and sound of theology from their particular contexts. Men do not have the experiential knowledge of women, knowledge that can offer a theological contribution.

11. Oduyoye, *Daughters of Anowa*, 19–21.

12. See Karl Barth, "The Word of God as the Speech of God," in *Doctrine of the Word of God*, vol. I/1 of *Church Dogmatics*, ed. G. W. Bromiley and T. F. Torrance (Peabody, MA: Hendrickson, 2010), 138–48.

13. Oduyoye, *Introducing African Women's Theology*, 51.

14. Ibid.

15. Ibid., 58.

16. Ibid., 51.

17. Ibid. Also, see Matthew 28:1–10. It even haunts the story of Mary Magdalene and Mary the mother of Jesus telling his disciples of an empty tomb where Jesus once lay. The notions of beginning and ending are blurred, confused, combined.

18. Oduyoye, *Hearing and Knowing*, 122.

19. Oduyoye, *Beads and Strands*, 21. Oduyoye interestingly names God as the one who rescued the Hebrew people "from childlessness and disease, famine and fire, from flood and from the deep sea, from disgrace and humiliation, so we find Jesus in the New Testament snatching women and men away from all domination, even from the jaws of death." To be clear, this statement does not cite a preference on Oduyoye's behalf, but signals the redemptive tradition in which Jesus is understood over time. Suffice it to say, childlessness is scripturally a concern from which to be redeemed.

20. Oduyoye, *Daughters of Anowa*, 62.

21. Oduyoye, *Introducing African Women's Theology*, 49. The experience of women is the palpable moment from which christological information can come. Oduyoye notes that African women's common and well-known fear of childlessness immediately puts them in, and connects them with, what is happening in the visitation moment, because "their [Jesus' and John's] expected births were due to special divine intervention, just what African women pray for in their dread of the reproach that accompanies childlessness."

22. See Oduyoye, "Coming Home to Myself," 119.

23. Oduyoye, *Introducing African Women's Theology*, 51.

24. Ibid., 16.

25. This question adds a feminine dimension to the inquiry found in the synoptic Gospels: Matthew 16:15; Mark 8:29; Luke 9:20.

26. Oduyoye, *Introducing African Women's Theology*, 52.

27. Ibid., 51.

28. Ibid., 52 (emphasis added).

29. Ibid., 28; Mercy Amba Oduyoye, "Unity and Freedom in Africa," *Ecumenical Review* 26, no. 3 (1974): 454–55.

30. Oduyoye, *Introducing African Women's Theology*, 26.

31. Ibid., 52.

32. Ibid., 55.

33. Ibid., 52.

34. Ibid., 57.

35. Ibid., 62.

36. Oduyoye, "Calling the Church to Account," 480. It is important to note that African theology often emphasizes race and class issues, but hardly gender and/or sexuality.

37. Oduyoye, *Introducing African Women's Theology*, 54.

38. Ibid., 54.

39. Ibid., 55.

40. To clarify, suffering is not a requirement for salvation, but often a feature present in salvation's narrative. I am in no way advocating for the necessity of suffering in order for salvation to be, but I am insisting on a close reading of what salvation means to the being who has experienced suffering. In this, I want to argue that salvation can be identified immediately; it can be recognized well by one who has undergone or experienced suffering. Suffering, in a way, serves as a lens to sharpen recognition of what can be categorized as good, as healing, and salvific.

41. Oduyoye, *Introducing African Women's Theology*, 54.

42. Hinga, "Jesus Christ and the Liberation," 191.

43. This distinction between embodiment as a whole and a particularized embodiment can be thought of in two ways, to the latter of which I'm referring. Jesus' particular embodiment can refer to his ontological status as both God and man or to the fact that Jesus connects most deeply (and arguably most readily) to those with severely marginalized identities, among whom are women (in patriarchal or patriarchal-adjacent societies).

44. It must be added that the question of the lowly solely claiming Jesus creates a misleading idea that suffering is the primary characterization of such persons. For example, this line of questioning might falsely solidify suffering as a permanent or primary feature of African womanhood at large.

45. Oduyoye, *Introducing African Women's Theology*, 28.

46. Oduyoye, "Calling the Church to Account," 479–80. This European-centered thinking has harmfully tried to impose a Western vision of womanhood onto African women.

47. Mercy Amba Oduyoye, "Feminist Theology in an African Perspective," in *Paths of African Theology*, ed. Rosino Gibellini (Maryknoll, NY: Orbis Books, 1994), 173.

48. Oduyoye, *Introducing African Women's Theology*, 31. Oduyoye asserts that for African women, theology is "a statement of faith enabling them to live their tomorrow today, as they await new life, the resurrection of the life of God in the midst of all creation beginning with . . . humans made in God's image."

49. Oduyoye, "African Experience of God," 500.

50. Oduyoye, *Introducing African Women's Theology*, 57.

51. Oduyoye, *Beads and Strands*, 22.

52. Oduyoye, *Hearing and Knowing*, 37.

53. Oduyoye, *Beads and Strands*, 22.

54. Oduyoye, *Hearing and Knowing*, 32.

55. Ibid.

56. See Aimé Césaire, *Discourse on Colonialism* (New York: Monthly Review Press, 1972).

57. See Thomas Pakenham, *The Scramble for Africa: White Man's Conquest of the Dark Continent from 1876 to 1912* (New York: Random House, 1991).

58. Oduyoye, *Daughters of Anowa*, 80.

59. See Oyèrónké Oyěwùmí, *The Invention of Women: Making an African Sense of Western Gender Discourses* (Minneapolis, MN: University of Minnesota Press, 1997), especially chapter 4, "Colonizing Bodies and Minds: Gender and Colonialism."

60. Oduyoye, *Beads and Strands*, 106.

61. Oduyoye, *Introducing African Women's Theology*, 26.

62. Ibid., 54.

63. Ibid., 63.

64. Ibid., 41.

65. Ibid., 15.

66. Ibid., 26.

67. Ibid., 51.

68. Looking through an African woman's theological lens, one might argue that the gathering of Mary, Elizabeth, Jesus, and John could be the first gathering of what would later formally become the Christian church.

69. Ada María Isasi-Díaz, *En La Lucha: Elaborating a Mujerista Theology* (Minneapolis: Fortress, 2004), 184.

70. Oduyoye, *Beads and Strands*, 21. Oduyoye notes that Israel, though a conquered nation, had few limits on their worship practices and their adherence to the law as long as they did not conflict with Roman rule. Their oppression was not complete, but still adverse in a number of ways.

71. Oduyoye, *Introducing African Women's Theology*, 52–53.

72. Oduyoye, *Beads and Strands*, 19.

73. Ibid., 20.

74. Oduyoye, *Introducing African Women's Theology*, 55.

75. The Christ figure can be interpreted in numerous ways according to whom one needs him to be. For the purposes of African women's theological thought, the Christ figure addressed both geographical and social colonialism and sexism as affiliated with the colonial presence.

76. Hinga, "Jesus Christ and the Liberation," 187.

77. Oduyoye, *Beads and Strands*, 70; For more on AICs, see "African Independent Churches," Patheos, https://www.patheos.com/library/african-independent -churches.

78. Oduyoye, *Introducing African Women's Theology*, 56.

79. Ibid., 54–55.

80. Oduyoye published *Introducing African Women's Theology* in 2001; thus her claims that a new form of Christianity emerged in the 1980s dates this conversation as happening across three decades.

81. Oduyoye, *Hearing and Knowing*, 34.

82. Oduyoye, *Beads and Strands*, 8.

83. Ibid., 23.

84. Oduyoye, "Unity and Freedom in Africa," 454.

85. Oduyoye, "Women's Presence," 82.

86. Oduyoye, *Introducing African Women's Theology*, 65.

87. Landman, "Mercy Amba Ewudziwa Oduyoye."

88. Oduyoye, *Introducing African Women's Theology*, 61.

89. Oduyoye, "Women's Presence," 83.

90. Ibid.

91. Ibid.

92. In these claims I am not equating womanhood or motherhood with the ability to reproduce or to physically create life but with something more in the vein of providing nurturance.

93. Oduyoye, "Women's Presence," 83.

94. Ibid. Though Oduyoye purports to speak a message of an antipatriarchal Christ attentive to the presence and needs of women, her rhetoric seems to be reaching in some places. She works hard to prove the full inclusion of women in every interaction Jesus has with women in the Gospels. She argues that Mary and Martha's relationship to Jesus was literally one of life and death as "Jesus was, for them, life." But what must be parsed out is *how* Jesus is life for them. Jesus is life for them in his ability to resurrect their brother. Does this send a message that is fundamentally patriarchal? That Jesus only matters to women only insomuch as he can make alive the males in their lives? Does Jesus only matter to Mary and Martha through Lazarus? Or is there a connection between kinship and how it serves as a life-form in itself in this culture? Is the message more cultural than patriarchal? Is the emphasis on family and relational living rather than patriarchal forms of relational living? Perhaps it can be argued that Jesus rejected Martha's domestic duties, to which Oduyoye asks, "Was Jesus downgrading domestic hospitality?" Perhaps there is an inversion, a reversal, happening here where women are the narrative's central characters: what is life—what Jesus resurrects—is community. Perhaps a feminist message is

present in Jesus' interactions with Mary and Martha. It is uncertain but certainly an objective of Oduyoye in this article.

95. Oduyoye, *Introducing African Women's Theology*, 64.

96. Oduyoye, "Women's Presence," 83.

97. Ibid., 89.

98. Ibid.

99. Ibid.

100. Oduyoye, *Introducing African Women's Theology*, 62.

101. Oduyoye, "God Alone Gives," 455.

Chapter Six

1. Oduyoye, *Hearing and Knowing*, 130.

2. Musimbi R. A. Kanyoro, *Introduction to Feminist Cultural Hermeneutics: A Key to African Women's Liberation Theology* (Cleveland: Pilgrim Press, 2002), 23.

3. When referring to God, I highlight the diverse ways in which Oduyoye understands and names God. For the purposes of this chapter, God is also known as "Nyame," "the Supreme Being," "the Source Being," and "the Creator."

4. David H. Kelsey, *Eccentric Existence: A Theological Anthropology* (Louisville: Westminster John Knox, 2009), 46.

5. Oduyoye, *Hearing and Knowing*, 56–57. Oduyoye is very clear that she does not call African belief "traditional," because "that word implies something 'customary,' something practiced without modification, or unthinkingly carried on just because that is how it has always been. 'Traditional' can imply a religion that is dying, being replaced by the new within which it is fruitlessly competing, a conservative and conserving religion bearing little relationship to the times." For reasons of consistency and clarity in this book, I will use terms such as "tradition/al," "customs," "thought," and "belief" to signify a claim—this logic and these practices belong to African communities who have been practicing and thinking, and continue to practice and think, in ways honoring the timelessness of such accounts and ways of thinking. I think of "tradition/al" and the subsequent terms as "ancestral."

6. Oduyoye, "Feminist Theology in an African Perspective," 167.

7. Ibid.

8. Oduyoye, *Hearing and Knowing*, 181. Oduyoye turns away from "hierarchical and oppressive terms like Omnipresent, Omniscient, Ruler, or All Mighty," because they "translate into race relations as racism and into gender relations as sexism."

9. Oduyoye, *Introducing African Women's Theology*, 126; Oduyoye, *Beads and Strands*, 71.

10. Oduyoye, *Introducing African Women's Theology*, 126; Oduyoye, *Beads and Strands*, 71. The "different but complementary" idea of complementarianism does not sit well with Oduyoye, however. She instead redefines complementarianism as more akin to "egalitarianism." Her definition accords better with a position of mutuality, equal collaboration, and true reciprocity. This is one way Oduyoye constructively overturns and repurposes the ideas of her culture.

11. Oduyoye, *Introducing African Women's Theology*, 74.

12. Ibid., 73.

13. Samuel Awuah-Nyamekye, "Salvaging Nature: The Akan Religio-Cultural Perspective," *Worldviews: Global Religions, Culture, and Ecology* 13, no. 3 (2008): 255.

14. Ibid., 255.

15. Ibid., 255–56.

16. Oduyoye, *Hearing and Knowing*, 52.

17. Esther Acolatse, *For Freedom or Bondage? A Critique of African Pastoral Practices* (Grand Rapids, MI: Eerdmans, 2014), 60. The ancestors are second only to the Supreme Being in Akan spirituality. Their intercession is the means of the Akan's experiencing favor in the earthly realm. Serving in mediating roles, the pantheon of gods is also a means of experiencing the favor of the Supreme Being.

18. Ibid., 61.

19. Awuah-Nyamekye, "Salvaging Nature," 256.

20. J. M. Assimeng, *Traditional Life, Culture and Literature in Ghana* (Owerri, Nigeria: Conch Magazine, 1976), 15. In assessing African traditional religion expert Kofi Asare Opoku's work, Assimeng asserts that Opoku's conceptions of Akan cosmology can be read as either dated or androcentric, since his identification with humanity is expressed through the gendered label of "man." Opoku also asserts that the life cycle is one of "birth, puberty, marriage, death and regeneration." This precludes a woman from holding a life purpose outside of that which her body is useful for: marriage in order to ensure reproduction.

21. Acolatse, *For Freedom or Bondage?*, 65. Subsequent citations of this work are in parentheses in the text.

22. The *kra* can also be known as *ɵkra*.

23. Rose Mary Amenga-Etego, "Gender and Christian Spirituality in Africa: A Ghanaian Perspective," *Black Theology: An International Journal* 10, no. 1 (2012): 15; Ursula King, "Religion and Gender," in *A New Handbook of Living Religions*, ed. John R. Hinnells (Cambridge: Blackwell, 1997), 647–66.

24. Oduyoye, *Hearing and Knowing*, 91. Oduyoye notes that Ananse Kokroko is a linguistic means to avoid calling God by God's personal name "Nyame," which can also be spelled "Onyame." (See also Awuah-Nyamekye, "Salvaging Nature," 265; Amenga-Etego, "Gender and Christian Spirituality in Africa," 21.)

25. Oduyoye, *Hearing and Knowing*, 91.

26. Although I have used this story to enter into conversations about gender division, Oduyoye's account does not assign sex to either being. The point is that they are unsexed and thus most importantly seen as beings who come to be because of Nyame/God.

27. Oduyoye, *Daughters of Anowa*, 19; Amba Oduyoye, "The Asante Woman: Socialization through Proverbs (Part I)," *African Notes: Bulletin of the Institute of African Studies, University of Ibadan* 8, no. 1 (1979): 5–6. Proverbs can also serve as a source of pursuing equality, as in the saying "Nnipa nyinaa Υε Onyame mma, obi nyε asaase ba," meaning, "All people are the children of God, no person is a child of the earth." But, as Oduyoye carefully notes, proverbs of this sort that uplift persons and promote "justice, peace and harmony are few and far between."

28. Oduyoye, "Asante Woman," 5.

29. See Samuel Kwesi Nkansah, "The Quest for Climactic Sanity: Re-Reading of Akan Creation Myth," *Language in India* 12, no. 8 (2012): 370. Though Nkansah labels these various accounts "creation myths," in Christian ideation they attend more to what Christianity would call "the fall" or original sin. They are not necessarily origin stories, but perhaps something more akin to proverbial stories explaining the course of divine-human relations. To collapse the lapsarian circumstances of humanity's separation from God into the creation account of humanity is to imply that God's creative initiation is embedded in sin, which can be a kind of theological mishandling. Nkansah's approach in his recounting the fundamentals of Akan culture is from an environmental standpoint, and not a theological one. I find his mythical accounts or proverbial accounts helpful to further demonstrate the narrative conceptions against which Oduyoye's work moves.

30. Oduyoye, *Introducing African Women's Theology*, 68; Nkansah, "Quest for Climactic Sanity," 376.

31. Nkansah, "Quest for Climactic Sanity," 376.

32. Oduyoye, *Daughters of Anowa*, 40.

33. Ibid.

34. Ibid.

35. Oduyoye, *Hearing and Knowing*, 181.

36. Oduyoye, *Daughters of Anowa*, 42.

37. Nkansah, "Quest for Climactic Sanity," 376.

38. Oduyoye, *Daughters of Anowa*, 82.

39. Ibid.

40. Oduyoye, *Introducing African Women's Theology*, 66; *Encyclopedia Britannica*, s.v. "Bemba people," https://www.britannica.com/topic/Bemba.

41. Oduyoye, *Introducing African Women's Theology*, 66.

42. Oduyoye, *Hearing and Knowing*, 121.

43. Oduyoye, *Introducing African Women's Theology*, 69.

44. Oduyoye, *Introducing African Women's Theology*, 68; Oduyoye, *Daughters of Anowa*, 9.

45. Oduyoye, *Introducing African Women's Theology*, 70. It is interesting to note how "female" and "male" descriptors (whether noun or adjective) are conflated with "feminine" and "masculine" adjective descriptors. This illustrates an understanding of sex that runs in step with notions of heteronormative sexuality in African theological circles. An account of Oduyoye's understanding of "sexuality" will be offered in chapter 8.

46. Nkansah, "Quest for Climactic Sanity," 377.

47. Oduyoye, *Introducing African Women's Theology*, 12.

48. Ibid., 17.

49. Ibid., 67, 69.

50. Ibid., 71.

51. Oduyoye, *Hearing and Knowing*, 127; Oduyoye, *Introducing African Women's Theology*, 72.

52. Oduyoye, *Hearing and Knowing*, 126.

53. Oduyoye, *Introducing African Women's Theology*, 69.

54. Oduyoye, *Hearing and Knowing*, 180.

55. Frantz Fanon, *Black Skin, White Masks* (New York: Grove Press, 1967), xii.

56. Oduyoye, *Introducing African Women's Theology*, 69. Though she names human sexuality as a topic that must be thoroughly treated, talked about, and vetted, Oduyoye primarily centers sex (biology) and gender (social labels assigned to particular sexes). I am not suggesting that her insight about sex or gender is not a form of sexuality (the expression of one's sexual disposition) discourse, but according to the trajectory of her logic, her attention is most centered on sex and gender formation, function, and misappropriation in theological discourse.

57. Oduyoye, *Hearing and Knowing*, 121.

58. Ibid., 131. Addressing biological critiques turned toward women's bodies, Oduyoye assesses a logic of sexism in theological anthropology through the interpretive lenses of the church fathers, particularly Tertullian and Gregory of Nyssa, who conceptualized women's bodies as parallel to a stumbling block for men and a "necessary evil." In these reflections around women's need for modest

dress, purity, and being the shattered image of man, women's embodiment is only considered in light of its relationship to men's understanding of them as well as men's own sexual shortcomings and limits. "Deemed to be a necessary evil," women's bodies as sexed bodies were considered agents that awakened sexual deviance in men; thus, women's embodiment, in the past and in the present, poses a problem for *men's* bodies and embodiment. The problem can be redirected in light of understanding the root of women's embodiment in theological anthropology: embodiment is characterized as aberrant and evil, but it is men's embodiment issues projecting themselves onto women that pose the greatest problem for the Christian imagination. Men's inability to correctly name and face their own bodies divides and positions female corporeality and male corporeality as contesting one another, instead of needing one another.

59. Oduyoye, "African Experience of God," 495.

60. Oduyoye, *Hearing and Knowing*, 92–93.

61. Oduyoye, *Introducing African Women's Theology*, 72.

62. Oduyoye, *Hearing and Knowing*, 120.

63. Ibid., 94.

64. Amenga-Etego, "Gender and Christian Spirituality in Africa," 17.

65. Ibid., 15.

66. A side note concerning this analogy would be helpful: the "problems" of home I note here exclude abuses and violence suffered at home. Oduyoye advocates working out problems within a system, but I conclude that should a system be death dealing, she would advocate for liberating oneself (away) from said system.

67. Oduyoye, *Hearing and Knowing*, 95.

68. Amenga-Etego, "Gender and Christian Spirituality in Africa," 13–15. One area for consideration is Akan culture itself. Oduyoye shows how the Akan worldview can contribute to a rich Christian theological anthropology. In Akan culture, the matrilineal importance of women can also be utilized to build a case for women's equality. What theological insight might surface if the Akan honored the heartbeat of their community—their women—in more expansive ways?

69. Oduyoye, *Hearing and Knowing*, 12–13. Though many argue that the feminist standpoint is Western in origin and nature, Oduyoye argues differently. Women have been speaking out about cultural values that harm or disadvantage them before what would be Westerly designated as "feminism" came into African women's consciousness. As I explored in chapter 2, Oduyoye's life was rooted in feminist expression for as long as she can remember. She was raised in what I want to name an expression of "Akan feminism." She learned early on that women not only were allowed to question their culture but should rightly do so for the well-being of the entire community. Thus, her Akan feminism was

an act of inclusion, because it dared to consider Akan women as part of the overall community and thus intrinsic to the determination of communal well-being, even if this reality had to move against culture in some ways.

70. Oduyoye, *Daughters of Anowa*, 82, 86.

71. Oduyoye, *Hearing and Knowing*, 95.

72. Oduyoye, *Introducing African Women's Theology*, 73.

73. Oduyoye, *Hearing and Knowing*, 135.

74. Oduyoye, *Introducing African Women's Theology*, 68–69.

75. Ibid., 69.

76. Ibid.

77. Oduyoye, *Hearing and Knowing*, 95.

78. Ibid., 94.

79. Amenga-Etego, "Gender and Christian Spirituality in Africa," 15.

80. Oduyoye, *Daughters of Anowa*, 202–5.

81. Ibid., 76.

82. Oduyoye, *Hearing and Knowing*, 129.

83. Ibid.

84. Oduyoye, *Daughters of Anowa*, 76.

85. Oduyoye, *Hearing and Knowing*, 76.

Chapter Seven

1. World Council of Churches, *The Church for Others*, in *A Reader in Ecclesiology*, ed. Bryan P. Stone (New York: Routledge, 2012), 292.

2. Oduyoye, *Introducing African Women's Theology*, 80.

3. Oduyoye, "African Family," 465.

4. Oduyoye, *Introducing African Women's Theology*, 80. For a more detailed exploration of hearth-hold as Oduyoye utilizes it, please see chapter 4 in the present volume.

5. Oduyoye, "African Family," 465.

6. Ibid., 466.

7. Oduyoye, *Introducing African Women's Theology*, 78. It is important to note that approximately ten years after Oduyoye published "The African Family as Symbol of Ecumenism" in *The Ecumenical Review*, she connected with different language and revised her use of "household" imagery. In her 2001 work *Introducing African Women's Theology*, Oduyoye admits her preference for "hearth-hold" imagery, because it frames God, Jesus, and the Holy Spirit in a more feminine and women-friendly light.

8. Oduyoye, "African Family," 467.

9. Ibid., 467–68.

10. Ibid., 468; Natalie Everts, "Incorporating Euro-Africans in Akan Lineages and a Modest Development towards a Euro-African Identity in Eighteenth Century Elmina," *Transactions of the Historical Society of Ghana*, n.s., 14 (2012): 85. Perhaps this contradiction signals an abuse of power from the Abusuapanini (who, Everts notes, is also called the *abusua mpanyin*), the head of the family, often a male "leader of the collective" who is treated as an authoritative figure.

11. Oduyoye, "African Family," 468.

12. Oduyoye, *Introducing African Women's Theology*, 81.

13. Ibid., 79.

14. Mercy Amba Oduyoye and Mary-John Manazan, "The Spirit Is Troubling the Water," *Ecumenical Review* 42, no. 3–4 (1990): 228.

15. Kwok Pui-lan, "Mercy Amba Oduyoye and African Women's Theology," *Journal of Feminist Studies in Religion* 20, no. 1 (2004): 20.

16. B. Diane Lipsett and Phyllis Trible, *Faith and Feminism: Ecumenical Essays* (Louisville: Westminster John Knox, 2014), 218.

17. Oduyoye, *Introducing African Women's Theology*, 81.

18. Ibid.

19. Oduyoye, "Calling the Church to Account," 484.

20. Mercy Amba Oduyoye, "The Passion out of Compassion: Women of the EATWOT General Assembly," *International Review of Mission* 81, no. 322 (1992): 314.

21. Oduyoye and Manazan, "Spirit Is Troubling the Water," 225.

22. Oduyoye, *Introducing African Women's Theology*, 83. Oduyoye notes that some women adopt this one-sided position, inflicting harm on themselves and others like them.

23. Ibid.

24. Oduyoye, *Daughters of Anowa*, 5–6; Oduyoye, *Beads and Strands*, 3.

25. Oduyoye, *Daughters of Anowa*, 5.

26. Ibid., 1.

27. Lipsett and Trible, *Faith and Feminism*, 218.

28. Ibid., 219.

29. Mercy Amba Oduyoye, "A Biblical Perspective on the Church," *Ecumenical Review* 53, no. 1 (2001): 44.

30. Ibid., 45.

31. Oduyoye, "Calling the Church to Account," 480; Oduyoye, *Hearing and Knowing*, 147.

32. Oduyoye, "Calling the Church to Account," 480.

33. Oduyoye, "Biblical Perspective on the Church," 45.

34. Oduyoye, "Calling the Church to Account," 480.

35. Ibid., 480. Oduyoye adds, "(Perhaps the morning ritual in our Methodist boarding school accomplished goals other than those sought by its leaders!)."

36. Oduyoye, *Who Will Roll the Stone Away?*, 46.

37. Oduyoye, "Biblical Perspective on the Church," 46.

38. Oduyoye and Manazan, "Spirit Is Troubling the Water," 225.

39. Oduyoye, *Who Will Roll the Stone Away?*, 3.

40. Ibid., 5.

41. Ibid., 14.

42. Mercy Amba Oduyoye, "The Search for a Two-Winged Theology: Women's Participation in the Development of Theology in Africa," in *Talitha, Qumi! Proceedings of the Convocation of African Women Theologians 1989*, ed. Mercy Amba Oduyoye and Musimbi Kanyoro (Ibadan, Nigeria: SWL Press, 1990), 55. Oduyoye offers a word of thanks to God for moving away the metaphorical stone of patriarchy and sexism in the church, "which blocks our chances."

43. Oduyoye, *Who Will Roll the Stone Away?*, 8.

44. Ibid., 53.

45. Oduyoye, "Unity and Mission," 342.

46. Oduyoye, "Church of the Future," 498.

47. Ibid.

48. Ibid., 499.

49. Ibid., 500.

50. Ibid., 501, 502–3.

51. Psalm 24:1.

52. Oduyoye, "Church of the Future," 501.

53. Ibid., 501.

54. Oduyoye, *Introducing African Women's Theology*, 85.

55. Oduyoye, "African Family," 471, 474. Oduyoye's conception of Christianity has a syncretic arc to it, but still holds fast to Christian identity as distinctly tied directly to Jesus Christ. On the one hand, she says, "In the Family [of God] members live and spread the 'good news' embodied in their chosen religion." On the other hand, she insists, "The church is home to those who accept Christ. Accepting Christ has become the criteria for belonging because the coming of Christ is the critical event that created the Christian family." She states again, "As a family, the church is concerned with the spirituality, traditions and preoccupations and predicaments of all who name themselves by Christ," and "The family of Christ whenever it is encountered might be accorded its proper name—the church." This assumes a specifically Christian understanding of church.

Unless Oduyoye is purposely moving through both territories of open inclusion and specificity, her syncretic move can appear confusingly broad and specific at the same time. A position that holds two seemingly opposing viewpoints muddies the narration of what the church is definitively—does it adhere to language of children of God and open itself up to differing religious positions, or does it assert itself as an extension of Christ? Assuming that the "church" she refers to is a Christian entity, full inclusion of those exercising an entirely different faith does not appear to fit—unless she is purposely asserting a new hybrid religious logic where a Christ-specific unit can also be religiously complex. In asserting both, Oduyoye may very well be expanding or challenging the possibilities of Christian understanding.

56. Oduyoye, *Beads and Strands*, 28.

57. Mercy Amba Oduyoye, "Troubled but Not Destroyed" (keynote address at the All African Council of Churches meeting, Addis Abba, Ethiopia, 1997).

58. Oduyoye, "Biblical Perspective on the Church," 45.

59. Oduyoye, "Search for a Two-Winged Theology," 46.

Chapter Eight

1. For a few examples of works that emerged from women who have been impacted by Oduyoye and/or who are Circle participants, see Oduyoye and Kanyoro, *Will to Arise*; Mercy Amba Oduyoye, ed., *Transforming Power: Women and the Household of God* (Accra, Ghana: SWL Press, 2007); Mercy Amba Oduyoye and Elizabeth Amoah, eds., *When Silence Is No Longer an Option* (Accra, Ghana: SWL Press, 2002); Phiri and Nadar, *African Women, Religion, and Health*.

2. Oduyoye, *Beads and Strands*, 88. In her comment, "Men and women are sexually distinct beings who do not necessarily need to have to be identified with the opposite sex in marriage or in other forms of complementarity," Oduyoye potentially cracks the door open for conceptualizing sexual expression on the spectrum, but again, it is not the primary manner in which she employs the term and concept of "sex/sexuality."

3. Ibid.

4. Ibid., 85–86. Oduyoye rightly names notions of the body, flesh, and purity/pollution as critical to examine in further research.

5. Oduyoye, *Daughters of Anowa*, 190.

6. Oduyoye, *Beads and Strands*, 87–88. Oduyoye does begin conversations around the double standards that exist in polygamous marriage for women; she problematizes monogamy as the "correct" sexual standard for them. She makes an interesting point on "correct sexual behavior" that bears further reflection: "A study of polygamy, which western Christians often view as a 'hangover' from 'primitive' lifestyles, may yield interesting information about its religious

imperatives." Perhaps the answer to sexual possibility can be found in thoroughly examining the kinship systems from which African women and men emerge.

7. Ibid., 88.

8. Ibid.

9. Ibid.

10. Oduyoye, *Introducing African Women's Theology*, 109. In her chapter "Hospitality and Spirituality" Oduyoye *does* offer a charge to men to sacrifice (or, as she puts it, "giving life in order to assure life or at least for the sake of assuring life"), and this charge could benefit from further elaboration. She states how in one of her previous books, *Daughters of Anowa*, she "calls on men to hold their end of the sacrificial bridge, so that all, especially the weak may cross from dying to living" (ibid.).

11. Oduyoye, "Story of a Circle," 99.

12. Ibid. (emphasis added).

13. Oduyoye, *Introducing African Women's Theology*, 25. Oduyoye would call this move one toward cultural and religious interdependence, which, in my opinion, both empowers and limits.

14. See Phiri and Nadar, *African Women, Religion, and Health*.

15. Oduyoye, "Be a Woman," 48. These women, the Mmabaawa (the millennial generation), are the generation coming after Oduyoye, who hold the hope of a theology equally voiced by women.

16. Amba Oduyoye, "Reflections from a Third World Woman's Perspective: Women's Experience and Liberation Theologies," in Fabella and Torres, *Irruption of the Third World*, 254.

17. Oduyoye, *Introducing African Women's Theology*, 112. Oduyoye asserts what she calls a theology of life, since, as she argues, "Africans are at home in life when they can celebrate life."

18. Ibid., 123.

19. Ibid.

20. Ibid., 126.

21. Ibid., 16.

22. Mary Elsbernd, "Social Ethics," *Theological Studies* 66, no. 1 (2005): 137–58.

23. The phrase "ways of knowing" speaks to a cultural framing or inherent cultural epistemology gained from the practices, values, principles, and beliefs of one's particular community. "African ways of knowing" thus gestures toward these similar values across cultures and peoples, such as the critical value of the many (the community) toward the wellness of the one (individual).

24. Oduyoye, *Daughters of Anowa*, 159.

25. Oduyoye, *Introducing African Women's Theology*, 17; Awa Thíam, "Feminism and Revolution," in *I Am Because We Are: Readings in Africana Philosophy*, ed. Fred Hord and Jonathan Lee (Boston: University of Massachusetts Press, 2016), 115. Awa Thíam articulates black African women's struggles as having two aspects, the second being "the struggle for the recognition of and respect for the rights and duties of men and women of all races."

26. Oduyoye, *Daughters of Anowa*, 171.

27. Interestingly enough, Christian values are said to express the same message of recognition of all and the full inclusion of the many.

28. Acolatse, *For Freedom or Bondage?*, 69.

Conclusion

1. See Alexis Shotwell, *Against Purity: Living Ethically in Compromised Times* (Minneapolis: University of Minnesota Press, 2016), especially chapter 1, "Remembering for the Future: Reckoning with an Unjust Past."

2. "Final Statement of the Fifth EATWOT Conference," 191.

3. 1 Corinthians 9:22b.

4. Oduyoye, "Be a Woman," 38.

5. Amba Oduyoye, "Reflections from a Third World Woman's Perspective," 254.

6. Oduyoye's doctrinal findings are one way that she pushes the boundaries of Christian and African cultural thought: God is father and mother who welcomes all into the fold. Jesus connects to the feminine. Humanity fails to know God if it does not know the fullness of itself. And, if it neglects all its members, the church is not the church. See Oduyoye, *Introducing African Women's Theology*.

7. Gustavo Gutiérrez, *A Theology of Liberation: History, Politics, and Salvation* (Maryknoll, NY: Orbis Books, 1988), xiv.

8. Fabella and Oduyoye, introduction, xi.

9. Ibid., xii.

10. Oduyoye, *Beads and Strands*, 45.

11. Oduyoye, "Spirituality of Resistance and Reconstruction," 167.

BIBLIOGRAPHY

Acolatse, Esther. *For Freedom or Bondage? A Critique of African Pastoral Practices.* Grand Rapids, MI: Eerdmans, 2014.

"African Independent Churches." Patheos. https://www.patheos.com/library /african-independent-churches.

Aidoo, Agnes Akosua. "Asante Queen Mothers in Government and Politics in the Nineteenth Century." *Journal of the Historical Society of Nigeria* 9, no. 1 (1977): 1–13.

Akyeampong, Emmanuel, and Ama de-Graft Aikins. "Ghana at Fifty: Reflections on Independence and After." *Transition* 98 (2008): 24–34.

Amadiume, Ifi. "Let My Work Not Be in Vain: Doing Matriarchy, Thinking 'Matriarchitarian' with Africa in the Twenty-First Century." In *Africa and the Challenges of the Twenty-First Century: Keynote Addresses Delivered at the 13th General Assembly of CODESRIA,* edited by Ebrima Sall, 57–66. Dakar, Senegal: Council for the Development of Social Science Research in Africa, 2015.

Amenga-Etego, Rose Mary. "Gender and Christian Spirituality in Africa: A Ghanaian Perspective." *Black Theology: An International Journal* 10, no. 1 (2012): 8–27.

Amoah, Elizabeth. Preface to Phiri and Nadar, *African Women, Religion, and Health,* xvii–xxii.

Apter, David E. *Ghana in Transition.* Princeton: Princeton University Press, 1972.

———. "Ghana's Independence: Triumph and Paradox." *Transition* 98 (2008): 6–22.

"As Decade of the Churches in Solidarity with Women 'Ends,' Participants Point the Way Forward for Continuing to Work: Letter to WCC's 8th Assembly Addresses Priorities, Divisive Issues of Human Sexuality." NCC News Archives, 1998. http://www.ncccusa.org/news/news107.html.

Assimeng, J. M. *Traditional Life, Culture and Literature in Ghana.* Owerri, Nigeria: Conch Magazine, 1976.

Awuah-Nyamekye, Samuel. "Salvaging Nature: The Akan Religio-Cultural Perspective." *Global Religions, Culture, and Ecology* 13, no. 3 (2008): 251–82.

Barth, Karl. "The Word of God as the Speech of God." In *Doctrine of the Word of God*, 138–48. Vol. I/1 of *Church Dogmatics*. Edited by G. W. Bromiley and T. F. Torrance. Peabody, MA: Hendrickson, 2010.

Bonhoeffer, Dietrich. "The Image of God on Earth." In *Creation and Fall: A Theological Exposition of Genesis 1–3*, edited by John W. de Gruchy, translated by Douglas Stephen Bax, vol. 3 of *Dietrich Bonhoeffer Works*, edited by Wayne Whitson Floyd Jr., 60–67. Minneapolis: Fortress, 2004.

Busia, Abena P. A. "Achimota: From the Story My Mother Taught Me." In Konadu and Campbell, *Ghana Reader*, 283–84.

Cambridge Inter-Collegiate Christian Union. "Who Are We?" https://ciccu.org.uk/whoarewe/.

Cannon, Katie. "Going Back before the Beginning." *Focus, the Magazine of Union Presbyterian Seminary*, Spring 2016, 9.

Césaire, Aimé. *Discourse on Colonialism*. New York: Monthly Review Press, 1972.

Coleman-Tobias, Meredith. "Dr. Mercy Amba Oduyoye: A Brief Bio." Speech introducing Mercy Amba Oduyoye before she spoke at Say Her Name! Africana Women as Interpreters, Healers, and Revolutionaries, Daughters of African Atlantic Fund, Atlanta, GA, July 12, 2016.

"The Community of Women and Men." *Ecumenical Review* 33, no. 4 (October 1981): 346–53.

Cone, James. *A Black Theology of Liberation*. Maryknoll, NY: Orbis Books, 2010.

Day, Keri. "Daughters, Arise." *Journal of Africana Religions* 2, no. 3 (2014): 385–94.

Dube, Musa Wenkosi. "Introduction: 'Little Girl, Get Up!'" In Njoroge and Dube, *Talitha Cum!*, 3–24.

Elsbernd, Mary. "Social Ethics." *Theological Studies* 66, no. 1 (2005): 137–58.

Everts, Natalie. "Incorporating Euro-Africans in Akan Lineages and a Modest Development towards a Euro-African Identity in Eighteenth Century Elmina." *Transactions of the Historical Society of Ghana*, n.s., 14 (2012): 79–104.

Fabella, Virginia, and Mercy Amba Oduyoye. Introduction to *With Passion and Compassion: Third World Women Doing Theology*, edited by Virginia Fabella and Mercy Amba Oduyoye, ix–xv. Maryknoll, NY: Orbis Books, 1988.

Fabella, Virginia, and Sergio Torres, eds. *Irruption of the Third World: Challenge to Theology*. Maryknoll, NY: Orbis Books, 1983.

Fallon, Kathleen M. "Transforming Women's Citizenship Rights within an Emerging Democratic State: The Case of Ghana." *Gender and Society* 17, no. 4 (2003): 525–43.

Fanon, Frantz. *Black Skin, White Masks*. New York: Grove Press, 1967.

Farley, Margaret A., and Serene Jones, eds. *Liberating Eschatology: Essays in Honor of Letty M. Russell.* Louisville: Westminster John Knox, 1999.

Fiedler, Rachel NyaGondwe. *A History of the Circle of Concerned African Women Theologians (1989–2007).* Mzuzu, Malawi: Mzuni Press, 2017.

"Final Statement of the Fifth EATWOT Conference, New Delhi, August 17–29, 1981." In Fabella and Torres, *Irruption of the Third World,* 191–206.

Fortunato, Laura. "The Evolution of Matrilineal Kinship Organization." *Proceedings: Biological Sciences* 279, no. 1749 (2012): 4939–45.

Gathogo, Julius. "Mercy Oduyoye as the Mother of African Women's Theology." *Theologia Viatorum: Journal of Theology and Religion in Africa* 34, no. 1 (2010): 1–18.

Gutiérrez, Gustavo. *A Theology of Liberation: History, Politics, and Salvation.* Maryknoll, NY: Orbis Books, 1988.

Hess, Janet Berry. "Imagining Architecture: The Structure of Nationalism in Accra, Ghana." *Africa Today* 47, no. 2 (2000): 34–58.

Hinga, Teresia M. "African Feminist Theologies, the Global Village, and the Imperative of Solidarity across Borders: The Case of the Circle of Concerned African Women Theologians." *Journal of Feminist Studies in Religion* 18, no. 1 (Spring 2002): 79–86.

———. "Jesus Christ and the Liberation of Women in Africa." In Oduyoye and Kanyoro, *Will to Arise,* 183–94.

Isasi-Díaz, Ada María. *En La Lucha: Elaborating a Mujerista Theology.* Minneapolis: Fortress, 2004.

Kanyoro, Musimbi R. A. "Beads and Strands: Threading More Beads in the Story of the Circle." In Phiri and Nadar, *African Women, Religion, and Health,* 19–42.

———. "Engendered Communal Theology: African Women's Contribution to Theology in the 21st Century." In Njoroge and Dube, *Talitha Cum!,* 158–80.

———. *Introduction to Feminist Cultural Hermeneutics: A Key to African Women's Liberation Theology.* Cleveland: Pilgrim Press, 2002.

Kelsey, David H. *Eccentric Existence: A Theological Anthropology.* Louisville: Westminster John Knox, 2009.

Kimble, David. *A Political History of Ghana: The Rise of Gold Coast Nationalism, 1850–1928.* Oxford: Clarendon, 1963.

King, Ursula. "Religion and Gender." In *A New Handbook of Living Religions,* edited by John R. Hinnells, 647–66. Cambridge: Blackwell, 1997.

Kobo, Ousman. "'We Are Citizens Too': The Politics of Citizenship in Independent Ghana." *Journal of Modern African Studies* 48, no. 1 (2010): 67–94.

Konadu, Kwasi, and Clifford C. Campbell, eds. *The Ghana Reader: History, Culture and Politics*. Durham, NC: Duke University Press, 2016.

———. "Independence, Coups, and the Republic, 1957–Present." In Konadu and Campbell, *Ghana Reader*, 299–300.

Kraus, Jon. "On the Politics of Nationalism and Social Change in Ghana." *Journal of Modern African Studies* 7, no. 1 (1969): 107–30.

Kumi, George Kwame. "Good Father-Mother God: The Theology of God from the Perspective of the Akan Matrilineal Society in Ghana." PhD diss., Fordham University, 1996.

Kwaku, Ken. "Tradition, Colonialism and Politics in Rural Ghana: Local Politics in Have, Volta Region." *Canadian Journal of African Studies/Revue Canadienne des Études Africaines* 10, no. 1 (1976): 71–86.

Landman, Christina. "Mercy Amba Ewudziwa Oduyoye: Mother of Our Stories." *Studia Historiae Ecclesiasticae* 33, no. 2. http://www.christina-landman .co.za/mercy.htm.

Lentz, Carola. "Ghanaian 'Monument Wars': The Contested History of the Nkrumah Statues." *Cahiers d'Études Africaines* 52, no. 3 (2017): 551–82.

Levine, Amy-Jill, Kwok Pui-lan, Musimbi Kanyoro, Adele Reinhartz, Hisako Kinukawa, and Elaine Wainwright. "Roundtable Discussion: Anti-Judaism and Postcolonial Biblical Interpretation." *Journal of Feminist Studies in Religion* 20, no. 1 (Spring 2004): 91–132.

Lipsett, B. Diane, and Phyllis Trible. *Faith and Feminism: Ecumenical Essays*. Louisville: Westminster John Knox, 2014.

Manuh, Takyiwaa. "Women and Their Organizations during the Convention People's Party Period." In Konadu and Campbell, *Ghana Reader*, 285–91.

Njoroge, Nyambura J. "The Missing Voice: African Women Doing Theology." *Journal of Theology for Southern Africa* 99 (1997): 77–83.

Njoroge, Nyambura J., and Musa Wenkosi Dube, eds. *Talitha Cum! Theologies of African Women*. Pietermaritzburg, South Africa: Cluster Publications, 2001.

Nkansah, Samuel Kwesi. "The Quest for Climactic Sanity: Re-Reading of Akan Creation Myth." *Language in India* 12, no. 8 (2012): 370–84.

Nkrumah, Kwame. "Independence Speech." In Konadu and Campbell, *Ghana Reader*, 301–2.

Nyengele, Mpyana Fulgence. *African Women's Theology, Gender Relations, and Family Systems Theory: Pastoral Theological Considerations and Guidelines for Care and Counseling*. New York: Lang, 2004.

Oduyoye, Mercy Amba. "The African Experience of God through the Eyes of an Akan Woman." *Cross Currents* 47, no. 4 (1997): 493–504.

———. "The African Family as Symbol of Ecumenism." *Ecumenical Review* 43, no. 3 (1991): 465–78.

———. *African Women's Theologies, Spirituality, and Healing: Theological Perspectives from the Circle of Concerned African Women Theologians.* New York: Paulist Press, 2019.

———. "Alive to What God Is Doing." *Ecumenical Review* 41, no. 2 (1989): 194–200.

——— [Amba Oduyoye]. "The Asante Woman: Socialization through Proverbs (Part I)." *African Notes: Bulletin of the Institute of African Studies, University of Ibadan* 8, no. 1 (1979): 5–11.

———. *Beads and Strands: Reflections of an African Woman on Christianity in Africa.* Maryknoll, NY: Orbis Books, 2004.

———. "Be a Woman, and Africa Will Be Strong." In Russell et al., *Inheriting Our Mothers' Gardens,* 35–53.

———. "A Biblical Perspective on the Church." *Ecumenical Review* 53, no. 1 (2001): 44–47.

———. "Calling the Church to Account." *Ecumenical Review* 47, no. 4 (1995): 479–89.

———. "Caught in a Whirlwind." *The Other Side* 36, no. 5 (2000): 51–52.

———. "Christianity and African Culture." *International Review of Mission* 84, no. 332/333 (1995): 77–90.

———. "The Church of the Future, Its Mission and Theology: A View from Africa." *Theology Today* 52, no. 4 (1996): 494–505.

———. "A Coming Home to Myself: The Childless Woman in the West African Space." In Farley and Jones, *Liberating Eschatology,* 105–20.

———. "Culture and Religion as Factors in Promoting Justice for Women." In *Women in Religion and Culture: Essays in Honour of Constance Buchanan,* edited by Mercy Amba Oduyoye and Constance H. Buchanan, 1–17. Ibadan, Nigeria: Sefer Books, 2007.

———. *Daughters of Anowa: African Women and Patriarchy.* Maryknoll, NY: Orbis Books, 1995.

———. "A Decade and a Half of Ecumenism in Africa: Problems, Programmes, Hopes." In *Voices of Unity: Essays in Honour of Willem Adolf Visser 't Hooft on the Occasion of His 80th Birthday,* edited by Ans J. van Bent, 70–77. Geneva: World Council of Churches, 1981.

———. "Feminist Theology in an African Perspective." In *Paths of African Theology,* edited by Rosino Gibellini, 166–81. Maryknoll, NY: Orbis Books, 1994.

———. "God Alone Gives and Distributes Gifts." In *Mystics, Visionaries, and Prophets,* edited by Shawn Madigan, 454–70. Minneapolis: Fortress, 1998.

———. *Hearing and Knowing: Theological Reflections on Christianity in Africa.* Eugene, OR: Wipf and Stock, 1986.

———. "Interview with Mercy Amba Oduyoye: Mercy Amba Oduyoye in Her Own Words." By Oluwatomisin Oredein. *Journal of Feminist Studies in Religion* 32, no. 2 (Fall 2016): 153–64.

———. *Introducing African Women's Theology.* Sheffield: Sheffield Academic, 2001.

———. "Jesus Christ." In Parsons, *Cambridge Companion to Feminist Theology*, 151–70.

———. "The Passion out of Compassion: Women of the EATWOT General Assembly." *International Review of Mission* 81, no. 322 (1992): 313–18.

———— [Amba Oduyoye]. "Reflections from a Third World Woman's Perspective: Women's Experience and Liberation Theologies." In Fabella and Torres, *Irruption of the Third World*, 246–55.

———. "Say Her Name! Africana Women as Interpreters, Healers, and Revolutionaries." Keynote address at Spelman College, Atlanta, GA, July 2016.

————. "The Search for a Two-Winged Theology: Women's Participation in the Development of Theology in Africa." In *Talitha, Qumi! Proceedings of the Convocation of African Women Theologians 1989*, edited by Mercy Amba Oduyoye and Musimbi Kanyoro, 31–56. Ibadan, Nigeria: SWL Press, 1990.

———. "Spirituality of Resistance and Reconstruction." In *Women Resisting Violence: Spirituality for Life*, edited by Mary John Mananzan, Mercy Amba Oduyoye, Elsa Tamez, J. Shannon Clarkson, Mary C. Grey, and Letty M. Russell, 161–71. Maryknoll, NY: Orbis Books, 1996.

———. "Standing on Both Feet: Education and Leadership Training of Women in the Methodist Church, Nigeria." *Ecumenical Review* 33, no. 1 (1980): 60–71.

———. "The Story of a Circle." *Ecumenical Review* 53, no. 1 (2001): 97–100.

———, ed. *Transforming Power: Women and the Household of God.* Accra, Ghana: SWL Press, 2007.

———. "Troubled but Not Destroyed." Keynote address at the All African Council of Churches meeting, Addis Abba, Ethiopia, 1997.

———. "Unity and Freedom in Africa." *Ecumenical Review* 26, no. 3 (1974): 453–58.

———. "Unity and Mission: The Emerging Ecumenical Vision." *Ecumenical Review* 39, no. 3 (1987): 336–45.

———. *Who Will Roll the Stone Away? The Ecumenical Decade of the Churches in Solidarity with Women.* Geneva: WCC Publications, 1990.

―――. "Women and Ritual in Africa." In Oduyoye and Kanyoro, *Will to Arise*, 9–24.

―――. "Women's Presence in the Life and Teaching of Jesus with Particular Emphasis on His Passion." *Ecumenical Review* 60, no. 1–2 (1970): 82–89.

Oduyoye, Mercy Amba, and Elizabeth Amoah, eds. *When Silence Is No Longer an Option*. Accra, Ghana: SWL Press, 2002.

Oduyoye, Mercy Amba, and Musimbi R. A. Kanyoro, eds. *The Will to Arise: Women, Tradition, and the Church in Africa*. Eugene, OR: Wipf and Stock, 1992.

Oduyoye, Mercy Amba, and Mary John Mananzan. "The Spirit Is Troubling the Water." *Ecumenical Review* 42, no. 3–4 (1990): 225–28.

Okali, Christine. *Cocoa and Kinship in Ghana: The Matrilineal Akan of Ghana*. London: Kegan Paul International, 1983.

Otieno, Tabitha, and Alberta Yeboah. "Gender and Cultural Practices: The Akan of Ghana and the Gushi of Kenya." *Journal of Intercultural Disciplines* 5 (2004): 108–27.

Owusu-Mensah, Isaac. "Promoting Local Governance in Ghana: The Role of Akan Queen Mothers." *Journal of Pan African Studies* 8, no. 9 (2015): 98–114.

Owusu-Mensah, I., W. Asante, and W. K. Osew. "Queen Mothers: The Unseen Hands in Chieftaincy Conflicts among the Akan in Ghana; Myth or Reality?" *Journal of Pan African Studies* 8, no. 6 (2015): 1–16.

Oyěwùmí, Oyèrónké. *The Invention of Women: Making an African Sense of Western Gender Discourses*. Minneapolis: University of Minnesota Press, 1997.

Pakenham, Thomas. *The Scramble for Africa: White Man's Conquest of the Dark Continent from 1876 to 1912*. New York: Random House, 1991.

Parsons, Susan Frank, ed. *The Cambridge Companion to Feminist Theology*. Cambridge: Cambridge University Press, 2002.

Pemberton, Carrie. *Circle Thinking: African Women Theologians in Dialogue with the West*. Leiden: Brill, 2003.

Phiri, Isabel Apawo, and Sarojini Nadar, eds. *African Women, Religion, and Health: Essays in Honor of Mercy Amba Ewudziwa Oduyoye*. Maryknoll, NY: Orbis Books, 2006.

Pobee, John S. *Religion and Politics in Ghana*. Accra, Ghana: Asempa Publishers, 1991.

Pui-lan, Kwok. "Mercy Amba Oduyoye and African Women's Theology." *Journal of Feminist Studies in Religion* 20, no. 1 (Spring 2004): 7–22.

Ruether, Rosemary Radford. "Liberation Theology and African Women's Theologies." In *Black Faith and Public Talk: Critical Essays on James H. Cone's*

"Black Theology and Black Power," edited by Dwight Hopkins, 167–71. Maryknoll, NY: Orbis Books, 1999.

Russell, Letty M., Kwok Pui-lan, Ada María Isasi-Díaz, and Katie Geneva Cannon, eds. *Inheriting Our Mothers' Gardens: Feminist Theology in Third World Perspective.* Louisville: Westminster, 1988.

Samuelsson, Tore. "'Behold, I Make All Things New': WCC's Fourth Assembly in Uppsala 4–20 July, 1968." World Council of Churches. https://www .oikoumene.org/en/press-centre/news/behold-i-make-all-things-new-wccs -fourth-assembly-in-uppsala-4-20-july-1968.

Shotwell, Alexis. *Against Purity: Living Ethically in Compromised Times.* Minneapolis, MN: University of Minnesota Press, 2016.

Smith, Yolanda. "Mercy Amba Oduyoye." Biola University. http://www.talbot .edu/ce20/educators/protestant/mercy_oduyoye/.

Stoeltje, Beverly J. "Asante Queen Mothers: A Study in Female Authority." *Annals of the New York Academy of Sciences* 810, no. 1 (1997): 41–71.

———. "Asante Queen Mothers: Precolonial Authority in a Postcolonial Society." *Research Review,* n.s., 19, no. 2 (2003): 1–19.

Student Christian Movement. "Who We Are." https://www.movement.org.uk /about-us/who-we-are.

Takyi, Baffour K., and Stephen Obeng Gyimah. "Matrilineal Ties and Marital Dissolution in Ghana." *Journal of Family Issues* 28, no. 5 (2007): 682–705.

Thíam, Awa. "Feminism and Revolution." In *I Am Because We Are: Readings in Africana Philosophy,* edited by Fred Hord and Jonathan Lee, 114–27. Boston: University of Massachusetts Press, 2016.

World Council of Churches. *The Church for Others.* In *A Reader in Ecclesiology,* edited by Bryan P. Stone, 291–96. New York: Routledge, 2012.

INDEX

abusua (house), 31, 142, 197n70
Achimota School, 16, 17, 22, 179n41
Acolatse, Esther, 122, 123
Africa: economic development, 22–23;
European political impact, 21–
22; religious belief, 54, 204n5;
social ethics, 163
African Christianity: emergence of,
77; European Christianity and,
56, 75, 77–78; hybrid identity,
77; traditional and ethnic culture
in, 2–3
African Christian theology: Akan cosmology and, 130–31; doctrine of
God in, 81; global nature of, 130;
interpretations of, 166; Oduyoye's
legacy in, 171–73; principles of,
80–81; scholastic recognition of,
3–4; women's contribution to,
2–3, 4, 5, 67–68, 69, 87–88
African culture: colonialism and, 22,
23, 103, 140, 144, 166; communal ideas of, 120; cosmological
thought, 81; European missionaries and, 76, 110–11; gendered
interpretation of, 81, 119–20;
holistic values of, 82; notion of
kinship in, 108; power structures in, 144; understandings of

redemption and salvation in, 76,
109
African feminism, 52, 57, 98, 167,
168, 189n19
African identity, 78
African Instituted Churches, 110
African men: accountability of, 154,
158–61; leadership of, 38
African ways of knowing, 163,
213n23
African women: advocacy for inclusiveness, 136; agency of, 184n54;
Christian church and, 69, 79,
86, 141, 146, 148, 149, 151–52,
168–69, 171; Christology of, 10,
91, 96–97, 116; cultural worldview, 124–25; discrimination of,
79; ecclesiological views of, 139–
41; education of, 26, 176–77n11;
employment of scripture, 146;
empowerment of, 25–27, 51, 52,
57, 65, 151, 160, 161; ethics of,
164; experiences of, 100–102,
120, 150, 153–54, 166; hybrid
identity of, 136, 146–47; liberation of, 116, 140, 145, 156, 167;
in matriarchal cultures, 31; motherhood of, 46, 94–95, 184n59,
200n21; Nkrumah's rule and, 27;

Oluwatomisin Olayinka Oredein is an assistant professor in
Black religious traditions, constructive theology, and ethics at
Brite Divinity School, Texas Christian University.

This book was selected as the recipient of the

2023 FIRST-TIME AUTHOR AWARD.

The First-Time Author Fund underwrites the promotion and production costs of one book per year and provides a grant directly to the author to aid their scholarship, professional development, or promotion of the book.

The University of Notre Dame Press and the author thank the following donors for their generous support:

Paul and Allegrita Ashenfelter	Richard H. Klein
James Bailey	Spyridon Kogkas
Teodolinda Barolini	Dennis Looney
William J. Becker	Steffi and Reed Marchman
Jennifer and Luis Bernal	Wendy and Joseph McMillen
Richard B. and Christine M. Bonfiglio	Daniel Milner
Laura Chmielewski	Natalie Meyers and Craig Cooksey
Prof. Lawrence and Cecilia Cunningham	Dr. Willard C. Morrey and J. B. Riley
Dr. Matthew and Amy Dowd	Kathleen Niehus
Thomas S. Gubanich and Maribeth Flynn	Dr. Anibal S. Pérez-Liñán
Fritz and Janet Heinzen	Kathryn D. Pitts
Paul and Joan Herrick	Christopher and Cody Rios-Sueverkruebbe
Evan and Rose Holguin	Professor Mark and Barbara Roche
Jieon Kim and Dr. Vittorio G. Hösle	Michelle Sybert and Jordan Allen
Harvey J. Humphrey, Jr.	John Thiel
David Juarez	Andrew W. Wendelborn
James M. and Joanne Kee	Stephen Wrinn
Dr. Terrence R. and Saskia Keeley	

CPSIA information can be obtained
at www.ICGtesting.com
Printed in the USA
LVHW040345280423
745466LV00001B/18